"Nolo's home page is worth bookmarking."
—WALL STREET JOURNAL

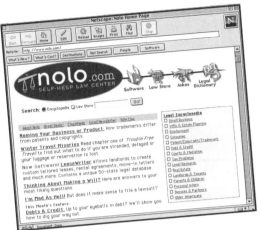

LEGAL INFORMATION ONLINE ANYTIME

24 hours a day

www.nolo.com

AT THE NOLO.COM SELF-HELP LAW CENTER ON THE WEB, YOU'LL FIND

- Nolo's comprehensive Legal Encyclopedia, with links to other online resources
- SharkTalk: Everybody's Legal Dictionary
- Auntie Nolo—if you've got questions, Auntie's got answers
- Update information on Nolo books and software
- The Law Store—over 250 self-help legal products including:
  Downloadable Software, Books, Form Kits and E-Guides
- Discounts and other good deals, plus our hilarious Shark Talk game
- Our ever-popular lawyer jokes
- NoloBriefs.com, our monthly email newsletter

Quality LAW BOOKS & SOFTWARE FOR NON-LAWYERS

Nolo.com legal books and software are consistently first-rate because:

- A dozen in-house Nolo legal editors, working with highly skilled authors, ensure that our products are accurate, up-to-date and easy to use.

- We know our books get better when we listen to what our customers tell us. (Yes, we really do want to hear from you—please fill out and return the card at the back of this book.)

- We are maniacal about updating every book and software program to keep up with changes in the law.

- Our commitment to a more democratic legal system informs all of our work.

KEEPING CURRENT

We update our books regularly to reflect changes in the law and in legal procedures. Use our **SPECIAL UPGRADE OFFER** to stay up-to-date. See the back of this book for details.

An Important Message to Our Readers

This product provides information and general advice about the law. But laws and procedures change frequently, and they can be interpreted differently by different people. For specific advice geared to your specific situation, consult an expert. No book, software or other published material is a substitute for personalized advice from a knowledgable lawyer licensed to practice law in your state.

1ST EDITION

THE
Trademark
Registration
Kit

BY ATTORNEYS PATRICIA GIMA & STEPHEN ELIAS

nolo.com
LAW FOR ALL

Keeping Up-to-Date

To keep its books up to date, Nolo issues new printings and new editions periodically. New printings reflect minor legal changes and technical corrections. New editions contain major legal changes, major text additions or major reorganizations. To find out if a later printing or edition of any Nolo book is available, call Nolo at 510-549-1976 or check our website at www.nolo.com.

To stay current, follow the "Update" service at our website at www.nolo.com. In another effort to help you use Nolo's latest materials, we offer a 35% discount off the purchase of the new edition of your Nolo book when you turn in the cover of an earlier edition. (See the "Special Upgrade Offer" in the back of the book.)

This book was last revised in: August 1999.

First Edition	AUGUST 1999
Editor	PERI PAKROO
Cover Design	TONI IHARA
Book Design	TERRI HEARSH
Index	SUSAN CORNELL
Proofreading	MIKE EDWARDS AND ROBERT WELLS
Printing	CONSOLIDATED PRINTERS, INC.

Gima, Patricia, 1964-
    The trademark registration kit / by Patricia Gima
        p.   cm.
        Includes index.
        ISBN 0-87337-434-7
        1. Trademarks—Law and legislation—United States—Popular works.
    I. Title.
    KF3181.Z9G56   1999
    346.7304'88—dc21   98-56071
                                                             CIP

Quantity sales: For information on bulk purchases or corporate premium sales, please contact the Special Sales department. For academic sales or textbook adoptions, ask for Academic Sales, 800-955-4775. Nolo.com, 950 Parker St., Berkeley, CA, 94710.

Acknowledgments

It's done, it's done, it's done! My biggest thanks goes to my family: my wonderful and patient husband, Joe, for hanging in there with me through thick, thin and thinner, and to my beautiful son, Jordan, who was eight months in utero when the idea for this book started and is now 2.5 years old. Thanks, too, to my parents, Ken and Aiko Gima, for encouraging me to pursue my dreams. Thanks to my Aunts Joan, Sue and Sandy for teaching me how to love books. Warm thanks to Sandra Maita for being Jordan's guardian angel while I worked on this book. Hugs and thanks to Steve Elias (AKA the heart and soul of Nolo) for being the inspiration for this book and for almost all work that I do at Nolo, for fending off those who may have wanted to announce the book before it was ready to be announced, for being an awesome co-author and editor and for knowing so much about trademark law. Thanks to Jake Warner for letting me do this book and for pushing me at key points. Thanks to Peri Pakroo for asking key questions, for pulling this book together and for reminding me day after day that there is a light at the end of the tunnel. Terri Hearsh, thank you for all your patience and hard work on the book's layout, graphics and charts. Thanks to anyone and everyone who never asked me, "How's that book going?"

Table of Contents

Appendixes

Introduction

This book explains the process for registering a trademark with the United States Patent and Trademark Office (PTO). Trademarks are used to identify products and services in the marketplace and include names, logos, packaging, slogans and product designs. Generally speaking, once you use a trademark in commerce, other businesses are not allowed to use it in a similar way that might confuse customers. Your legal rights to the trademark exist as soon as you use it; registration is not necessary. Registration will, however, greatly enhance your rights to your trademark and increase your power to prevent others from using it.

This book provides detailed instructions for the registration process from start to finish, including information on how to prepare for the process and how to deal with problems that may arise while your application is pending. You'll also learn how to maintain your trademark once it's registered in order to keep it strong and protected.

A. Who Should Use This Book

This book is for individuals or businesses who:
- have decided on a mark for their business or product (that is, a name, logo, slogan, distinctive packaging or other means of distinguishing the product or service in the marketplace)
- have decided that it makes sense to register the mark with the U.S. Patent and Trademark Office to protect it from being copied by others, and
- have already done a trademark search to find out whether the mark has already been registered or is in use by others in a context where your use of the same or similar mark would likely confuse consumers.

Recommended Reading: If you are in the process of deciding upon a mark or logo and want to learn about the legal impact of using particular marks, *Trademark: Legal Care for Your*

Business & Product Name (Nolo), written by attorneys Stephen Elias and Kate McGrath, is the best book for you. This book will also take you step-by-step through the trademark search process if you need to find out whether your proposed mark is already being used by someone else.

B. What This Book Does Not Cover

While this book covers a lot of information about the trademark registration process, it does not cover the following issues:
- how to choose a mark, including what factors entitle a mark to maximum legal protection
- how to do a trademark search, or
- how to assess your legal position in the case of a trademark dispute.

These issues are covered in *Trademark: Legal Care for Your Business & Product Name,* by Stephen Elias and Kate McGrath (Nolo).

This book also doesn't cover:
- how to sue or defend a federal or state court lawsuit for trademark infringement or unfair competition without a lawyer
- how to accomplish and record transfers or assignments of trademarks or business names, or
- international trademark registrations.

For these issues, you will find information about helpful resources in Chapter 14, Help Beyond This Book.

C. How to Use This Book

To get the most from this book, we recommend you begin by reading Chapters 1 through 3. These chapters will give you a basic understanding of trademark law and will prepare you for filling out the registration application and choosing the specimens you will need to file with it. If you're in a hurry, or if you're already familiar with the big picture of trademark law, you can skip Chapter 1 and proceed directly to Chapter 2.

Once you've oriented yourself with the preliminary information provided in the first three chapters, and decided which type of application you will file (a use application or an intent-to-use application, as explained in Chapter 2), you will read either Chapter 4 or Chapter 5, which both provide step-by-step instructions for use applications and intent-to-use applications, respectively. Chapter 6 provides valuable information about the drawing you will need to submit along with your application. Chapter 7 explains how to file your application, specimens and drawing with the PTO.

Problems do often arise after the initial application has been filed, and Chapters 8 through 10 cover the most common ones. Chapter 11 outlines the follow-up activity required for intent-to-use applicants. Chapter 12 covers the very important period directly preceding registration, known as publication and opposition. Finally, Chapter 13

explains how to maintain your mark once registered.

New rules governing the trademark registration process are being proposed as this book goes to print (May 1999). These rules will likely affect the most basic trademark application requirements including signature, specimen and drawing requirements. The good news is that it looks like the PTO is poised to relax some of its more strict rules regarding trademark applications. The bad news is that we really don't know what the final rules will be until sometime between now and October 30, 1999. If you are using this book after October 30, 1999, please visit Nolo's website at http://www.nolo.com/ for the most updated information about the PTO's new rules and how they affect trademark registrations. To receive e-mail notification of when these changes go into effect, subscribe to *NoloBriefs*, Nolo's email newsletter, at http://www.nolo.com/ newsletter/join.cfm. ■

PART I

Your Trademark Application

Trademark Basics

People have used marks to identify items of value and services for centuries. One of the earlier "trademarks" was the watermark used on sheets of paper to identify the manufacturer of the paper. Today, corporations invest millions of dollars creating whole corporate identities, the purpose of which is to create a distinctive look and feel to products and/or services, thereby sealing their name or logo in the consumer's mind and ensuring the consumer's repeat business. Its power to identify products and services in the marketplace is what makes a trademark so valuable. This commercial aspect is a core, defining characteristic of trademarks.

A trademark is also a legal creature. In general, the legal aspects of trademarks have to do with who owns a trademark and to what degree an owner can prevent others from using that mark. Trademark owners have certain rights established in the vast body of trademark law. As this chapter explains, an owner of a trademark who registers it with the United States Patent and Trademark Office (referred to as the PTO) will have stronger rights than the owner of an unregistered trademark, and will have more power to enforce those rights. While this book is devoted to explaining the trademark registration process step by step, this chapter gives an overview of the legal meaning of trademarks and how trademark registration fits into the big picture.

➡ **The explanation of the trademark registration process begins in the next chapter.** If you feel adequately educated about trademark law in general and are ready to learn the trademark registration process, you may skip this chapter and start with Chapter 2, Preparing to File Your Trademark Application.

State Registration Systems

Trademark registration systems are maintained at both the federal and the state level. The federal government maintains the Federal Trademark Register. In addition, each state maintains its own trademark register which affords statewide protection to trademarks. This book explains the federal trademark registration process only. For information on your state's registration system, contact your state's trademark agency, which is often found within the Secretary of State's office.

A. Federal Trademark Register

The Federal Trademark Register is overseen by the U.S. Patent and Trademark Office (PTO), which keeps two lists of all trademarks registered with the federal government, along with the names of their owners, dates of registration, class of goods or services in which the names are used, and other information. The two lists are known as the Principal Register and the Supplemental Register. Placement on the Principal Register is only for marks that are distinctive (see Section C1, below, for information about what makes a mark distinctive) and gives a mark the important protections that make federal registration worthwhile. When a mark is said to be "federally registered," it generally means that it's included in the Principal Register. This book is primarily concerned with registration on the Principal Register.

The main benefits of federal registration are as follows:

- The trademark owner obtains the right to recover up to triple damages and attorneys' fees from an infringer.
- The trademark owner gets exclusive nationwide ownership of the mark (except as

against those who actually used the mark first).

- Registration provides official notice to all would-be users of the mark that the mark is already taken.
- The trademark owner obtains the right to put an ® after the mark.
- The trademark owner obtains the right to make the mark "incontestable" (explained in Chapter 13) by keeping it in continuous use for five years after the date of registration.
- The trademark owner obtains the presumption of ownership in case of litigation (lawsuits) involving the mark.

Placement on the Supplemental Register is for all other marks which are not distinctive enough to qualify for placement on the Principal Register. While not as beneficial as placement on the Principal Register, the Supplemental Register still provides some protection:

- Registration provides official notice to all would-be users of the mark that the mark is already taken.
- The trademark owner obtains the right to put an ® after the mark.
- Registration on the Supplemental Register allows the owner to apply for registration on the Principal Register, despite the fact that the mark is not distinctive, if the mark has been in continuous and substantially exclusive use for five years.

B. Trademark and Service Mark Defined

Trademark law has two fundamental goals:

1. To prevent businesses from stealing or riding off the goodwill that rightfully belongs to other businesses who have creatively named and distinguished their services and products in the marketplace.
2. To prevent customers from being misled by the use of confusingly similar marks on products and/or services.

As with so many things in life, there's more to a trademark than meets the eye. The term "trademark" has a real-world meaning and a legal (or other-worldly) meaning.

1. The Commercial Meaning of Trademark

Trademarks, as that term is used in the commercial world, are typically names and symbols that are used to identify and market products. Similarly, service marks are names or symbols used to identify and market services. For example, one famous trademark for a brand of film and cameras is Kodak. McDonald's is a famous service mark for a brand of fast food service. The swoosh symbol is a trademark for Nike athletic gear. But trademarks don't necessarily have to be names or symbols. Under the right conditions, a trademark can be any one of the following:

- a color
- a sound
- a product's packaging (sometimes called trade dress).

2. The Legal Meaning of Trademark

The term "trademark" also has a legal meaning. To own a trademark means to have the exclusive right to use that mark to identify your goods and/or services. Court decisions made and written down by judges over time have established that the first person or business to use a mark in commerce gets exclusive use of that mark to identify his, her or its goods or services. This is a basic and fundamental principle of trademark law and you will find the term "first use" used throughout this book. There are, of course, exceptions (see sidebar "Who Is the First User?" below). But the purpose of this principle is to keep others from copying a trademark and using it in the marketplace to confuse the consumer into buying their product.

Who Is the First User?

As a general rule, there are two ways to qualify as a first user:

- by being the first to actually use the trademark on products or the first to market a service;
- by being the first to apply for registration of the trademark on the federal Principal Register (described in Section A) on the grounds that you intend to use it in the future.

What it actually means to use or intend to use a trademark is discussed in detail in Chapter 2.

Although ownership is determined by first use, it's possible for two or more separate businesses to own the same mark. This will only be true if there is no likelihood of customer confusion by the two (or more) uses of the mark. This often depends on the geographic scope of each business' use of the mark. For instance, if one business uses a trademark in New York and another business uses that same trademark in California, each business may be considered the first user and owner of the mark in its respective territory. But what happens if the New York owner wants to move into California, or vice versa? Or if one business used the mark on sportswear and the other on lawn mowers and they both moved into gardening clothes? In these examples, a court deciding the respective rights of the owners would consider the following facts when making its decision:

- Did the second business to use the mark know of the first business's previous use?
- Is the first user's mark federally registered? If yes, did the second use begin before or after the date of registration?
- Is the second user's mark federally registered?
- How broad were the first user's marketing efforts when the second use began?

Likelihood of customer confusion is further discussed later in this Chapter in Section D, and in Chapter 10, Section B.

Trademark law protects both trademarks and service marks equally and it is common to use the term "trademark," or just "mark," when referring to either. We use all of these terms more or less interchangeably. See "Marks You Might Recognize" below for examples of trademarks and service marks.

Marks You Might Recognize

Trademark Examples:

Apple	Kodak
Coca-Cola	Nike
Exxon	Xerox

Service Mark Examples:

ACLU	Kinko's
Blockbuster	McDonald's
CBS	UPS

C. What Trademark Law Protects

A central and fairly complex aspect of trademark law is that only certain marks are protectible. In a nutshell, only memorable marks (sometimes called "distinctive" marks) are eligible for trademark protection. Marks can be memorable for two reasons:

- They are arbitrary, unusual, unique, evocative, surprising or otherwise effective in setting the product or service off from others; or
- They have become familiar over time and through continuous use—that is, customers have come to associate the name with the business. The legal principle that protects this type of mark is called the "secondary meaning rule."

By contrast, marks consisting of common or descriptive words, personal names and geographic terms (called "descriptive" marks) won't receive much, if any, protection—unless they have become distinctive under the secondary meaning rule (mentioned above).

Because distinctive marks receive the most protection that the law has to offer, they are also commonly known as "strong marks." Not surprisingly, descriptive marks are known as "weak marks." The following two sections offer some more detail on what makes a mark distinctive or merely descriptive.

1. Distinctive Marks

The ability of a mark to stand out in a customer's mind—its distinctiveness in the trademark context—can derive from a number of different characteristics. Distinctive marks include:

- Coined terms—words that are made up, such as Exxon, Kodak or Rackafrax.
- Fanciful or surprising terms—words that are common in one context but distinctive in another. This usually occurs when the term is imaginative, unexpected or arbitrary in the context of its use, such as Apple computers, Cherokee clothes, *Time* Magazine and Double Rainbow Ice Cream.
- Evocative or suggestive terms—marks such as Greyhound bus lines, Suave shampoo and Jaguar cars all fit this category.

Distinctive marks have little or no descriptive function but rather operate primarily to set the product or service off from others. Their uniqueness is what gives them their legal strength. One of our favorite examples of a distinctive mark is the name used by a local bookstore—Diesel, A Bookstore. The "Diesel" part of the name is so surprising in the context that once you see it, you're unlikely to forget it.

The question of what makes one mark strong and another mark weak is at the heart of trademark law and must be understood to handle your own trademark issues. To learn more about what makes an effective trademark, see *Trademark: Legal Care for Your Business & Product Name,* by Stephen Elias and Kate McGrath (Nolo).

2. Descriptive Marks

While trademark law serves to protect distinctive or strong marks, it doesn't protect commonly used words or words that many similar businesses might use to describe the types of services or products they provide. For example, most adjectives (like soft, fluffy, tasty, accurate, fast, easy, tough, reliable) are available for anyone to use. Common words don't do a good job of distinguishing one product or service from others anyway. Weak, descriptive trademarks often either describe the nature of the service or product they identify (Unfinished Furniture or A-Z Hardware); or they describe where the service is located (Southside Liquors); or they praise the product or service's quality (Blue Ribbon Dairy); or they use personal names (Tom's Barber Shop).

The law keeps these ordinary terms available for everyone's use by classifying them as weak, descriptive or even generic. In trademark law, "generic" means that the name of one brand of a service or product becomes so common that it merges with the service or product itself, as happened with the formerly strong trademarks "escalator" and "aspirin."

What Is Infringement?

Infringement is a term of art which, in the trademark realm, refers to a situation where a mark is used in violation of another's valid trademark rights. Consider the following example:

Adam owns a trademark over his film editing software's name, "DigiReel," which he has used in commerce for two years. Adam was the first anywhere to use this mark. Owen starts to use the mark "DigiReel" for his sound editing software. Since Owen's software is likely to be marketed in the same channels as Adam's software and Adam has superior rights to use the mark because he was the first to use it, Owen is infringing on Adam's trademark.

The issues involved in trademark disputes are covered in depth in *Trademark: Legal Care for Your Business & Product Name,* by Stephen Elias and Kate McGrath (Nolo). That book will tell you how to deal with these issues and how the courts are likely to resolve them in specific fact situations.

D. What Qualifies for Trademark Protection

Before being placed on the Principal Register, a trademark must meet certain legal criteria, including the following positive factors:

- It must be used in or affect commerce between two or more states (also known as interstate commerce); between a state and a territory or between a territory and another territory (also known as territorial commerce); or between a state or territory and another country (international commerce). (See Chapter 2, Section B1, for a detailed discussion of the commerce requirement.)
- It must be sufficiently distinctive to operate reasonably as a product or service identifier.

On the negative side:

- It can't be so similar to an existing federally registered trademark that your average, everyday consumer would confuse the two.
- It can't be the U.S. flag or other federal or local governmental insignias; the name of a living person without his or her consent; the name or likeness of a dead U.S. President without the widow's consent; a word or a symbol that disparages living or dead persons, institutions, beliefs or national symbols; or a mark that is judged immoral, deceptive or scandalous.
- It can't consist primarily of a surname or geographical name unless the mark has become well known over time or the geographical name is obviously used in an arbitrary or evocative way without deceptively implying that the goods came from a specific place. For instance, South Pole Fishing Equipment is okay as a trademark since customers are unlikely to believe that the equipment actually came from the South Pole. (See *Trademark: Legal Care for Your Business & Product Name* for more on when surnames and geographical names can be registered.)
- It can't be the title of a book, play, record or movie that is a single-issue artistic work (as opposed to a series or serial) until it has become very well known over time.

E. The Application Process

To apply for registration, you will need to submit an application, a drawing of your mark (Chapter 6), three specimens showing your mark in use (for use applications), and pay a filing fee of $245 per application, per mark. There are two types of applications—use applications and intent-to-use applications—which involve significantly different procedures. Because the procedures are so different, we explain them in different chapters. Chapter 4 covers use applications and Chapter 5 explains intent-to-use applications, both in step-by-step detail. In addition, Chapter 11 explains the extra follow-up tasks that must be completed for intent-to-use applications. For an outline of all the steps involved in each of these types of applications, refer to the beginning of Chapters 4 and 5.

According to the PTO's own current timetables, it will take approximately one year from the date of your application to obtain a registration certificate (assuming your registration is successful).

 Do not use the ® symbol unless you have achieved trademark registration for your mark. You've likely seen the ® symbol on packaging and advertising for goods and services in the marketplace. This symbol stands for "registered trademark" and can only be used when the mark has, in fact, been registered with the PTO. Unless you have the certificate of registration in hand, never use the ® symbol next to your mark. Instead, use the ^{TM} symbol, which indicates to all who see it that you are claiming trademark rights based on first use of the mark (not based on actual registration of the mark).

Trademark Law Sources

Trademark laws are governed by the following federal and state resources:

- **Federal:** Federal trademark laws are governed by the Lanham Act, found in Title 15 of the United States Code (USC), Sections 1051-1127.
- **State:** State resources include state agencies and statutes. For a state-by-state list of these resources, see Appendix A.

A similar and related body of law governing unfair competition is based in federal and state statutes and cases. While there are subtle differences between trademark and unfair competition law that will concern those engaged in a lawsuit, the main principles that underlie them are very similar.

F. Other Business Names and Marks

In addition to trademarks and service marks, following are other types of business names of which you should be aware.

1. Trade Names

A trade name is the name a business uses as its formal business name. A trademark/service mark is the name a business uses to market its products or services. The difference between trademarks/service marks and trade names can be confusing because businesses often use at least part of their trade name as a trademark/service mark.

For example, every time a small business named something like Pete's Graphic Designs, Elmwood Copymat or Good Taste Organic Foods puts its name on a store sign, window display or brochure, it is using its trade name as a mark—in this case, a service mark.

On the other hand, large businesses commonly use different names for each type of activity. For instance, Walt Disney Pictures (service mark) created the movie *The Little Mermaid* (trademark) for the Walt Disney Company (corporate name and trade name), which operates Disneyland (service mark).

2. Corporate and Fictitious Business Names

A corporate name is simply the official name of a corporation as it appears on its Articles of Incorporation, which is the legal document filed with the state that creates the corporation. A fictitious business name is any business name that does not contain the legal name(s) of its owner(s). If the owner is a person, then the legal name of the owner is simply the person's last name, and if the business name does not contain that name, it would be considered a fictitious business name.

The name of a business owned by a number of people such as a partnership would be considered to be a fictitious business name if it did not contain all the last names of the owners. If the owner is a corporation, the legal name of the owner is the corporate name.

3. Certification and Collective Marks

Used less frequently than trademarks and service marks, certification and collective marks distinguish groups of products and services from other general groups. Because use of these marks is relatively rare, registration of these marks is not covered in this book. We do, however, provide a brief explanation of each type below. To file for registration of one of these types of marks, you'll probably need a trademark attorney. See Chapter 14, Help Beyond This Book.

Certification marks are used only to certify that products or services which are manufactured or provided by others have certain qualities associated with the mark. For example, Good Housekeeping Seal of Approval, Roquefort (a region in France), Stilton cheese (a product from the Stilton locale in England), and Harris Tweeds (a special weave from a specific area in Scotland) are all certification marks. Among the characteristics that this type of mark may represent are regional origin, method of manufacture, product quality and service accuracy.

A collective mark is a symbol, label, word, phrase or other distinguishing mark that members of a group or organization use to identify the goods they wish to produce or the services they render. For example, the letters "ILGWU" on a shirt is a collective mark identifying the shirt as a product of members of the International Ladies Garment Workers Union. It distinguishes that shirt from those made by non-union shops. Only members of the group are entitled to use the collective mark in order to indicate, for example, membership in a union, association or other organization.

G. Should You Apply for Trademark Registration? Strategies for Small Businesses

You may be operating under the assumption that applying for trademark registration is your best option. But let's take a look at your other options and why registration may not be your best one at this point.

If you own or operate a small business, chances are you are on a tight budget. Although registering a trademark may be a priority for you, the $245 filing fee—not to mention any search fees you may need to incur—may not be within your immediate budget, even if you do it on your own with this book. If you cannot afford to make trademark registration a top priority, there's no need to be overly concerned. When you register to do business in your local community, the name of your business is placed on your region's list of local businesses. This serves as a limited notice to others locally who might try to use the same name. They won't be able to register this name with your local government authority.

The same is true on a state level if you are incorporating in your state of operation. When you incorporate, your corporate name is usually put on the state's register of corporations. No other corporation may use that same name in that state. The list of corporate names provides notice to others that the name is unavailable because you are using it.

The final important thing to remember is that your first use of the mark has ultimate priority, at least in your region. So if you cannot file an application now for registration, do your best to gather and keep all documentation proving and showing the actual date you first used your mark in commerce. ■

2

Preparing to File Your Trademark Application

Before you start filling out your trademark application, it's important to get your ducks in a row and assemble all the important facts about your mark and how you plan to use it. Don't wait until you've started filling out the forms to figure out these details. Some of your preliminary tasks include:

- determining whether your mark is for a good (a product), a service or both
- determining what type of trademark application you will file, and
- choosing one or more official categories (called classes) that apply to the goods or services associated with your mark.

This chapter covers all of these tasks in detail and will help you gather much of the information you'll need to fill out your trademark application.

A. Goods, Services or Both?

Before starting to fill out your trademark application, you will need to determine whether your mark is a mark for a good, for a service or both. When your mark is placed on a good, it is typically called a trademark. When your mark is used in connection with a service, it is typically called a service mark. We will refer to all marks in this book as trademarks for the sake of efficiency.

Goods are tangible products, items you can touch—for example, cans of soup, pens, cookies, cars, oxygen canisters, calendars, computers and clothing. Even creative works, such as software, music and inventions, are goods since they are marketed in a tangible form (floppy disks, tapes, CDs). Downloadable forms of these works are also considered to be goods, even though they exist only in electronic form.

Services are activities performed for customers. Examples of services are: professional advice or consultation; physical maintenance and/or repair (for instance, fixing washing machines or typewriters or caring for gardens); performances (such as those by actors, rent-a-clowns or singing

telegram services); delivery (such as overnight mail services, bicycle courier services, trucking or busing companies or airlines); financial services (such as banking, lending, real estate or credit); and selling items (such as food, products or services).

It is important to understand that many businesses provide both a service and a product under the same mark. For example, Weight Watchers and Jenny Craig are used as marks both for diet foods (goods) and for weight-loss counseling (services). Xerox and IBM are used as marks both for office machines (products) and for machine repairs and maintenance (services).

On the other hand, it's also common for businesses to use one mark for their service and another mark for their product. For instance, Sears Roebuck & Co. uses Sears as a service mark for its department store services and Craftsman as a trademark for its line of tools (products).

B. Actual Use vs. Intent to Use

One of the most fundamental distinctions you need to understand up-front is the difference between a "use" (sometimes called "actual use") and an "intent-to-use" application. When you file an application for trademark registration, you will either file on the basis that you have already begun using the mark, or on the basis that you intend to use the mark in the future. This distinction is important because the application process and the rules governing it are different for each type of application. Although we refer to each basis as a type of application, both are, in fact, choices on one application form. These choices appear on the official trademark application form which is shown below.

This section discusses the precise meanings of "use" and "intent to use," which you'll need to understand in order to proceed with the appropriate type of application. The specific rules and procedures for each are discussed in their own chapters, Chapters 4 and 5.

BASIS FOR APPLICATION: (Check boxes which apply, **but never both the first AND second boxes,** and supply requested information related to each box checked in.)

[ ]	Applicant is using the mark in commerce on or in connection with the above identified goods/services. (15 U.S.C. 1051(a), as amended.) Three specimens showing the mark as used in commerce are submitted with this application. • Date of first use of the mark in commerce which the U.S. Congress may regulate (for example, interstate or between the U.S. and a foreign country):_____ • Specify the type of commerce:_____ (for example, interstate or between the U.S. and a specified foreign country) • Date of first use anywhere (the same as or before use in commerce date):_____ • Specify manner or mode of use of mark on or in connection with the goods/services:_____ (for example, trademark is applied to labels, service mark is used in advertisements)
[ ]	Applicant has a bona fide intention to use the mark in commerce on or in connection with the above identified goods/services. (15 U.S.C. 1051(b), as amended.) • Specify intended manner or mode of use of mark on or in connection with the goods/services:_____ (for example, trademark will be applied to labels, service mark will be used in advertisements)

1. "Use" Defined

What, you may ask, constitutes actual use? Like so many terms utilized in the trademark context, the term "use" has a specific definition apart from its plain English meaning. For a trademark to be officially in use, the PTO requires that it be "in use that Congress may regulate." Technically speaking, this definition has two parts: the trademark must be "in use," plus the use must be "in commerce that Congress may regulate." If either of these elements is not true for your trademark, then you may not file a use application to register it.

a. "In Use"

As a general rule, "in use" means that the mark is being utilized in the marketplace to identify your goods or services. This doesn't mean that you need to have actually sold the product or service, just that the product or service associated with the mark is available for sale in the marketplace. The criteria used to determine whether a trademark is in use are different depending on whether the trademark is being used for a product or a service.

For products (tangible goods), your mark is in use if the mark appears on the goods or on labels or tags attached to them, and the goods have either been shipped to a store for resale or use as a sample, or are available for sale by mail or over the Internet. However, a token sale made only for the purpose of getting your mark "in use" doesn't count. The use has to be a true attempt (sometimes called a "bona fide" attempt) to identify and distinguish your goods or services in the marketplace.

EXAMPLE 1: Ben sent a sample of his No-Knees pants to a department store potentially interested in selling them. This counts as a use of his mark No-Knees.

EXAMPLE 2: Emily's earrings were shipped in a box carrying the label All Ears, for the legitimate purpose of resale by a local street vendor. This counts as a use of her mark All Ears.

EXAMPLE 3: Peter developed a system for taking orders and processing credit card payments over the web, and launched the sale of his Bearware software online. He used the mark Bearware prominently on his website. Making his software available for sale online counts as a use of his mark.

For services, your mark is in use if the services are actually being marketed under the mark and you can legitimately deliver them to end users.

EXAMPLE 1: Toby purchased a 900 line for providing sports trivia under the name Sports R Us. As soon as his lines were up and running and he had advertised his services under the name Sports R Us, his mark was in use.

EXAMPLE 2: Helen decided to call her house-cleaning service Mrs. Clean. When she first advertised her services under that name on a bulletin board at a local market, she put her mark into use.

EXAMPLE 3: Alice started her own Internet service provider business under the mark CosmoNet. She set up her system and prepared all of the equipment she would need to offer her services. The day she first started advertising her services under her mark and with all of her systems in place and ready to go, she put her mark into use.

b. "Use That Congress May Regulate"

For the PTO's purposes, being in use isn't enough—federal registration is allowed only for marks that are being used in commerce that Congress may regulate. "Commerce that Congress may regulate" means a business or trade which the federal government, through the U.S. Congress, may control. Technically, Congress may control interstate commerce, territorial commerce and international commerce. In practice, this means that to qualify for federal trademark registration, your business must do at least one of the following:

1. Ship a product (upon which the mark is used):
   - across state lines
   - between a state and a territory or a territory and another territory, or
   - between a state or territory and another country.

2. Use the mark to advertise in other states services offered by your business in your state.
3. Use the mark in connection with or to advertise a service business that you conduct:
   - across state lines
   - in more than one state, or
   - across international or territorial borders.
4. Use the mark in connection with or to advertise a business that you operate catering to interstate or international travelers.

Examples of the activities listed above are provided in the chart below.

2. "Intent to Use" Defined

If your mark is not in actual use as defined above, you may file as an intent-to-use (ITU) applicant. As an ITU applicant, you will have to state that you have a bona fide intention to use your mark within six months of the date your application is approved by the PTO. "Bona fide intention" simply means that you genuinely and sincerely intend to use the mark in commerce. An example of an insincere intent is if you were to file an application for a mark in order to keep a competitor from using that mark, even though you don't really intend to use it. You are not allowed to put the mark out of commission for a competitor and simply hold it hostage.

If you are unable to put the mark into actual use within six months of your application's approval, you can purchase additional six-month extensions, one at a time, until three years have passed, assuming you are able to convince the PTO that the reasons for the delays are legitimate. As a practical matter, then, the initial requirement that you put your mark into actual use in commerce within six months is expandable to a total period of three years. Only after you put the mark into actual use will you be able to accomplish your ultimate goal—to register your mark.

Types of Commerce That Congress May Regulate

Commerce That Congress May Regulate	Example
Shipping across state lines	Shipping products from California to Virginia
Shipping between a state and a territory or a territory and another territory	Shipping products from New York to Puerto Rico or Puerto Rico to the Virgin Islands
Shipping between a state or territory and another country	Shipping products from California to Hong Kong or Puerto Rico to Cuba
Using the mark to advertise in other states services offered by your business in your state	Advertising in a national magazine a business that performs services in Illinois
Using the mark in connection with or to advertise a service business that you conduct across state lines	Advertising a business that performs services nationwide
Using the mark in connection with or to advertise a service business that you conduct in more than one state	Advertising a business that maintains several locations nationwide
Using the mark in connection with or to advertise a service business that you conduct across international or territorial borders	Advertising a business that performs services internationally
Using the mark in connection with or to advertise a business that you operate catering to interstate or international travelers	Advertising a business aimed at tourists from outside the U.S.

3. Why File an Intent-to-Use Application?

You may be wondering: If you're not using your mark yet, why bother to file an application based on an intent to use the mark some time in the future? Why not just wait until you are actually using the mark in commerce and then file a use application? Simply, if you file an intent-to-use application and then later go on to put your mark into use, your intent-to-use application filing date will be considered as the date you first used the mark anywhere. This date of first use is often the deciding factor when two different people or businesses claim ownership of the same basic mark. (Determining your date of first use is explained in Chapters 4 and 5, which walk you through completing a use or an ITU application.) That is, the first to use a mark will often be determined to be the owner of the mark. So the purpose of filing an intent-to-use application is to secure that early filing date.

Once you decide to file on this basis, you should do so as quickly as possible to obtain the earliest possible date of first use. But remember, for the filing date also to serve as your date of first use you have to complete the registration process by going ahead and using the mark in commerce that Congress may regulate.

While reserving a mark for future registration may be a good strategy for some marks—especially marks consisting of words and phrases—it may not be a good strategy for many other types of marks. For example, if you reserve a mark for a specific distinctive design and then later on want to change the design when it gets around to putting the mark into use, you may have to reapply and pay a new application fee. And, you may lose the ability to claim your early filing date if a conflict develops.

An ITU application usually is not advisable for these types of marks:

- marks with unique graphic designs (see Chapter 5, Section A, sidebar: "Strategies for Successful ITU Applications")
- marks consisting of trade dress and product configurations
- marks that include highly specific colors.

For more on these issues, see Chapter 5.

4. Potential Costs of Intent-to-Use Applications

Assuming that you ultimately put your mark into actual use and complete the registration process, the intent-to-use approach will be more expensive than simply filing a use application—at least $100 more expensive, plus $100 for each additional six-month extension that is needed. Therefore, it's best to use the intent-to-use application when you have come up with a truly distinctive name or you plan to spend lots of money "tooling up" to use the mark and you don't want to lay out the cash until you know that the mark will be yours and yours alone.

On the other hand, if your mark uses common words, or is descriptive of the products or services, you may be better off waiting until your actual use begins and then submit an application at that time. You may forfeit the advantage of the early use date, but since your mark is weak, that date is not as important.

For more information about what makes a mark weak or strong, see Chapter 1, Trademark Basics.

Multiple Marks and Multiple Uses

If you wish to obtain trademark protection for more than one mark, you will need to file a separate application for each. However, if you plan to use the same mark as both a service mark and a trademark, you need not file a separate application. Instructions for how to specify that your mark is both a trademark and a service mark on the same application are in Chapter 4 for use applicants (those who wish to register a mark they are already using) and Chapter 5 for intent-to-use applicants (those who wish to reserve a mark for use in the near future). But even though you would be filing one application in this circumstance, you would have to pay a double fee. See Chapter 7, Section B1, for more information about filing fees.

C. Choosing a Class

All registered trademarks fall into one or more classes of goods or services. The main purpose of the PTO's classification system is to group marks by type and enable the Examiner (the PTO attorney who will evaluate your application) to determine whether a proposed mark may conflict with another registered mark in the same or a similar class. This section explains how the classification system works and what you need to know about it before submitting your application.

1. What Are Classes?

Classes are legal categories of goods or services. For trademark registration purposes the PTO uses the International Schedule of Classes of Goods and Services which contains 42 classes: 34 for goods and eight for services. When you register your mark with the PTO, you can (but need not) specify which class or classes correspond to the goods or services on which you use (or intend to use) your mark. If you do not specify a class in your application, one will be chosen for you by the PTO Examiner. The Examiner will base his or her class choice on the description of goods and/ or services you provided in your application.

Because deciding which class your goods or services belong in can sometimes be confusing, we list a variety of resources in Section C3 below to help you effectively choose a class (or classes) under which to register your mark.

2. The Role of Classes in the Trademark Registration Process

Before registering your mark, the Examiner will look at all other previously registered and pending marks (applications that have been filed but which are awaiting official action), to answer this question: Does your mark look like, sound like or have a similar meaning as another registered or pending mark? If not, then the mark will have cleared this particular registration hurdle. If, however, a similarity is found between your mark and an existing mark, the Examiner will go on to another question: Will customers likely be confused by the use of the two marks? If so, then registration will be denied. If, however, the marks are being used in widely divergent marketing contexts, then registration may be approved, since customer confusion would be unlikely.

The PTO's classification system helps the Examiner figure out the likelihood of confusion between the two marks by indicating whether the two marks will be used in similar marketing contexts. Generally speaking, the more similar the goods or services represented by the two marks, the more likely that they will be marketed in similar contexts—and the greater the chance of customer confusion.

The purpose of the International Schedule of Classes of Goods and Services is to group together in the same class goods or services that are offered through the same channels of trade and to the same general types of consumers. The International Schedule helps the PTO determine whether or not the specific goods or services associated with conflicting marks are so closely related to each other (for example, they are likely to be marketed in the same channels and sold to the same consumers) that the likelihood of confusion is too high—which would mean the last mark seeking registration would be rejected.

EXAMPLE: Mark is a jeweler with a line of handmade jewelry (necklaces, bracelets and earrings) which feature small, black rubber parts with an industrial look. He calls this special line of jewelry The Rub. Jackie's Tool Shop, Inc., has designed and manufactured a line of hand tools with rubber handles for three years and has a registered trademark for the name of the line, The Rub, under Class 8, for hand tools. Mark would like to register the mark, The Rub, for his line of jewelry. Can he still do so, even though Jackie's has already registered it?

Mark will likely succeed in registering his mark if Jackie's mark is the only obstacle to registration. Mark's line of jewelry would be registered under Class 14, for jewelry. The fact that Jackie's mark is registered under Class 8 and Mark's mark for the jewelry line would be registered under Class 14 indicates that these goods are not marketed in the same channels and to the same consumers. Jackie's hand tools are marketed to hardware stores, home improvement stores and the hardware section of department stores. Mark's jewelry is marketed to jewelry and clothing boutiques.

The fact that the marketing contexts do not overlap indicates that consumers would not likely be confused by the use of the same mark on both goods.

To summarize, if your mark proves to be too similar to another mark that is already registered with the PTO, and the marks belong in the same class or in related classes, your application will likely be rejected. Likewise, if your mark proves to be relatively unique and distinctive and is not too similar to any other registered marks in the same class or a related class, your mark will be registered and applications filed after yours containing marks too similar to yours will be rejected.

3. How to Choose the Appropriate Class

It may take a little study to pick the best class for your good or service. For instance, does a belt made of woven cord belong under Class 22, which includes cordage and fibers? As it turns out the answer is no because the cord is made into clothing, which belongs in Class 25.

Similarly, if a mark represents a new type of service or product, it may be difficult to decide how to categorize it. For example, about 30 years ago the service mark Synanon was registered for use in connection with drug rehabilitation services. At the time, drug rehabilitation was a novel service and placed in the miscellaneous category, Class 42. But today the same service would be assigned to Class 41, education services.

To place a product or service within its appropriate classification, follow these steps:

Step 1: Study the list of classifications in the International Schedule of Classes of Goods and Services in the Appendix. See whether the goods or services for which the mark is being used naturally fits into one of the groupings.

Step 2: If you are unsure, use the resources listed below.

Considering Potential Conflicts When Choosing a Class

As mentioned in Chapter 10, Section B, the PTO typically views marks which are identical or very similar to one another, and which are also in the same class as each other, as potentially confusing to customers, which means the mark will be rejected for registration. For example, the owner of Titan brand cigarettes was able to stop a cigar maker from using the Titan mark. Cigars and cigarettes are in the same PTO class, Class 34, which also encompasses "tobacco, raw or manufactured, smoker's articles, and matches." It is therefore important for you to know that if you conduct a search for registered trademarks that are the same or similar to your mark and you find one or more that are also registered in the same class as your mark would be, then you are running a high risk of rejection.

It's also important to understand that two products or services in the same or different classes does not, by itself, establish that the two marks are legally in conflict or free of conflict. For example, because the international classification system has packed all goods and services into only 42 classes, combining for example, abrasive cleansers and cosmetics, products within the same class may be marketed in totally different ways. So, in evaluating a conflict, you may at least argue that a trademark for a scouring powder that is similar to a trademark for lipstick won't confuse customers.

However, even if your proposed mark falls into a different class than another mark, we recommend that you not use your mark if it is very similar to the other mark and would appear in the same marketing channels. Even if the PTO registers your mark and your mark is in a different class, the existing mark owner may still sue you for infringement (using his mark without permission and in conflict with his rights). Keep in mind that the prohibitive cost of litigation usually makes borderline decisions too risky.

Step 3: If you are still not sure, pick the three most likely classes and use these as possibilities. You can then discuss these possibilities with a PTO clerk at the Trademark Assistance Center (703-308-9000). Alternatively, you can leave Block 2 for Class in your application blank, and the PTO Examiner will fill it in for you.

If after using the International Schedule of Classes of Goods and Services you still aren't sure which class to choose, there are a number of resources available to help you.

a. Acceptable Identification of Goods & Services Manual

Probably the best source for finding the right class or classes for your goods or services is the list of approved descriptions the PTO has prepared for its Examiners to use when reviewing applications. This list is found in the *U.S. Patent & Trademark Office Acceptable Identification of Goods and Services Manual.* This manual contains an alphabetical listing of goods and services, their descriptions, the proper class for each, a designation of "A," "D" or "M" indicating that the listing was either added, deleted or modified and the date of the change. The "added" designation means that the class is a new class on the list. The "deleted" designation means that the class is no longer available (so you can't use it). The "modified" designation means that the class was somehow changed recently. Perhaps it was broadened to include more types of goods or services, or perhaps its scope was pared down to include fewer goods or services.

The manual is available for browsing and searching on the PTO's website (its address is listed below where we provide searching tips). Searching is recommended, since browsing can be cumbersome with such a large document. Instructions for searching the manual on the web are given below. You can also order a hard copy edition of the manual for $40 plus shipping costs from the International Trademark Association, New York, N.Y. (212-986-5880). Your nearest Patent and Trademark Depository Library (see Appendix B for a listing) should also have a copy. This manual is not available in hard copy from the PTO. The manual has over 13,000 listings and if you are only planning to prepare one application, purchasing it is probably unnecessary.

The hard copy version of the manual is organized into two categories—goods or services—and within each category the common names used for the goods and services are in alphabetical order. To find the appropriate class for your product or service, you would look in the relevant category (goods or services) and then look for the common description of your product or service. For example, if you designed and manufactured snowboard boots and wished to register a trademark for the boots, you would look under the goods list for "snowboard boots" (or, for a broader category, simply "boots"). Under the listing for "snowboard boots," you would find "G 025 Snowboard boots A 1997-01-02." The "G" stands for "Good" (as opposed to a service). The number "025" is the international class number given to snowboard boots by the PTO. "A," as explained above, stands for "Added." The date "1997-01-02," is the date this listing was added to the manual, January 2, 1997.

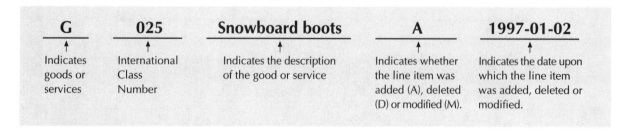

To search the PTO's website for the same information, simply go to its website at http://www.uspto.gov/web/offices/tac/doc/gsmanual/, and choose the "Search" button at the bottom of the page. Enter a word or words in the "Search For" box that you would use to identify your good or service—for example, "wrench," "accounting," or "telephone"—using an "and" or "or" between words. This technique is sometimes termed "Boolean searching." By using the "and" between words, you search for listings in the manual that contain all of the words you type in. By using the "or" between words, you search for listings that contain any one of the words you

type in, but not necessarily all of them. After you click on the "Search" button on the left of the screen, the search engine will return a list of class information for the product or service you entered. (Samples appear below.)

For example, if you wanted to register a trademark for your website design and hosting service and you wanted to find out what class the PTO considers appropriate for this service, you could use the search words, "computer and network." Using the general terms, "computer" and "network" provides you with a broad base of possible results, making your search more fruitful.

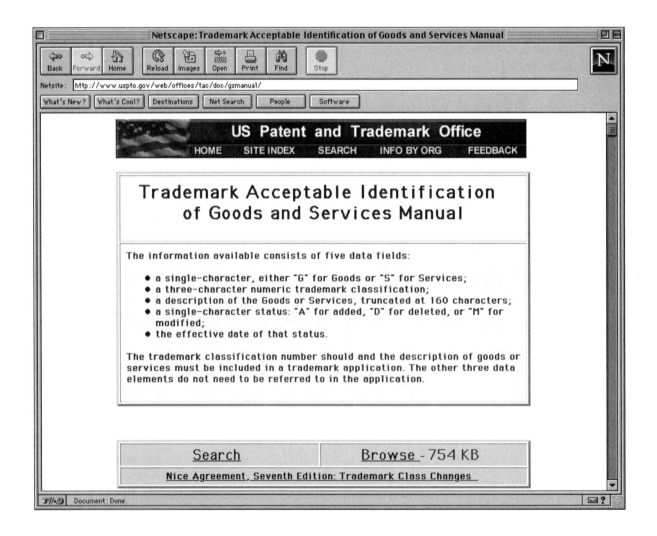

The results you would find are shown below.

The second listing from the top (with an arrow pointing to it) shows the correct information for your website design service. The appropriate class is Class 42. The fourth listing from the top (also pointed to with an arrow) demonstrates the correct information for your website hosting service. The appropriate class is, again, Class 42.

Suppose, as another example, that you have created a line of designer paper coffee filters for use in automatic drip coffee makers. Your filter paper is printed with retro, playful and unique designs to make your coffee filters more interesting to look at and fun to use. You want to register

the mark for your line of paper coffee filters, Zoo Filters. To find out what class the PTO deems correct for this product (good) and what description to use for your application, you could simply do a search using the word "coffee."

Your search would produce the results shown on the next page. About two-thirds down this list, indicated by an arrow, is the item you would be looking for. It states, "G 016 Filters for coffee makers (Paper) A 1991-04-02." From this line item, you can see that the PTO considers Class 16 as the appropriate class for paper coffee filters. Note that a simple search using "coffee and filter" would have produced only the line item highlighted

---

Trademark Acceptable Identification of Goods and Services Manual
Search Results

The S field indicates the status of the record: A=added, M=modified, D=deleted. The Date field indicates the date of that status. Minor corrections to an entry, e.g., typos, are not considered changes in status.

T IC GOODS S DATE

Result of search for "computer and network":

S 038 Broadcasting programs via a global computer network A 1997-01-02

→ S 042 Computer services, namely, designing and implementing network web pages for others A 1997-01-02

S 042 Computer services, namely, providing search engines for obtaining data on a global computer network A 1997-01-02

→ S 042 Hosting the websites of others on a computer server for a global computer network A 1997-01-02

S 041 Programming [scheduling of programs] on a global computer network A 1997-01-02

S 035 Promoting the goods and services of others by preparing and placing advertisements in an electronic magazine accessed through a global computer network A 1995-09-01

S 041 Providing a computer game that may be accessed network-wide by network users A 1995-01-01

S 042 Providing computer software [indicate specific subject or function] that may be downloaded from a global computer network D 1997-01-02

S 042 Providing multiple-user access to a global computer information network for the transfer and dissemination of a wide range of information A 1994-10-01

S 038 Providing telecommunications connections to a global computer network A 1996-02-20

above, and not the rest of the items, making your search more efficient and useful. However, we recommend using the more general search, such as our search for "coffee," as it may turn up items that are relevant to your product but that don't contain more specific wording.

b.   Search for Classes Used by Competitors

If the *U.S. Patent & Trademark Office Acceptable Identification of Goods and Services Manual* doesn't do the trick for you, you might consider examining the database of marks registered with the PTO to find out what classes have been assigned to the marks registered by your competitors. Also, once you conduct a trademark search in the course of adopting your mark, the report generated by that search may provide some good tips as to what class you should use.

If you have access to the World Wide Web, you also have access to a free database of marks that have already been registered with the PTO. This database is updated every two months and is available at http://www.uspto.gov/. Once you get to the PTO's homepage, choose the "Trademarks" button to your left. This will lead you to the Trademarks Information page. Choose "Search U.S. Trademarks" at the top of this page. This link will lead you to the PTO's Web Trademark Database page.

Once you get to that page, follow these steps to find out what classes have been assigned to a competing mark:

- Use the "Combined Marks" search.
- Select the "Registered Marks" database.
- To the right of the "Words in the Marks" line, type in one of the distinctive words used as a mark on a competing product.
- Use the pull-down menu located next to the "Results must contain:" line. Choose the "All of these words" option.
- Click the "Search" button to the right.
- Repeat this process for each competing product.

EXAMPLE: You have created a new kind of coloring crayon that makes the colors brighter when applied to any type of paper or poster board. You know that Crayola has been making crayons for decades. You type in the word "Crayola" in the "Words in the Marks" box, select the "All of these words" choice in the Results menu and click on the Search button. You will get a 31-item list of all the registered trademarks containing the term "Crayola." If you look at registration number 1279429—Crayola, you will learn that crayons have been assigned to international class 016.

Again, for more complete instructions on all aspects of trademark searching, see *Trademark: Legal Care for Your Business and Product Name* by Stephen Elias and Kate McGrath.

c.   Trademark Assistance Center

If after reading this section you are still in doubt about the proper class or classes for your product or service, you can call the Trademark Assistance Center of the PTO (703-308-9000), describe the product or service and ask them which class or classes may be involved. The trademark information specialist will answer your question and normally give you sound advice. Unfortunately, you don't have the legal right to rely on this opinion. If the person who eventually examines your application in the Patent and Trademark Office disagrees with the answer you were given, you will have to assign a different class to the product or service.

Record the details of all advice you receive from the PTO. Always write down the date you called and the full name of the person who provided you with advice, in case the Examiner later disagrees with what you were told. You may not convince the Examiner that you are right, but he or she will probably be impressed with your attempts to get correct information, and may consequently treat you with more respect.

**Trademark Acceptable Identification of Goods and Services Manual
Search Results**

The S field indicates the status of the record: A=added, M=modified, D=deleted. The Date field indicates the date of that status. Minor corrections to an entry, e.g., typos, are not considered changes in status.

T IC GOODS S DATE

Result of search for "coffee":

G 030 Chicory based coffee substitute A 1991-04-02

G 030 Coffee beans A 1996-02-20

G 021 Coffee cups A 1991-04-02

G 021 Coffee grinders (Hand-operated) A 1991-04-02

G 007 Coffee grinders for commercial use (Electric) A 1991-04-02

G 007 Coffee grinders for commercial use (Power-operated) A 1991-04-02

G 007 Coffee grinders for domestic use (Electric) A 1991-04-02

G 011 Coffee makers for commercial use (Electric) A 1991-04-02

G 011 Coffee makers for domestic use (Electric) A 1991-04-02

G 021 Coffee measures [domestic] A 1991-04-02

G 011 Coffee percolators (Electric) A 1991-04-02

G 021 Coffee percolators (Non-electric) A 1991-04-02

G 011 Coffee pots (Electric) A 1991-04-02

G 014 Coffee pots of precious metal A 1991-04-02

G 021 Coffee pots, not of precious metal (Non-electric) A 1991-04-02

G 011 Coffee roasting ovens A 1991-04-02

G 021 Coffee servers not of precious metal (Non-electric) A 1991-04-02

G 014 Coffee servers of precious metal (Non-electric) A 1991-04-02

G 021 Coffee services not of precious metal A 1991-04-02

G 014 Coffee services of precious metal A 1991-04-02

G 021 Coffee stirrers A 1991-04-02

G 030 Coffee substitutes [grain or chicory based] A 1991-04-02

G 030 Coffee A 1991-04-02

G 021 Cups (Coffee) A 1991-04-02

→ G 016 Filters for coffee makers (Paper) A 1991-04-02

G 021 Grinders (Hand-operated coffee) A 1991-04-02

G 007 Grinders for commercial use (Electric coffee) A 1991-04-02

G 007 Grinders for domestic use (Electric coffee) A 1991-04-02

G 011 Ovens (Coffee roasting) A 1991-04-02

G 011 Percolators (Electric coffee) A 1991-04-02

G 021 Percolators (Non-electric coffee) A 1991-04-02

G 011 Pots (Electric coffee) A 1991-04-02

G 021 Pots not of precious metal (Coffee) A 1991-04-02

G 014 Pots of precious metal (Coffee) A 1991-04-02

G 021 Stirrers (Coffee) A 1991-04-02

S 040 Coffee roasting and processing A 1991-04-02

4. Multiple Class Applications

It is possible to apply for registration of a mark under more than one class. The PTO does not like to register marks that are identical to registered marks in the same classes—which means you can prevent registration of conflicting marks by expanding the number of classes you register under. Also, by registering in a number of classes, potential users of the same or similar mark for goods or services in those classes will be discouraged because of your broad registration.

> **EXAMPLE:** Etta, who both sells computer software and offers consulting services under the mark Quick-Bytes, registers the mark under Class 9 (electrical and scientific apparatus). This registration may keep the same or similar marks used on computer software and other related products from being registered by the PTO. But it may not keep the PTO from registering the mark in connection with computer services. If Etta also registers the Quick-Bytes mark under the appropriate service class (Class 35 or Class 41), she may be able to achieve some protection against the registration of the same mark for computer services. Also, Etta will discourage would-be users of her mark for services within that additional service class.

The number of classes you should include in your initial application depends on your circumstances. The down side of registering under more than one class is that an additional application fee (currently $245) must be paid for each additional class. For instance, the fee for a use application seeking to register a mark under three classes will be $735 (three times $245). For this reason, applicants sometimes apply under one class and then wait to see if the mark (and their business) is successful enough to warrant broadening the scope of their registration by applying under other classes as well.

> **EXAMPLE:** Maria and Conner started their business six months ago publishing and digitally delivering a zine (a web-based magazine) called *Boardz. Boardz* is a zine devoted to snowboarding, snowboarders and snowboarding equipment. Maria and Conner have decided to name their publishing business Boardz as well. Since Maria and Conner are providing the service of publishing a zine that is both educational and entertaining, the proper class for registering the mark *Boardz* as used for the name of their publishing service is International Class 41. To register the mark Boardz as used for the zine itself, the proper class would be International Class 16. But Maria and Conner only have enough money budgeted to pay for registration under one class. Since their main concern is reserving the name of the zine (because it is their flagship publication), Maria and Conner have decided to pursue registration only under Class 16 for now. They will apply to register under Class 41 at a later time, when their budget allows.

Applicants who can afford the additional fees occasioned by a multiple class registration may wisely register in more than one class with the idea that this will block future applicants as much as possible. The ability to block future applicants is a powerful use of multiple class applications because it keeps others from registering the mark before you. Nonetheless, it is best to remember that simply filing for registration under multiple classes does not, by itself, protect you in an infringement lawsuit. (See Chapter 1, Section C, for an explanation of what infringement means.) This is because registration alone does not give you superior rights over everyone else to use your mark. The first *to use* the mark anywhere has superior rights. See Chapter 1, Section B2, for more information about first use.

EXAMPLE: Toyco has developed a new line of video games based on a character named Torchier. Each game is labeled with the name Torchier. The games are just about ready to ship, well before Toyco has had a chance to develop its line of Torchier action figures, toy planes, toy cars, shirts, gloves, hats and costumes. Toyco is prepared to register the mark for its video games under International Class 9. Because it wants to reserve the mark for all of the related toys and clothing items, it decides to apply for registration of the mark under Classes 25 and 28 as well. Doing so will more likely keep competitors from trying to register the mark under those classes or possibly keep them from using the Torchier mark for toys and clothing items.

If you have decided that you will apply under more than one class, the next decision you need to make is whether or not to file a multiple class application (one application with more than one class listed on the application) *or* to file separate applications for each class. The filing fees will be the same regardless of which strategy you choose, since you must pay the $245 filing fee per class (not per application). Of course, if you are planning to file under some classes now and some classes later, you will necessarily file separate applications.

Despite the extra paperwork, we recommend that you file separate applications, and here's why:

- By doing so, each application will be examined separately, and it's possible that one or

more of the applications will be ready for publication and registration before the others. (For a brief explanation of the examination process, including publication and registration, see the introductory section of Chapter 4 or Chapter 5.) If you file a multiple class application, publication and registration for the mark will be delayed until all classes have been cleared.

- Delays caused by opposition to registration will apply only to the mark in a particular class, rather than to the whole application with multiple classes. (See Chapter 12, Section B, for more information about oppositions.)

- For intent-to-use applications, delays in filing an Allegation of Use for all classes could be avoided if one or two classes were ready for such a filing. (See Chapter 11, Sections B and C, for more information about the Allegation of Use form.)

EXAMPLE: Janice owns her own business designing and manufacturing handbags and other accessories from recycled rubber products (such as tires). The name of her manufacturing and design service and product line is PetroWear. Janice decides to apply for trademark registration under Class 42 for her design and manufacturing services and under Classes 17 and 22 for her rubber handbags and accessories. Since the mark is already in use for all classes, she will file an Actual Use Application (see Section B, above, and Chapter 4). Janice decides to file separate applications for each class (one application each for Classes 42, 17 and 22) in case filing under one particular class proves problematic. That way, the applications for the remaining, problem-free classes can move forward.

If you decide that you'd rather file a multiple class application, you'll find more information about how to prepare a multiple class application in Chapter 4 (if you are applying based on use) or Chapter 5 (if you are applying on an intent-to-use basis).

D. Special Considerations for Special Marks

When your mark includes a special typeface, graphic design or product configuration, you will have additional issues to consider before filling out your application.

1. Name Marks Combined With Unusual Typefaces

If your name mark uses an unusual typeface, your mark has two important aspects—the words that constitute the name, and the look and feel of the typeface. If money is no object, register both separately. But if funds are short—as they usually are—you will probably want to choose one or the other. As a general rule you will be better off registering the unadorned name. This way, you can use the name in many different configurations and be assured the name (though not the design element) is fully protected. If the only registration for your name is in the unusual typeface, then only that exact image is protected. In other words, if someone else used the name without the unusual typeface, you would not be able to stop them from doing so. For the broadest possible protection for a name with a particular typeface, you will need to make new registrations each time your name is used in a different configuration.

2. Name Marks Combined With Graphic Designs

If you use your name with a graphic image, you will have the same issues discussed above in the previous section. You have several choices when it is time to register:

- **register the name alone:** this provides protection for the name in whatever configuration you use it, but it does not protect any graphic that you use with it.
- **register the combined name/graphic image:** this protects the mark in its entirety and in the specific way that it is represented. It will not offer protection for the words alone, without the graphic aspects.
- **register both the name and name/graphic image combination:** if money is no object, this option is the best. You will then have protection for the entire name/graphic image you've developed, as well as the name by itself and any other configuration you use it in.

What if money is tight and you must choose between the first two options above? If money counts, you should probably start with the combination name/graphic image *if* the graphic image is distinctive. If you've developed a really unique and great graphic for your mark, you certainly want to protect it as soon as possible to keep others from trying to copy you. If the graphics are not particularly distinctive, however, then register the name by itself. The idea is to get the most mileage for your initial registration and if you are limited to one mark, it is wise to register the mark that has the most distinctive elements.

3. Product Configurations

Product configurations can be registered trademarks by themselves, such as the unique design of the Coca-Cola bottle and the fish shape of Pepperidge Farm's goldfish crackers. Here are some important tips for you to consider if what you want to register is a product configuration. More information is available to you in either Chapter 4 (for use applicants) or Chapter 5 (for intent-to-use applicants).

1. If you want to register your product configuration as a trademark, be prepared to furnish the following information (upon

request) to the trademark Examiner, along with a cover letter which closely follows the format of the example given in Chapter 8, Section D2:

- whether the design is also the subject of a design or utility patent (if it is, you'll have a hard time getting it registered as a trademark)
- similar designs used by competitors, and
- your advertising and promotional material.

2. If your product design is novel, then you should research patent law to determine if the design is entitled to a patent. (See the caution below, "Product Configurations: Proceed With Caution.") For more information about design patent protection, see *Patent It Yourself* by David Pressman (Nolo).

3. Avoid using product configurations that are unique to competitors—especially competitors who have invested time and money in the promotion of those product shapes or containers.

4. When possible use the product configuration in combination with your name—for example, Levi's distinctive brass buttons always feature the name "Levi's."

⚠ **Product Configurations: Proceed With Caution.** Because there is some uncertainty as to the protectibility of patentable product configurations under trademark laws, we suggest you consult an attorney if you are seeking trademark protection for a product configuration that you believe might also be patentable.

E. Tips to Keep In Mind

Now that you're familiar with some basic issues involved in the registration process, you're just about ready to learn the details of each type of application. Before you move on, store these tips in your memory bank:

- There is a time factor involved in the registration process. Once you decide to register your mark, it is wise to do so as quickly as possible. Life is full of coincidences. If someone else is in a hurry to register a mark that is the same as or similar to yours, your application will receive priority if the PTO receives it first.
- You will be happy to learn that attorneys are seldom needed to accomplish a federal registration. It is quite common for non-attorneys to apply for and receive certificates of registration. In fact, the trademark attorneys at the PTO are usually friendly and helpful to non-attorneys.
- You can reach the PTO's automated trademark information line at 703-308-HELP. The number for the Trademark Assistance Center (where you will receive one-on-one help from a staff person) is 703-308-9000.

F. The Application Form

You may use one of three different types of application forms to register your trademark: an office application, an online application, or a non-office application. This section explains these three different options.

1. PTO Form 1478: Office Application

The registration application form issued by the PTO, Form 1478—"Trademark/Service Mark Application, Principal Register, With Declaration" —is commonly called an office application. The form must be completed in English. It will be accepted if it is neatly handwritten, but the PTO prefers it to be typed. The form does not have numbered blanks, but is divided into several blocks of information.

A copy of the application form is in the Appendix of this book. Simply tear it out and make several photocopies, so if you make a mistake on one copy, you'll still have several more to use.

You can also download Form 1478 from the PTO's website at: http://www.uspto.gov/. From the home page, choose "Download Forms" from the menu on the left side of the homepage. Click on the link, "Trademark Related Forms" or scroll down the page until you reach the pink section titled, "Trademark Related Forms." Look at the column on the far right of the chart. Choose the form marked "PTO/TM/1478" and named "Trademark/Service Mark Application, Principal Register, with Declaration."

You will need Adobe's free Acrobat reader in order to view the forms on your computer and print them on your printer. If you do not have the reader, simply click on the term, "Adobe's free Acrobat reader" in the first paragraph of the home page and you will receive further instructions on how to obtain the reader you need for free. Keep in mind that with this type of application, you will not be able to fill out the form(s) online. (To fill out the form online, you'll need to use the online application, discussed below.) To fill the form(s) out, you must first print them out, and then either type the information using a typewriter, or legibly handwrite the information onto the form.

2. Online Application

The Trademark Electronic Application System (TEAS) is a streamlined system for applying for trademark registration. The PTO offers two types of electronic applications. One, called PrinTEAS, allows you to fill out the form online, print it out and send it to the PTO via U.S. mail. The other method, e-TEAS, is similar, except that to submit it you don't need to print it out and mail it, you simply file it electronically. To use PrinTEAS and e-TEAS, you must have access to the Internet and use either Netscape Navigator (Version 3.0 or most recent) or Microsoft Internet Explorer (Version 4.0 or most recent) as your browser. If

you have the access outlined above, we recommend you try one of these online application systems.

While the PrinTEAS and e-TEAS systems are simple to use, you will still need to do the same preparations for filing as you would to file a regular application. Before going to PrinTEAS or e-TEAS, you should complete the chapter for your type of application (either use or intent-to-use), and jot down the information on a scratch piece of paper or onto the blank application form in the back of this book. Then use the information you've entered to help your online application experience go faster. The PTO offers online help for questions you may have about using the system itself.

The PTO's website also offers other trademark forms for downloading. You will find a list of these forms in the Appendix.

3. Non-Office Application

While you may simply fill in the PTO's standard trademark registration form (Form 1478, office application), you may also submit the same information on clean sheets of letter-size paper, as long as you follow certain guidelines. This is called a non-office application. Putting together a non-office application with your word processor can be a lot easier than trying to fill out the PTO's office form with a typewriter. Your written application must be in English, plainly written or typed on one side of letter-sized paper. The information must be double-spaced with at least a one and one-half inch margin on the left-hand side and top of the page. The pages should be consecutively numbered. You will find a sample non-office application at the end of this chapter. The instructions in Chapters 4 and 5 apply equally to office, online and non-office applications unless otherwise noted. Special tips for non-office applications are marked by a special icon.

PTO Form 1478: Office Application, Page 1

TRADEMARK/SERVICE MARK APPLICATION, PRINCIPAL REGISTER, WITH DECLARATION	MARK (Word(s) and/or Design)	CLASS NO. (If known)

TO THE ASSISTANT COMMISSIONER FOR TRADEMARKS:

APPLICANT'S NAME:

APPLICANT'S MAILING ADDRESS:

(Display address exactly as it should appear on registration)

_____

_____

_____

APPLICANT'S ENTITY TYPE: (**Check one** and supply requested information)

	Individual - Citizen of (Country)
	Partnership - State where organized (Country, if appropriate):_____ Names and Citizenship (Country) of General Partners:_____
	Corporation - State (Country, if appropriate) of Incorporation:
	Other (Specify Nature of Entity and Domicile):

GOODS AND/OR SERVICES:

Applicant requests registration of the trademark/service mark shown in the accompanying drawing in the United States Patent and Trademark Office on the Principal Register established by the Act of July 5, 1946 (15 U.S.C. 1051 et. seq., as amended) for the following goods/services (SPECIFIC GOODS AND/OR SERVICES MUST BE INSERTED HERE) :

_____

_____

_____

_____

_____

BASIS FOR APPLICATION: (Check boxes which apply, **but never both the first AND second boxes,** and supply requested information related to each box checked in.)

[ ] Applicant is using the mark in commerce on or in connection with the above identified goods/services. (15 U.S.C. 1051(a), as amended.) Three specimens showing the mark as used in commerce are submitted with this application.
- Date of first use of the mark in commerce which the U.S. Congress may regulate (for example, interstate or between the U.S. and a foreign country):_____
- Specify the type of commerce:_____ (for example, interstate or between the U.S. and a specified foreign country)
- Date of first use anywhere (the same as or before use in commerce date):_____
- Specify manner or mode of use of mark on or in connection with the goods/services:_____

(for example, trademark is applied to labels, service mark is used in advertisements)

[ ] Applicant has a bona fide intention to use the mark in commerce on or in connection with the above identified goods/services.(15 U.S.C. 1051(b), as amended.)
- Specify intended manner or mode of use of mark on or in connection with the goods/services:_____

(for example, trademark will be applied to labels, service mark will be used in advertisements)

[ ] Applicant has a bona fide intention to use the mark in commerce on or in connection with the above identified goods/services, and asserts a claim of priority based upon a foreign application in accordance with 15 U.S.C. 1126(d), as amended.
- Country of foreign filing:_____ • Date of foreign filing:_____

[ ] Applicant has a bona fide intention to use the mark in commerce on or in connection with the above identified goods/services and, accompanying this application, submits a certification or certified copy of a foreign registration in accordance with 15 U.S.C 1126(e), as amended.
- Country of registration:_____ • Registration number:_____

NOTE: Declaration, on Reverse Side, MUST be Signed

PTO Form 1478 (REV 6/96)   U.S. DEPARTMENT OF COMMERCE/Patent and Trademark Office
OMB No. 0651-0009 (Exp. 06/30/98) There is no requirement to respond to this collection of information unless a currently valid OMB Number is displayed.

PTO Form 1478: Office Application, Page 2

DECLARATION

The undersigned being hereby warned that willful false statements and the like so made are punishable by fine or imprisonment, or both, under 18 U.S.C. 1001, and that such willful false statements may jeopardize the validity of the application or any resulting registration, declares that he/she is properly authorized to execute this application on behalf of the applicant; he/she believes the applicant to be the owner of the trademark/service mark sought to be registered, or if the application is being filed under 15 U.S.C. 1051(b), he/she believes the applicant to be entitled to use such mark in commerce; to the best of his/her knowledge and belief no other person, firm, corporation, or association has the right to use the above identified mark in commerce, either in the identical form thereof or in such near resemblance thereto as to be likely, when used on or in connection with the goods/services of such other person, to cause confusion, or to cause mistake, or to deceive; and that all statements made of his/her own knowledge are true and that all statements made on information and belief are believed to be true.

_____   _____
DATE   SIGNATURE

_____   _____
TELEPHONE NUMBER   PRINT OR TYPE NAME AND POSITION

INSTRUCTIONS AND INFORMATION FOR APPLICANT

TO RECEIVE A FILING DATE, THE APPLICATION MUST BE COMPLETED AND SIGNED BY THE APPLICANT AND SUBMITTED ALONG WITH:

1. The prescribed **FEE ($245.00)** for each class of goods/services listed in the application;
2. A **DRAWING PAGE** displaying the mark in conformance with 37 CFR 2.52;
3. If the application is based on use of the mark in commerce, **THREE (3) SPECIMENS** (evidence) of the mark as used in commerce for each class of goods/services listed in the application. All three specimens may be the same. Examples of good specimens include: (a) labels showing the mark which are placed on the goods; (b) photographs of the mark as it appears on the goods, (c) brochures or advertisements showing the mark as used in connection with the services.
4. An **APPLICATION WITH DECLARATION** (this form) - The application must be signed in order for the application to receive a filing date. Only the following persons may sign the declaration, depending on the applicant's legal entity: (a) the individual applicant; (b) an officer of the corporate applicant; (c) one general partner of a partnership applicant; (d) all joint applicants.

SEND APPLICATION FORM, DRAWING PAGE, FEE, AND SPECIMENS (IF APPROPRIATE) TO:

**Assistant Commissioner for Trademarks
Box New App/Fee
2900 Crystal Drive
Arlington, VA 22202-3513**

Additional information concerning the requirements for filing an application is available in a booklet entitled **Basic Facts About Registering a Trademark,** which may be obtained by writing to the above address or by calling: (703) 308-HELP.

This form is estimated to take an average of 1 hour to complete, including time required for reading and understanding instructons, gathering necessary information, recordkeeping, and actually providing the information. Any comments on this form, including the amount of time required to complete this form, should be sent to the Office of Management and Organization, U.S. Patent and Trademark Office, U.S. Department of Commerce, Washington, D.C. 20231. Do NOT send completed forms to this address.

Non-Office Application

Mark: _____

Class No.: (If known) _____

TO THE ASSISTANT SECRETARY AND COMMISSIONER
OF PATENTS AND TRADEMARKS:

(Name of corporation)

(State or country of incorporation)

(Business address of corporation)

The above identified applicant has adopted and is using the trademark shown in the accompanying drawing for the following goods *[or services]*: _____ ,
and requests that said mark be registered in the United States Patent and Trademark Office on the Principal Register established by the Act of July 5, 1946.

The trademark was first used on the goods on *[Date]*; was first used on the goods in _____ *[Type of commerce]* commerce on _____ *[Date]*; and is now in use in such commerce.

The mark is used by applying it to _____ *[Specify mode and manner of use]* and three specimens showing the mark as actually used are presented here with this application.

_____ *[Name of officer of corporation]* being hereby warned that willful false statements and the like so made are punishable by fine or imprisonment, or both, under Section 1001 of Title 18 of the United States Code and that such willful false statements may jeopardize the validity of the application or any registration resulting therefrom, states that he/she is _____ *[Official title]* of applicant corporation and is authorized to execute this instrument on behalf of said corporation; he/she believes said corporation to be the owner of the mark sought to be registered; that said mark is in use in the type of commerce specified in this application; to the best of his/her knowledge and belief no other person, firm, corporation, or association has the right to use said mark in commerce either in the identical form thereof or in such near resemblance thereto as to be likely, when applied to the goods of such other person, to cause confusion, or to cause mistake, or to deceive; that the specimens or facsimiles accompanying this application show said mark as actually used in connection with the goods; the facts set forth in this application are true; and that all statements made of his/her own knowledge are true and all statements made on information and belief are believed to be true.

_____
[Name of Corporation]

By:_____
    [Signature of Officer of corporation, and official title of officer]

_____
[Date]

A Note About Trademark Form Updates

While this book will almost always contain the most current forms, there may be times when the PTO's release of new forms precedes a new printing or edition of this book. To make sure you have the most up-to-date forms, you can:

- visit the PTO's website at http://www. uspto.gov/.
- call the Trademark Assistance Center at 703-308-9000 (office hours are 8:30 a.m. to 5:00 p.m., Monday through Friday, except federal holidays).
- call the PTO's automated information system for patents and trademarks (operating 24 hours a day, seven days a week, including holidays) at 703-557-INFO.

- visit your local Patent and Trademark Depository Library (a list is in the Appendix). Look for a booklet titled "Basic Facts About Registering a Trademark." This booklet should contain the most current version of the trademark registration application form.

To check on the date of your form, look at the bottom left-hand corner of the form. You will see, in small type, "PTO Form 1478 (REV 6/96)." This tells you that this particular Form 1478 was last revised June 1996. Check this date against any other Forms 1478 that you find online or at the library, or ask the service representative at the Trademark Assistance Center about the current version date. The form with the later date of the two is the one you should use.

Choosing Your Specimens

When filing a use application, you must submit three specimens of your mark being used in commerce (defined in Chapter 2, Section B). If you plan to apply for registration under more than one trademark class (see Chapter 2, Section C), you will need to submit specimens showing use for each class. Picking the right specimens is very important, and can have a significant effect on the ultimate success or failure of your application. The Examiner will compare the information you provided in your application with the specimens which show how you're actually using your mark. In conjunction with the application form, the specimens will help the Examiner answer various questions about your application. In particular, the Examiner is interested in:

- whether or not the mark you want to register is in fact a mark
- whether or not you are actually using the mark
- whether the mark as shown on the specimen is exactly the same in form, color and style as the mark shown in the drawing you submit with your application (drawings are discussed in Chapter 6)
- the goods or services on or in connection with which the mark is being used, and
- whether other different, and possibly related, companies are also using the mark.

We recommend you pick your specimens now, before you start filling out your application, because doing so will ensure that you match the description of your mark in your application and the accompanying drawing with the specimens you've chosen. This is an important step, and one that the Examiner will most likely scrutinize when he or she receives your application.

This chapter will explain in more detail what a specimen is, how to choose the right specimens and how to choose the right format for the specimens.

Intent-to-use applicants do not need to send in specimens until the mark is put into actual use. The chapter that covers that process (Chapter 11) refers you back to this discussion for guidance in selecting your specimens. If you haven't yet read Chapter 5 on filling out your ITU application and Chapter 11 on what happens after you've filed the ITU application, you should do so before reading this chapter.

A. Showing That the Mark Is a Mark

One fundamental requirement for your specimens is to show that your mark is actually being used as a mark. What does that mean? Simply placing a catchy word or graphic on a product does not necessarily mean you are using it as a mark. A mark is distinguished from a merely ornamental graphic or display of words by its purpose, which is to identify the source of the goods or services to the consumer.

For example, the Nolo logo on this book consists of a small box containing a block-style representation of the scales of justice in black, white and red, and the name Nolo below the block. This logo is placed on every Nolo product, not as a decorative feature of the cover, but to tell the consumer that these products are published by Nolo. Thus, this logo is being used as a mark. But suppose, for example, that the cover of this book contained an illustration of the planet Earth as a design feature of the cover. Attempting to register this image as a trademark would be inappropriate because it is not being used to identify the source of this book, but is merely an ornamental feature of the cover.

Do not use photocopies, sketches or mock-ups —for a specimen, you must send the real thing. An exception to this rule is allowed when your specimen is too large or appears on a product that is too large to send to the PTO. In this case, you may take a photograph of the specimen and send it. (See Section C below.) This requirement serves to prove that you are actually using the mark.

B. Conforming the Specimen With the Drawing

The Examiner will look for consistency between the mark represented on your specimens and the drawing of the mark which must accompany your application. Drawings are covered in Chapter 6, but for now, just keep in mind that the drawing you submit with your application must match the mark shown in your specimens. If your trademark drawing shows the mark in plain, block letters, do not provide a specimen showing the mark with a distinct or unusual style or design. Likewise, if your drawing shows the mark in a distinctive design or in certain colors, your specimens should match that design or those colors.

C. Specimens for Marks on Goods (Trademarks)

A fundamental requirement for your specimens is that they show a direct connection between the mark itself and the goods you recite in your application. For example, if you are offering a new blend of coffee as a product and you have named your coffee Blast-Off Blend, your specimen should show the mark Blast-Off Blend along with information clearly showing that Blast-Off Blend is a coffee product as stated in your application. A good specimen would be the label on the bag containing the coffee.

Acceptable specimens usually include labels, tags or containers showing the mark. Specimens must be flat, so if you submit a container such as a box or a display, it must be flattened. Obviously, there may be many degrees of flatness, depending on the container and materials. Simply do the best you can under the circumstances. If you are dealing with an item that simply won't flatten, like a baseball, take a photograph. (See discussion below on photos.)

All three specimens may—but don't have to—be the same. Even specimens submitted for different classes may be the same. The specimens may

not exceed 8½ inches (21.6 cm) wide and 13 inches (33 cm) long, and must be flat. There is no minimum size.

Displays As Specimens for Goods

Displays such as banners and window displays may also be used as specimens, but with caution. The display must be meant to catch the buyer's attention where the sale is made (for instance, at the store), and the mark must be prominent and clearly connected to the goods. For example, if a window sign in a drugstore said, "See our All Ears earrings special!" that would probably qualify as an appropriate specimen. However, the line between displays and advertising can be fuzzy, and advertising is not sufficient for specimens of marks used for goods. (See the discussion below on unacceptable specimens for goods.) If you have a choice, use another type of specimen.

---

1. Photographic Specimens

If it's impractical to provide a specimen of the mark, three copies of a photograph showing the mark in use may be used. The photo may not exceed 8½" by 11". For example, if your Solve-it Solvent mark was used in connection with 55-gallon drums of solvent and printed only on the drums, you could submit a photograph of a drum or drums clearly showing the whole mark. The photograph must show the whole item, or enough of it so the Examiner can clearly see what is shown in the picture (for example, enough to make it clear that it is a storage drum), and all writing on the item must be visible. If a photograph of the whole item does not show the mark in enough detail, send one photo of the whole item and another photo close-up of the writing including the mark. The two photos together will constitute one specimen. If there is writing on more than one side, either send more than one photo, or place several items in one photo so they show all sides of the item on which writing appears.

> **EXAMPLE:** Suppose your mark, Solve-it Solvent, appears on the front and back of a 55-gallon drum in large type, surrounded by other writing describing the contents. Your first photo should portray three or four drums, each showing a different part of all the writing (Solve-it Solvent and the description). You would then want a few more photos from a closer range showing the Examiner all of the writing that appears on a typical drum. Keep in mind that all these photos together would constitute one specimen. If the writing could not be made legible for some reason, (maybe the writing is too small to photograph well), a separate piece of paper including all text on the drum should also be submitted.

The reason why all the writing has to be visible is that the PTO wants to see the context in which your mark is used to be sure it is consistent with the class under which you are registering the mark. (See Section B, above.)

2. Small Specimens

If the specimens are very small (such as clothing tags), put them in an envelope which is labeled "Specimens" and which contains your name and address, the mark and the date the application was signed. That should prevent their loss from the PTO file.

3. Movies and Video Tapes

Normally, the name of a movie or videotape will appear on the container. But sometimes marks appear only in the actual film or tape. In this situation, submit a film strip negative or a photo of a frame depicting the mark. If your mark includes motion, such as the NBC peacock with tail feathers spreading, submit a videotape of the mark.

Rubber Stamps and Stencils

If you place your mark on your goods by using a rubber stamp or stencil, you may submit a specimen of an impression of the stamp or stencil on a piece of paper. However, the Examiner may ask for proof that the goods themselves are imprinted in that manner. You may save yourself some trouble, avoiding an inquiry from the Examiner, if you submit a photograph showing the mark imprinted on the goods, along with an impression on paper for the close-up view.

4. Unacceptable Specimens for Marks on Goods

Unacceptable specimens of marks on goods include:

- advertising material, including anything that is produced for the sole purpose of telling potential buyers about your product, even if you package it with the goods (such as cards packaged with a new pen telling how wonderful it is and what it's made of)
- price lists, catalogs, trade directories and publicity releases
- instruction sheets
- internal company documents, including invoices and memos sent within an applicant company
- specimens showing the mark with the ® symbol. It is illegal to use the ® symbol until after your mark is officially registered

with the PTO (see Chapter 1); however, using the ™ next to the mark is okay

- any use of the mark merely to identify your business (not in direct connection with particular goods), including letterhead stationery, labels carrying only a company name and return address and bags and boxes used at store cash registers to carry sold merchandise.

D. Specimens for Marks Used for Services (Service Marks)

When offering a service, you obviously have no product to which you can affix a label. Acceptable specimens for services can include a variety of advertising and marketing materials such as newspaper and magazine ads, brochures, billboards, direct mail pieces and restaurant menus.

Like specimens for goods, all three specimens may—but don't have to—be the same. The specimens may not exceed 8½ inches (21.6 cm) wide and 13 inches (33 cm) long, and must be flat. There is no minimum size.

Letterhead stationery and business cards showing the mark may be used if the services are plainly reflected on them, since the name or symbol being claimed as a mark would, in that context, be used to identify the services provided—that is, as a mark rather than as a trade name. Trade names as such are not registrable. (See sidebar below on trade names.)

EXAMPLE 1: Etta's business cards for her personal computer consulting services include her mark Quick-Bytes and the text, "Consulting services for the PC user." The business cards would be accepted as specimens.

EXAMPLE 2: Toby's sports trivia 900-line grew and he had stationery printed including the line, "Sports R Us Gives You the Latest Sports Trivia 24 Hours a Day." The stationery would be accepted as a specimen.

A letter on stationery will even be accepted as a specimen for a service mark if the mark appears and the services are described in the letter. Assume Toby's letterhead only said "Sports R Us" and gave the address and phone number. He could submit a copy of a letter sent to a national sports magazine asking that his 900-number be listed in their directory, as long as the letter described the services.

Sports R Us
555 First Street
Sonoma, CA 95476

Dear Sirs:

As you may know, our sports trivia line, 900-555-7777, has been providing customers with sports trivia twenty-four hours a day for the past year. We would be honored if you would consider listing our trivia line and phone number in your directory of Sports Specialists.

---

1. Audio Tapes

Most marks appear in writing somewhere. If your mark represents a service, and it appears only in radio ads or in some other audio form, you may submit three audio tapes of the mark being used. You do not need to include any radio programming actually aired before or after your ad. You can just submit the working copy of the ad itself.

EXAMPLE: If Etta decides to advertise her computer consulting service only by radio, she would submit as specimens three copies of an audio tape of her ad.

2. Unacceptable Specimens for Services

The following items are unacceptable specimens for services:

- news releases or articles based on news releases
- documents showing trademark rather than service mark usage (use of the mark in connection with goods rather than services)
- invoices or similar documents such as packing slips
- specimens showing trade name usage only (use of the mark to identify a company, such as on letterhead); as discussed earlier, one exception to this is if the letterhead or the text of the letter printed on the letter-head stationery identifies the services repre-sented by the mark.

Trade Names

A trade name is the formal name a company uses to identify itself as a business. Trade names are not registrable as marks unless they are also used to market the company's goods or services —that is, identify the goods the company sells (trademark), or promote the company's services (service mark). It is, in fact, very common for a company's trade name and the mark used in promoting the company's services to be the same, which therefore makes the trade name registrable in its capacity as a mark. For example, a business known as Reliance Electric Repair almost surely uses that same name to market its services.

E. Websites as Specimens

You can submit a printout of a screen shot of your website as a specimen. The rules for presenting website specimens are the same as for any other specimens. Read Sections A and B above for a discussion of those considerations. Keep in mind that websites may not always make the best specimens. The look, feel and design of a website are often driven by aesthetic considerations, and not necessarily by the desire to satisfy the PTO's requirements for consistency, discussed above in Section B.

In the next paragraph, we discuss the types of design elements that make for strong website specimens. If your website does not exactly match our examples, don't fret. As long as it is clear from your website that a connection exists between the mark you wish to register and the goods and/or services you stated in your applica-tion, then using the website as a specimen should be okay.

If your mark is for a good, the mark should be prominently displayed along with the product— for example, a thumbnail photo of the product packaging with a label clearly showing the mark and a product description next to the photo which uses the mark prominently. If your mark is for a service, use it in close proximity to the introduction to and description of your services. For example, if your business provides home security installation services under the service name VigilEase Home Security, prominently display the service name at the top of your website and then use it in the body of your service description. For instance, "VigilEase Home Security services are designed to secure your home without imposing complicated procedures for you to learn." ■

Completing a Federal Trademark Use Application

If you are basing your application on your intent to use it within the next six months, you should skip this chapter and start with Chapter 5 which discusses intent-to-use applications.

This chapter walks you through the steps involved in completing an application for a trademark that's already been put into use. The process for use applications can be broken down as follows:

Step 1: You complete one application form.

Step 2: You file the application form with the U.S. Patent and Trademark Office, along with a drawing page, specimens of how your mark is being used and a fee of $245 (as of July 1999).

Step 3: You will likely be asked to make some changes in your application based on specific suggestions by the trademark Examiner.

Step 4: If all goes well and the trademark Examiner becomes satisfied that your application is complete and your mark is sound enough to register, your application will be approved for publication in the *Official Gazette*, which gives notice to the public of your application. The public then has 30 days to oppose your registration. If there is no opposition (only 3% of published marks are opposed), then your application will enter the next stage in the process.

Step 5: Assuming your application has not been opposed, the PTO will register the mark, issue a Certificate of Registration, and send the certificate to you about 12 weeks after the date the mark was first published. The Certificate of Registration contains most of the information you included in your application.

What Happens in an Opposition?

Companies intent on protecting their mark or marks and pursuing competing marks may hire an attorney or trademark monitoring service to routinely review the *Official Gazette*. If the company is alerted to any pending marks that may potentially conflict with their own, they may oppose the registration of that mark. An opposition begins with the filing of Form 4-17a, Opposition to the Registration of a Mark, With Declaration, along with a $200 filing fee. The rest involves a proceeding before the Trademark Trial and Appeal Board. We discuss oppositions in more detail in Chapter 12, Publication, Opposition & Registration.

 Are you really ready to file? If you have not already done so, read Chapter 2 to learn:

- the difference between an application based on actual use and one based on intent to use
- whether your product is a good, a service or both
- about the trademark classification system used by the U.S. Patent and Trademark Office
- the different rules for simple words, special typefaces, graphic designs and product configurations, and
- which type of application form to use.

You also should read Chapter 3 for information on the specimens you must submit with your application, and upon which you will base the descriptions in the application.

Finally, refer to Chapter 1 for a brief overview of trademark law and some instruction as to whether or not your proposed mark might qualify for trademark registration. For more in-depth information on trademark law in general, read

Trademark: Legal Care for Your Business and Product Name, by Stephen Elias and Kate McGrath (Nolo).

⚠ **New rules governing the trademark registration process are being proposed as this book goes to print (May 1999).** These rules will likely affect the most basic trademark application requirements, including signature, specimen and drawing requirements. The good news is that it looks like the PTO is poised to relax some of its more strict rules regarding trademark applications. The bad news is that we really don't know what the final rules will be until sometime between now and October 30, 1999. If you are using this book after October 30, 1999, please visit Nolo's website at http://www.nolo.com/ for the most updated information about the PTO's new rules and how they affect trademark registrations. To receive e-mail notification of when these changes go into effect, subscribe to *NoloBriefs,* Nolo's e-mail newsletter, at http://www.nolo.com/newsletter/join.cfm.

A. Completing the Use Application

This section goes step-by-step through the process of completing your registration application. As you follow our instructions, keep one point firmly in mind: consistency is key. You will be describing your mark, the goods and/or services upon which the mark is used and the manner or mode of use. You will also be submitting a drawing of your mark and specimens of its use with your application. (Drawings are discussed in Chapter 6, and specimens in Chapter 3.) The descriptions, drawings and specimens must be consistent with each other. If your application contains inconsistencies, it will be delayed while you are asked to make the necessary corrections.

For example, suppose you apply for registration of the mark "Eatwell" and describe your services as "Distribution of snack foods to school campuses." If your specimens seem to show a narrower use than your description implies, you may run into trouble. If your specimens are fliers directed to preschools, and the flyers all describe one cookie, it may appear as though the proper services description should be "Distribution of a particular cookie to preschools." The Examiner may ask for specimens proving that you distribute a variety of snack foods in addition to the cookie and that you distribute to school campuses other than preschools.

While we recommend consistency throughout this book to avoid delay, you should also keep in mind that a delay in the application process will not necessarily hurt your registration chances. Pending applications are published in most trademark databases and are thus available to anyone who chooses to conduct a preliminary search before they file their own application. Seeing that a registration application for your mark is pending will discourage others from applying to register conflicting marks. This is because they will know that the PTO will not consider their application until and unless your application is, for some reason, finally rejected.

1. Block 1: Mark (Words and/or Design)

➡ If your mark consists entirely of words (no designs or graphics) and the letters are not stylized, skip to subsection a, below, and follow the brief instructions there.

▣ If you are creating a non-office application based on our sample in Chapter 2, use all caps and bold type to set your mark apart from the rest of the text in your application. If you aren't sure what a non-office application is, or what kind of application to use, review the information in Chapter 2, Section F.

This block is where you describe your mark. Marks may be composed of many different elements: words, graphics, colors and combinations of these items. If your mark is made up of words only, the space in Block 1 should be big enough. But if your mark includes a graphic image, your description may be too long for the space. If this occurs, simply begin the identification in the box and state "continued on attachment." Then follow the instructions in the "continuation pages" sidebar set out below to prepare the attachment. If you are using the non-office form template or PrinTEAS, space should not be a problem.

a. Marks Consisting Entirely of Words

The mark should be typed exactly as you want it to appear. Make sure it is consistent with your specimens. (See Chapter 3 for more information about specimens.) Use all capital letters unless you specifically want it to be case sensitive, in specific upper and lower case letters.

> EXAMPLE **(Text only):** If your mark includes no distinctive style or design, then you may describe it in the application by typing it in capital letters. For example, if your mark is "Dynomat," you simply type in "DYNOMAT" in block one of the application.

b. Marks Consisting of Graphic Images

If all or part of the mark is a design or graphic image, do not draw it in this space (the drawing, described later in this chapter, will show the PTO what the mark looks like). Instead, use words to describe the mark as accurately as you can. Don't agonize about your description; the PTO will suggest a different one if they don't like yours. If you disagree with theirs, discuss the matter with the Examiner at that time; an acceptable description

will likely emerge. Following are examples of some common types of marks and their descriptions.

EXAMPLES:

Text with graphics: The mark below, which is owned by the Walt Disney Company, could be described as "Walt Disney World, with a mouse head inside the D."

Stylized text: If your mark consists of text with stylized letters, your description can be fairly simple. For example, using the ABA mark as shown below, the description would be as follows, "The stylized letters ABA."

Graphics only: One of the most famous graphic marks is owned by The Quaker Oats Company. It could be described as "The face of a smiling, white-haired older man wearing a hat of a type common in America in the early 17th Century."

Trademark/Service Mark Application (Page 1)

TRADEMARK/SERVICE MARK APPLICATION, PRINCIPAL REGISTER, WITH DECLARATION	MARK (Word(s) and/or Design)	CLASS NO. (If known)

TO THE ASSISTANT COMMISSIONER FOR TRADEMARKS:

APPLICANT'S NAME:

APPLICANT'S MAILING ADDRESS:

(Display address exactly as it should appear on registration)

APPLICANT'S ENTITY TYPE: (**Check one** and supply requested information)

	Individual - Citizen of (Country)
	Partnership - State where organized (Country, if appropriate): _____ Names and Citizenship (Country) of General Partners: _____
	Corporation - State (Country, if appropriate) of Incorporation: _____
	Other (Specify Nature of Entity and Domicile): _____

GOODS AND/OR SERVICES:

Applicant requests registration of the trademark/service mark shown in the accompanying drawing in the United States Patent and Trademark Office on the Principal Register established by the Act of July 5, 1946 (15 U.S.C. 1051 et. seq., as amended) for the following goods/services (SPECIFIC GOODS AND/OR SERVICES MUST BE INSERTED HERE) :

BASIS FOR APPLICATION: (Check boxes which apply, **but never both the first AND second boxes,** and supply requested information related to each box checked in.)

[ ]	Applicant is using the mark in commerce on or in connection with the above identified goods/services. (15 U.S.C. 1051(a), as amended.) Three specimens showing the mark as used in commerce are submitted with this application. • Date of first use of the mark in commerce which the U.S. Congress may regulate (for example, interstate or between the U.S. and a foreign country): _____ • Specify the type of commerce: _____ (for example, interstate or between the U.S. and a specified foreign country) • Date of first use anywhere (the same as or before use in commerce date): _____ • Specify manner or mode of use of mark on or in connection with the goods/services: _____ (for example, trademark is applied to labels, service mark is used in advertisements)
[ ]	Applicant has a bona fide intention to use the mark in commerce on or in connection with the above identified goods/services (15 U.S.C. 1051(b), as amended.) • Specify intended manner or mode of use of mark on or in connection with the goods/services: _____ (for example, trademark will be applied to labels, service mark will be used in advertisements)
[ ]	Applicant has a bona fide intention to use the mark in commerce on or in connection with the above identified goods/services, and asserts a claim of priority based upon a foreign application in accordance with 15 U.S.C. 1126(d), as amended. • Country of foreign filing: _____ • Date of foreign filing: _____
[ ]	Applicant has a bona fide intention to use the mark in commerce on or in connection with the above identified goods/services and, accompanying this application, submits a certification or certified copy of a foreign registration in accordance with 15 U.S.C 1126(e), as amended. • Country of registration: _____ • Registration number: _____

NOTE: Declaration, on Reverse Side, MUST be Signed

PTO Form 1478 (REV 6/96)   U.S. DEPARTMENT OF COMMERCE/Patent and Trademark Office
OMB No. 0651-0009 (Exp. 06/30/98) There is no requirement to respond to this collection of information unless a currently valid OMB Number is displayed.

Graphics only with color: The New York Statue of Liberty Celebration Foundation developed the mark shown below, lined for the colors red and blue. This mark would be described as follows, "A circle generally containing the outline of the upper portion of the Statue of Liberty, the mark including the colors red and blue." For more on describing colors, see Section d, below.

Marks presented in the context in which they appear: Sometimes, a mark appears on and is an integral part of the product it represents. Your drawing and specimens will show the mark as it appears on the product and you will describe the mark in its context. For example, the stripes on the shoe shown below would be described as follows, "Two bands having a color contrasting with the color of the shoe, the bands being applied diagonally from the instep of the upper edge of the shoe, the lower extremity of the bands being closest to the front of the shoe."

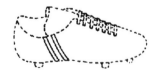

Using Continuation Pages

You can always use a blank piece of paper as a continuation page if you don't have enough room on the form. The top of each continuation page should have the following information in case it gets separated from your application:

- Applicant's complete name.
- Applicant's mailing address.
- Mark (use the words or description of your mark that you have developed here in this Section).
- Goods or services with which mark is used.
- Which answer you are continuing.

EXAMPLE:

APPLICANT NAME: Quick-Byte, Inc.

APPLICANT BUSINESS ADDRESS:
1001 Badger Rd., Badger, VT, 98765

MARK: QUICK-BYTES

GOODS OR SERVICES: Computer consulting services

CONTINUATION OF APPLICATION

MARK, Continued: similar thick horizontal stripe, in golden yellow.

APPLICANT BUSINESS ADDRESS, Continued: Address in state of incorporation, 11 Pinkham Square, Denver, CO, 80100

---

c. Marks Consisting of Trade Dress and Product Configurations

A mark can be a word, symbol, scent or color. A mark can also be the presentation or packaging of a product, such as the unique design of the Coca-Cola bottle. This is called "trade dress." When the mark manifests itself in the physical shape or appearance of a product, such as the shape of a Pepperidge Farm goldfish cracker, then it is known as "product configuration."

If you plan to register a product shape, you must submit a description that clearly defines the configuration. For example, acceptable language would be "The mark consists of the configuration of the blade portion of a fly swatter," or "The mark consists of the configuration of a cologne bottle and cap, both having a "V" shape as viewed from above." If the configuration constitutes a portion of the product, the statement should reflect that. For example, "The mark consists of a red button positioned on the lower front area of a shirt."

For more information about registering product configurations, see Chapter 2, Section D3.

d. Marks That Include Specific Colors

If the mark always appears in one specific color that you intend to be an integral part of the mark, describe the color in this block. For example, the Visa credit card trademark could be described as a white background with the word "Visa" in the middle in royal blue, a thick horizontal stripe above the word "Visa" in the same blue, and a similar thick horizontal stripe below the word "Visa" in golden yellow. (See also Graphics only with color example, above.)

Mark contains lining or shading not intended to indicate color: If your mark contains some lining or shading that it is not intended to indicate color (see Chapter 6, for a discussion of lining and shading in relation to color), such as IBM's blue, lined mark, then you should include a phrase like the following in your description, "The lining and stipling are features of the mark and do not indicate color."

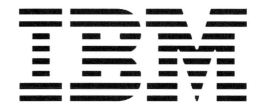

The fact that your mark will sometimes appear in color when you use it on your products or in connection with your services doesn't mean that the color is part of the mark for the purpose of this block. Only if you intend to always use the same color and treat the color as an inseparable part of the mark should you indicate the color or colors when you fill in this block.

The Visa logo described above is a good example of how color is used as an inseparable part of the logo. The colors, royal blue, white and golden yellow, are always used with the Visa logo whenever it is presented in color. These colors help to make the logo even more recognizable. Even different shades of the same color can be used to make your mark unique and thus an inseparable part of your mark. A special shade of blue may be the finesse that distinguishes your mark from others.

Be consistent. Remember, the mark you put here should be consistent with the specimen and the drawing you plan to submit.

2. Block 2: Class Number

Assign at least one class to the product or service for which you are using the mark. (Remember, each additional class will cost an extra $245.) If, after using the resources we describe in Chapter 2, you aren't sure which class to use, call the PTO's

Trademark Assistance Center at 703-308-9000 to get their opinion, or leave the block blank. The PTO will fill it in for you. Filling in the class yourself is better because you will have more control over what class is ultimately used.

3. Block 3: Applicant's Name

➡ If you are seeking registration under your own name as a sole proprietor and owner of the mark and you know for certain that no one else is going to claim ownership over your mark, then simply insert your full, legal name in block three and go on to the next section. If you are a sole proprietor doing business under a fictitious business name, then simply insert your full, legal name followed by: "a sole proprietorship doing business as" (or "a sole proprietorship DBA"), and then your fictitious business name. You can also use "AKA" (also known as) or "TA" (trading as). Example: "James T. Smith, DBA Software Works."

The applicant is the person or business who owns the mark when the application is filed. Whether or not you own the mark you're seeking to register should not be an issue that overwhelms you at this point. As long as you, or the business you own, determines or controls the quality of the goods or services represented by the mark, then you should be fine to move ahead with your application.

For goods, this is usually the person or business identified on the specimens as the source of the goods. For example, the container for a pint of Ben & Jerry's ice cream contains the registered trademark "Ben & Jerry's," on the lid. The container itself gives information about the source of the ice cream, "Ben & Jerry's Homemade, Inc." To register the mark Ben & Jerry's, the applicant name would be Ben & Jerry's Homemade, Inc.

Following are the general rules that apply to different types of entities and examples of how different business entities would list their names in the Applicant Name box. Sole proprietors are

discussed in the Fast Track box above. partnerships, corporations, limited liability companies and joint ventures are discussed below.

a. Partnerships

If the partnership doesn't have a fictitious business name—that is, it does business using the partners' legal names—these names should be listed in the order they normally appear.

EXAMPLE:
APPLICANT NAME: Kim Bunch, Gloria Grant & Nancie Valle.

If the partnership uses a fictitious business name, then the partners' full legal names should be listed, followed by "a partnership doing business as," and then the fictitious business name. You can also use "AKA" (also known as) or "TA" (trading as).

EXAMPLE:
APPLICANT NAME: Kim Bunch, Gloria Grant & Nancie Valle, a partnership doing business as AB Company.

Another way to fill out this blank as a partnership using a fictitious name is to list the fictitious name first, followed by the legal names of the partners.

EXAMPLE:
APPLICANT NAME: AB Company, a partnership composed of Kim Bunch, Gloria Grant & Nancie Valle.

b. Corporations

The official name of the corporation should be listed in the Applicant Name box. Officers of the corporation should not be listed here, but an officer will have to sign the application at the end.

EXAMPLE:
APPLICANT NAME: Quick-Byte, Incorporated.

Divisions of corporations should not be listed here. Instead, list the parent corporation. If the mark is used only by a division, that may be stated in the second part of Block 7 (Basis for Application) or in a cover letter submitted with the application. For example, M&M/Mars distributes M&M chocolate candies and is a division of Mars, Inc. "M&M" is a registered trademark for the candies, but is not owned by the division, M&M/Mars. Rather, it is owned by the corporation, Mars, Inc. Therefore, Mars, Inc., would be the applicant for the trademark registration of "M&M."

c. Limited Liability Companies

Limited liability companies should state their official business name, whether it be a fictitious name or the names of the company's owners.

EXAMPLE:
APPLICANT NAME: Bridgeworks Design.

d. Joint Ventures

A joint venture is a single business entity and its official business name should go in the Applicant Name box.

EXAMPLE:
APPLICANT NAME: The Shacter/Alberts Company.

⚠ Has ownership of the mark changed? Extra care should be taken to explain any ownership changes if you submit a specimen (see Chapter 3) that includes the name of a former owner—that is, a person other than you, or a company other than yours.

For instance, suppose the specimen is a computer-related newsletter, at the bottom of which is printed "Quick-Bytes is a service mark of Etta Linton." Perhaps after the newsletter was printed Etta was doing so well she formed a corporation, Quick-Bytes, Inc. If the application lists the corporation as the owner of the mark, the Examiner will probably notice the discrepancy between the owner listed on the application and the owner noted at the bottom of the newsletter, and want to know which is correct.

More Than One Owner

Usually there is only one owner of a mark, such as a sole proprietorship, a partnership, a limited partnership, a corporation, a limited liability company, an association or a joint venture. However, if two separate individuals who are not partners, or two unrelated businesses, agree that both own the mark, joint applicant status may be accepted by the PTO if both owners would together jointly offer the goods or services designated by the mark and jointly control their nature and quality. For instance, two separate businesses may agree to perform a specific service that requires the active and joint involvement of each. Joint ownership issues can be tricky. If you are not sure, you should consult with an attorney for advice on how to list yourself and the other applicant.

4. Block 4: Applicant's Mailing Address

Use an address at which mail is received, whether a physical location or a post office or private mail box service (the PTO prefers a street address). If you need more room, continue on an extra page. (See "Using Continuation Pages" in the sidebar above.) If your mailing address changes at any time during the application process, you must send a written request to the PTO to have your correspondence address changed. The PTO will not change it over the phone.

For applicants applying as individuals: list both a home and a business address. They may both be the same.

If you are filing your own non-office application, you can add this information after the identification of the applicant. For example, "James Bonner, an individual and a citizen of the United States of America, whose business address is 2435 Marina Circle, Berkeley, CA 94712, and whose residence address is 5712 Adeline Ave., Berkeley, CA 94721," or "whose business and residence addresses are 5712 Adeline Ave., Berkeley, CA 94721."

For joint applicants: list the business addresses for all parties involved, specifying which address belongs to which applicant.

If you are filing your own non-office application, your statement would look something like, "Alice Kamamoto and Anthony Phillips, joint owners, both citizens of the United States of America. Alice Kamamoto's business address is 79 Jones Street, San Francisco, CA 94118, and Anthony Phillips's business address is 7689 Park Village Avenue, San Diego, CA 92129."

For sole proprietorships, partnerships, limited liability companies, corporations, joint ventures and associations: list the business address. If the corporation also has an address in its state of incorporation (different from its business address), list both.

If you're filing your own non-office application, your statement would look similar to the following example, "MindSet, Inc., a corporation of the State of California, whose corporate address is 2345 West End Blvd., Los Angeles, CA 90061, and whose business address is 45 Tailor Street, Virginia Beach, VA 23454."

5. Block 5: Applicant's Entity

Check one appropriate box and fill in the information requested.
- Individual applicants: Give your country of citizenship.
- Partnerships: Give the state and country under which the partnership was formed. Then list the names and countries of citizenship of the general partners. Silent, limited or inactive partners need not be listed.
- Corporations: Give the state (or country if outside the U.S.A.) of incorporation.
- Other: If the applicant is not an individual, partnership or corporation, check this box. For example, you would check this box if the applicant(s) was a sole proprietorship, an association, joint applicants, a limited liability company or a joint venture.

If a sole proprietorship, specify the national citizenship of the applicant.

EXAMPLE:
"Other: (Specify Nature of Entity and Domicile) Sole Proprietorship of the state of California. Leslie Ganes is the individual owner and a citizen of the United States."

If an association, specify the state or country where the association is organized or existing.

EXAMPLE:
"Other: (Specify Nature of Entity and Domicile) Association of the state of Texas."

If joint applicants, specify the national citizenship of each joint applicant.

EXAMPLE:

"Other: (Specify Nature of Entity and Domicile) Joint Applicants composed of Alice Abrams and Betty Bertrand, both citizens of the United States.

If a Limited Liability Company (LLC), specify the state or country where the LLC is organized or existing.

EXAMPLE:

"Other: (Specify Nature of Entity and Domicile) Limited Liability Company of the state of Michigan.

If a joint venture, specify the state or country where the joint venture is organized and list the members by name.

EXAMPLE:

"Other: (Specify Nature of Entity and Domicile) Joint Venture of the state of Ohio, composed of Sabreen Hurt, Marn Reich and Sonja Eriksson."

Use the precise legal description of your business form. If you're not sure, call the local Small Business Administration office (check in your phone book). They may be able to provide some guidance. Whatever you do, don't simply use the word "firm" or "company" to describe your legal entity. These words are not specific enough for the PTO and could cause a delay in processing your application.

6. Block 6: Goods and/or Services

In this portion of the application, you are asked to identify the goods and/or services with which you are using the mark in commerce. Describe the goods or services as clearly and succinctly as possible. Use ordinary English and be as accurate as you can. Here are some important guidelines to use when describing your goods or services.

a. Make Your Description Appropriately Inclusive

Subject to the other hints offered in this section, it is important to make your initial description broad enough to include all the goods or services for which you want your mark to be protected. This is because of a PTO rule that, for the most part, doesn't permit the expansion of a description to include additional products or services once the application has been filed.

For example, assume you're a citrus fruit grower and your initial description lists "grapefruit, oranges, lemons, and limes." If you later realize that you should have included kumquats in this list, the chances are pretty good the Examiner won't let you amend your application to include them. Instead, you will probably be required to file another application—and pay another application fee—to extend your registration to the additional goods or services.

Beware of using labels, stationery, menus, signs and containers. If you are planning to describe your goods or services by reference to a label, menu, sign, stationery or container because that is where you think your mark will appear, then stop. You must not describe the mode or method by which you are using the mark in this section. The mode or method of use means the manner in which you affix the mark to the goods you are describing or in association with the services you are describing (for example, placing the mark on labels, signs, stationery, etc.). The labels, signs, stationery, etc., are not the goods or services themselves, and that is what you are being asked to describe here. Section 7c below explains where to place information about the manner or mode of use. If you mistakenly identify the goods or services as a label, stationery, menu, sign or container here, you will not be allowed to amend the application later to specify the actual goods or services. This means you will have to file another application and pay another fee.

b. Avoid an Overly Broad Description

In the previous section, we discussed how to make your description broad enough to include the goods and/or services under which you want your mark to be protected. The flip side of making your description broad enough is avoiding a description that is so broad, it actually encompasses more than the classes you intended. For example, for acrylic paints, you should use the specific phrase "artists' paints" rather than "artists' materials," since "materials" could mean paint brushes, canvasses, easels, etc., all of which could be listed in different classes.

A good rule of thumb is that the goods and services covered by your description should fall within the number of classes for which you want to pay. (Remember from Chapter 2 that you must pay $245 for each class under which you wish to register.) If the Examiner thinks that your description is too broad, he or she will give you an opportunity to amend it. Remember, however, that if you amend your description to reduce the number of goods or services included in it, you won't later be able to add those goods or services back in if you change your mind.

If you find yourself using indefinite terms, such as "accessories," "components," "devices," "equipment," "food," "materials," "parts," "systems" or "products," then try using the words "namely" or "consisting of" afterwards and then list the goods or services by their more common commercial names. This will keep your description from inadvertently falling into an unintended class. For example, "Computer equipment, namely computer keyboards, computer monitors and modems."

> **EXAMPLE:** You produce a desk set that includes pens, pencils and scissors, and your trademark budget dictates that you register under only one class. Since scissors are in a different class than pens and pencils, your description should be "a desk set with pens and pencils" (Class 16), or, "a desk set with scissors" (Class 8), but not "a desk set with

pens, pencils and scissors." If you inadvertently describe goods and/or services in more than one class, the trademark attorney examining your application at the PTO will likely allow you to amend your application to narrow your description so that it encompasses only one class, as intended.

c. Be Consistent

The description you use for your goods or services must match the mark as shown on the specimens you provide with your application. After you decide which specimens to use you may have to come back to this section of the form and modify your description accordingly.

d. Avoid Using Open-Ended and Indefinite Terms

Don't use open-ended, indefinite terms such as "including," "and the like," "such as," "and so on" or "for example."

- Unacceptable: Office supplies (pens, pencils and the like).
- Acceptable: Office supplies consisting of pens and pencils.
- Unacceptable: Typing paper including copy machine paper.
- Acceptable: Paper—namely that suitable for use in offices for typing and copy machines.

Indefinite phrases are not acceptable because they are not specific and could lead to the types of classification problems mentioned above in subsections b and c. For example, suppose you are applying for a mark which is to appear on a line of goods falling under Class 16, which includes Office Requisites. You wrote in Class 16 on your application and then described the goods as "pens, pencils and the like." The Examiner may decide the description is unacceptable because "pens, pencils and the like" could include items in more than one class (Class 16 for pens and pencils, Class 8 for scissors). If that were the case, you would have to pay double the filing fee, one for each class. (See subsection b. above.) When descriptions of goods and services are specifically defined or stated, the Examiner feels more certain that the proper class has been designated and the proper filing fee has been paid.

e. If You're Still Having Trouble

The PTO understands that, in our rapidly changing world, the number of possible goods and services (and descriptions of them) is limitless. Often when a good or service is first created it is difficult to describe it with common language. For example, when Ford first began making cars, the words "motor car" and "automobile" had not yet become common language. Similarly, in the mid-1970s there was no common language for describing consulting services in the field of personal computers (since personal computers had not existed before that time).

Fortunately, the PTO will help answer your questions about how to word the description of your goods or services. To speak with the Managing or Senior Attorney handling the class you plan to register under, call 703-308-9101 and follow the instructions on the recording. For example, if your mark is used in connection with mailbox rental services (Class 39, transportation and storage services), follow the instructions to get to the PTO office which handles Class 39 applications. Explain that you need help articulating a description for your goods or services. The lawyer will give you some suggestions based on your description of the good or service involved. Don't feel bound by the Examiner's first suggestion, especially if it would reduce the number of goods and services included in your description or change the class you will register under. It is usually possible to discuss the goods or services and make counter-suggestions until a description that satisfies you and the Examiner is found.

Resources to Help You Describe Your Goods or Services

There are a number of resources available to help you decide how to describe your goods or services. Probably the best source is the list of approved descriptions the PTO has prepared for its Examiners to use when reviewing applications, called the *U.S. Patent & Trademark Office Acceptable Identification of Goods and Services Manual*. You may recall from Chapter 2 that this manual is also an excellent resource for choosing the appropriate class for your goods or services. Besides class information, this manual contains a list of descriptions the PTO deems acceptable for each type of product and service.

You can search the manual for free at the PTO's website (http://www.uspto.gov/) or you can order it for $40 plus shipping costs from the International Trademark Association, New York, N.Y. (212-986-5880). You can also find a copy at your nearest Patent and Trademark Depository Library (see Appendix for a listing). It is not available in hard copy from the PTO. This manual has over 13,000 listings, and if you are only planning to prepare one application it's probably not cost effective to purchase it.

For a complete explanation of how to search the hard copy manual and the online manual, see Chapter 2, Section C3 which explains search techniques for choosing a class. The same techniques will help your search for acceptable descriptions of your goods and/or services.

You can also use the International List of Classes for Goods and Services to find more terms to describe your goods or services. You will find this list in the Appendix. The International Classification of Products and Services (under the Nice Agreement, 7th Edition) is helpful for the same purpose. You will find it published on the World Intellectual Property Organization's (WIPO) website at http://www.wipo.org/eng/clssfctn/nice/enmn01.htm.

Another way you can get help from the PTO is by reading this section, consulting the resources discussed in the sidebar above and putting your own description on your application. If the PTO finds your description unacceptable, they will call or write you and suggest another description, sometimes after they get more information about your goods or services. Be aware, however, that this may cause some delay in getting your registration accomplished.

One final suggestion: You can search the federal trademark database for marks used by competitors and then examine the goods and services description used for those marks. See Chapter 2, Section C3, for a quick way to do this on the Internet.

This block also mentions an "accompanying drawing" being submitted with the application. Basically, this means a literal representation of the mark you are registering. Drawings are explained in Chapter 6.

7. Block 7: Basis for Application

In this block you indicate the basis for your application. Because you are reading this chapter (for use applications) you will want to check the first box, "Applicant is using the mark in commerce on or in connection with the above identified goods/services," and fill in the blanks as we instruct below.

If you choose to file a non-office application, use the samples in the Appendix which demonstrate what the appropriate language is to designate the basis for your application as a use application. The disk contains a template for the use application with the appropriate language establishing the basis for the application included.

After checking the first box you may notice that the application states, "Three specimens showing the mark as used in commerce are submitted with this application." In Chapter 3, we provide precise instructions for completing this important part of

the trademark registration process. You'll want to check back here after you are through reading that material, if you haven't already done so.

a. Date of First Use

At this point, you'll need to determine these two dates:

- the date you first actually used your mark anywhere in connection with the goods or services upon or for which you are using the mark. The term "anywhere" does not include use within a company. The use must be external—out in the public marketplace.
- the date you first used your mark in "commerce that Congress may regulate." In a nutshell, this includes interstate and international commerce.

(See Chapter 2, Section B, for a full discussion of the definitions of "use" and "commerce that Congress may regulate.")

The date of the first use anywhere obviously can be a different date than when you first used the mark in commerce that Congress can regulate. For example, you may have used the mark just in your neighborhood for years and then decided to expand nationwide. The date the mark was first used in your neighborhood would be the date of first use. The date you marketed your product or service in a second state (or territory or outside the country) would be the first use in commerce that Congress can regulate.

It's important to understand that the date of first use anywhere—not the date of first use in commerce that Congress can regulate—establishes the beginning of your legal rights to the mark. Therefore, it's crucial to know and be able to prove this date because, as we've seen, the business that has been using the mark the longest generally gets priority in case a conflict develops. No matter how careful your trademark search, there is always the possibility that someone else in the country was using the same mark (or a similar one) before you. It is also possible that someone who started using the mark after you has also applied to have their mark registered. (See *Trademark: Legal Care for Your Business & Product Name* by Stephen Elias and Kate McGrath for more information about conflicts between marks.)

Document Your Use

If possible, we suggest you document the first use of your mark. This is important not only for the registration process but also in case you become involved in a trademark dispute. Some examples of documentation include:

- copies of cover letters or invoices that show the mark sent with product shipments (for goods)
- copies of advertisements offering services under the mark (for services), and
- photos of displays, signs or other marketing materials if the business doesn't advertise (services and, in some instances, goods).

Since many advertisements and other marketing materials don't include the date(s) when they appeared, it is helpful to write the date(s) of publication on the back of the ad, photo or display. Even better would be a letter from the publication confirming that your ad will appear on or by a certain date or that your business will attend a trade show on a certain date.

We also suggest you keep examples (or photographs) of the first use of your mark in commerce that Congress may regulate.

It's possible that you've been using a mark for years before you decide to register it and may not know the exact date of its first use anywhere or in commerce that Congress may regulate. Do your best to determine the correct dates. If necessary, it is okay to use imprecise dates, such as "before March 25, 1998" or "on or about January 16, 1975."

You may also give a month or year without a date, such as "in 1966" or "in February 1984." If you are unsure as between two dates, use the earliest possible date that you can reasonably assert as the correct one. Use dated documents that you have gathered over the years (such as old advertisements or business licenses) to help jog your memory.

b. Type of Commerce

After you list the two dates, indicate the type of commerce in which the mark was used (interstate, international or interterritorial), as discussed in Chapter 2.

If your first use anywhere was in commerce which the U.S. Congress may regulate, both dates (the first two lines in block 7) will be the same. Even so, you still must fill in both blanks.

c. Manner or Mode of Use

In Section 6, above, we discuss the different ways a mark may be used with goods and services. In this blank you must describe at least one such way your mark is being used. You need not describe all the ways it is used.

Examples of how marks are used to identify goods:

- If your mark is employed on items such as books, jeans, hats or other goods on which a mark might appear, your manner or mode of use may be: "The mark is placed directly on the goods and used in other ways customary to the trade."
- If your mark is used in connection with items such as window glass, jewelry or other goods on which it is impractical to place the mark directly, try this or similar wording: "The mark is used on labels attached to the goods and on packaging."
- If your mark is used in connection with services, you may state something like: "The

mark is used in letters, advertisements and signs used to promote the services."

Consistency Reminder

The PTO will look to see if the manner or mode of use you describe is consistent with the specimen you submit. If it isn't, the PTO will ask for clarification. Since you may be using the mark in several different ways, the ones you describe here should be consistent with all of your specimens. For instance, suppose you describe the manner or mode of use as follows: "The mark is used in newsletters used to promote the services." If the specimens you submit are copies of phone book advertisements rather than newsletters, the PTO will logically conclude that your specimens are inconsistent with the manner or mode of use you are claiming and send your application back for clarification. For this reason, it is often best to first decide which specimens you plan to use and then fill in this box. Read Chapter 3 for a full discussion of choosing specimens.

---

8. Block 8: Declaration (Back Side of the Application)

By signing the Declaration, you are stating under oath that you:

- understand that willful false statements are punishable by fine, imprisonment or both under federal law, and that such willful false statements may jeopardize the validity of the application or any resulting registration;
- are authorized to "execute" (sign) the application on behalf of the applicant (if the applicant is a business entity);
- believe the applicant is the owner of the mark for which registration is sought;

- believe no other person, firm, corporation or association has the right to use the mark or a mark so similar that consumers could be confused or deceived; and
- know all statements in the application are true or that you have been informed and believe that they are true.

This declaration is mostly to warn you that you had better be telling the truth. The PTO rarely, if ever, takes the time to figure out if people are lying or to prosecute them for making false statements. However, if you ever get into a dispute, any lies you make in your application may come to light and cause you to lose. The bottom line is that you should not file an application if any of the following is true:

- You are not sure whether you are the owner of the mark. (See Section 3, above, regarding who can apply for registration.)
- You know of a clear conflict with a mark used by someone else. (See Chapter 1, Section D.)
- You are making some other statement in the application that you believe is not true.

Be consistent. Make sure your signature (and title) is consistent with information you entered in Block 3.

If you are filing as an individual, simply sign your name, print your name, give the date and provide a phone number where you can be reached. If you are filing as another entity, skip to the appropriate section below and follow those instructions.

The rules for who should sign the declaration are as follows:

Individuals: If the applicant is an individual, sign here. If a wife and husband, or any other individuals, are applying together as separate individuals rather than as a partnership, each must sign as joint owners (see below).

Sole Proprietorships: If you are the sole owner of a business you must sign the application. On

Trademark/Service Mark Application (Page 2)

DECLARATION

The undersigned being hereby warned that willful false statements and the like so made are punishable by fine or imprisonment, or both, under 18 U.S.C. 1001, and that such willful false statements may jeopardize the validity of the application or any resulting registration, declares that he/she is properly authorized to execute this application on behalf of the applicant; he/she believes the applicant to be the owner of the trademark/service mark sought to be registered, or if the application is being filed under 15 U.S.C. 1051(b), he/she believes the applicant to be entitled to use such mark in commerce; to the best of his/her knowledge and belief no other person, firm, corporation, or association has the right to use the above identified mark in commerce, either in the identical form thereof or in such near resemblance thereto as to be likely, when used on or in connection with the goods/services of such other person, to cause confusion, or to cause mistake, or to deceive; and that all statements made of his/her own knowledge are true and that all statements made on information and belief are believed to be true.

_____   _____
DATE   SIGNATURE

_____   _____
TELEPHONE NUMBER   PRINT OR TYPE NAME AND POSITION

INSTRUCTIONS AND INFORMATION FOR APPLICANT

TO RECEIVE A FILING DATE, THE APPLICATION MUST BE COMPLETED AND SIGNED BY THE APPLICANT AND SUBMITTED ALONG WITH:

1. The prescribed **FEE ($245.00)** for each class of goods/services listed in the application;
2. A **DRAWING PAGE** displaying the mark in conformance with 37 CFR 2.52;
3. If the application is based on use of the mark in commerce, **THREE (3) SPECIMENS** (evidence) of the mark as used in commerce for each class of goods/services listed in the application. All three specimens may be the same. Examples of good specimens include: (a) labels showing the mark which are placed on the goods; (b) photographs of the mark as it appears on the goods, (c) brochures or advertisements showing the mark as used in connection with the services.
4. An **APPLICATION WITH DECLARATION** (this form) - The application must be signed in order for the application to receive a filing date. Only the following persons may sign the declaration, depending on the applicant's legal entity: (a) the individual applicant; (b) an officer of the corporate applicant; (c) one general partner of a partnership applicant; (d) all joint applicants.

SEND APPLICATION FORM, DRAWING PAGE, FEE, AND SPECIMENS (IF APPROPRIATE) TO:

Assistant Commissioner for Trademarks
Box New App/Fee
2900 Crystal Drive
Arlington, VA 22202-3513

Additional information concerning the requirements for filing an application is available in a booklet entitled **Basic Facts About Registering a Trademark,** which may be obtained by writing to the above address or by calling: (703) 308-HELP.

This form is estimated to take an average of 1 hour to complete, including time required for reading and understanding instructions, gathering necessary information, recordkeeping, and actually providing the information. Any comments on this form, including the amount of time required to complete this form, should be sent to the Office of Management and Organization, U.S. Patent and Trademark Office, U.S. Department of Commerce, Washington, D.C. 20231. Do NOT send completed forms to this address.

the line below, print your name and show your position as "sole proprietor."

Partnerships: Any partner of a general (as opposed to a limited) partnership may sign. You need not provide proof that the signer is a general partner with power to make business decisions binding the partnership, but such proof should be available in case the Examiner requests it.

Joint Ventures: Any principal member of the joint venture may sign.

Limited Liability Companies: Any officer of the limited liability company may sign. The following titles are acceptable: president, vice-president, secretary, treasurer, CEO, CFO (or controller or comptroller). Modifications such as VP of Sales or Executive VP are also acceptable.

Corporations (profit and nonprofit) and unincorporated associations (such as labor unions and community groups): The following corporate titles are acceptable: president, vice-president, secretary, treasurer, CEO, CFO (or controller or comptroller). Clerk is acceptable for mass corporations. Also acceptable are chairman or chairman of the board of directors (but not a director). Modifications such as VP of Sales or Executive VP are also acceptable. If you decide to use someone with another title not typically considered to be a corporate officer, you must provide proof that the person is in fact an officer. For example, if you decide to have the corporate General Counsel sign the application, you should provide a

declaration (statement under penalty of perjury) explaining that the person is an officer, and attach a copy of the corporate minutes in which the person was made a corporate officer. A corporate employee such as an executive director, publisher or managing director may not sign unless she is also a corporate officer.

Put the date on the line to the left of the signature line. The application must be filed with the PTO within a reasonable time after it is signed and dated. Eight weeks or less is considered reasonable by the PTO, but we recommend that the application be filed as soon as possible. Remember to add your phone number and printed name. Following is an example of how to complete the Declaration block of the application.

December 7, 1998	*Ken Andres*
Date	Signature

510-441-9100	Ken Andres, Treasurer
Telephone Number	Print or Type Name and Position

B. What's Next?

You have completed your trademark application. But you are not finished yet! Now you must prepare your drawing and then file your application along with your specimens. Chapters 6 and 7 will take you through each procedure. ■

Completing a Federal Trademark Application Based on Intent to Use

I f you don't qualify to file a trademark application based upon actual use, you can file what's called an intent-to-use (ITU) application if you plan to put your mark into use within a certain time period. (Use applications for marks already being used are covered in Chapter 4.) This chapter provides the nuts and bolts for completing the application for a trademark or service mark on an intent-to-use basis with the PTO.

Are you really ready to file? If you haven't already done so, read Chapter 2 to learn what information you will need to complete this chapter. Also in that chapter we discussed the differences between a use application and an intent-to-use application. You may also want to read Chapter 1 for an overview of trademark laws and for some instruction as to whether or not your proposed mark would qualify for trademark registration.

If the PTO approves (or "allows," in PTO-speak) the mark that is the subject of your intent-to-use application, you will have reserved the right to use the mark in the manner claimed in your application, even though you've never used it at all. The initial reservation period lasts for six months from the time the PTO issues a Notice of Allowance on the mark. Due to delays that are common in the PTO, your initial reservation may, as a practical matter, last a year or more. And, if you have good reasons why you haven't put your mark into use by the time this initial period expires, you can reserve your mark for up to five additional six-month periods (at $100 a period). See Steps 1 through 6 in the trademark application process below.

It's important to understand that filing an ITU application will not by itself lead to registration of your trademark. There are more steps to take before registration will be complete, which include:

- putting your mark into actual use in commerce that Congress may regulate, and

- following up your initial application with an Allegation of Use documenting the circumstances of your use.

The entire process for intent-to-use trademark applications can be fairly complex. In general, the steps go as follows:

Step 1: You complete the application form.

Step 2: You file the application with the U.S. Patent and Trademark Office, accompanied by a drawing and the trademark registration fee of $245 per class claimed for the mark (as of July 1999).

Step 3: You will usually be asked make some changes in your application based on specific suggestions by the trademark attorney looking over your application (the Examiner).

Step 4: The PTO publishes your proposed mark in the *Official Gazette* so that the public has an opportunity to oppose your application.

Step 5: If there is no opposition filed within 30 days of the date of publication, and your mark otherwise qualifies for registration, you will receive a Notice of Allowance from the PTO.

Step 6a: At any time after you file your ITU application, but *before* the PTO authorizes publication of your mark in the *Official Gazette*, you may file a form called an Allegation of Use once you actually use the mark in commerce that Congress may regulate.

EXAMPLE: Penny filed her ITU application September 1, 1998. Penny started using her mark in commerce November 23, 1998. Penny has not, at this point, received any notice from the PTO that her mark has been approved for publication in the *Official Gazette*. Because Penny has started using her mark before notification of approval for publication, she will file an Allegation of Use form to notify the PTO that she is now using her mark.

The Allegation of Use Form

This form tells the trademark attorney examining your application the date when you first started using the mark in commerce that Congress may regulate, and the date when you first started using the mark anywhere. You also submit specimens with your Allegation of Use to show the trademark attorney how you are actually using the mark. The attorney compares the specimens with the drawing you submitted with your intent-to-use application to make sure they are consistent with one another. To file an Allegation of Use you must pay a $100 fee. (For more information about Allegations of Use, see Chapter 11.)

or:

Step 6b: If you first use the mark in commerce that Congress may regulate within six months after the date the PTO issues the Notice of Allowance, you may file an Allegation of Use proving you have used the mark in commerce and are ready for final registration. Keep in mind that you may not file an Allegation of Use form during the period of time which occurs after the PTO authorizes your mark for publication and before the PTO issues a Notice of Allowance. If you begin to use your mark during this time, wait until the PTO issues you a Notice of Allowance before submitting your Allegation of Use form. The only difference between Step 6a and this step (6b) is timing. The form is the same, but the timing is different. Because the timing is different, the PTO treats these two situations a little differently.

or:

Step 6c: If you haven't used the mark in commerce within six months after the PTO issues a Notice of Allowance, you may file for a six-month extension of time to file an Allegation of Use. You must file for the extension *before* the six-month period has expired. (For more information about the Allegation of Use form, see Chapter 11.)

Strategies for Successful ITU Applications

Here is a short list of rules that we advise you to keep in mind while you are preparing your ITU application.

1. **Keep it simple.** The PTO's rules for ITU applications do not allow the applicant to make a material alteration to the mark as shown on the application during the time the application is pending. The safest course of action for ITU applicants with word marks is to go with a mark presented in plain, block letters. That way, you will have reserved the word mark and you can later use it in any way you wish without objection from the trademark Examiner. If your mark is a logo without any words, present it in its current design, but keep in mind that the mark you present now will need to be substantially the same as the mark you later show the PTO on the specimens you submit with your Allegation of Use. When you do finally settle on the final design of the mark, you can file another application showing the mark in its final form (for an extra fee, of course).

   EXAMPLE: Etta couldn't decide whether or not her mark Quick-Bytes should always be printed in her favorite color, green. She also thought she wanted to use a drawing of a computer terminal as her logo with the mark, but she wasn't sure. Unless she firmly decides, she should file her application without the logo, and without the green coloring of the mark. That way, she can request protection for the most important part of her mark, the words Quick-Bytes. If she later decides the color or logo are so important that they need federal trademark protection, she can file a new application. And of course there is nothing to stop her from displaying her mark in green against a background featuring a computer terminal in the meantime.

2. **Make sure your drawing is in order.** A 1990 notice from the PTO, published in the *Official Gazette*, listed the six most common problems with ITU applications—and four of them involved the drawing. Make sure your drawing conforms to the PTO's requirements in the following ways:
   - the drawing is the correct size
   - the drawing has a heading, and
   - the drawing contains the mark you seek to register.

   Some of these requirements may seem pretty obvious, but they are evidently not obvious enough, judging from how many applicants get them wrong. For specifics about the drawing, see Chapter 6.

3. **Follow the preparation and filing instructions to the letter.** Sometimes, even little technical errors in the filing procedure can cause unwanted and unnecessary delays.

4. **Mind your manners.** Follow the instructions in Chapter 8 for communicating with the PTO, including the advice regarding courtesy and promptness. If problems do arise during the prosecution of your application, it's always the best policy to treat the Examiner with courtesy and respect and to return phone calls or send correspondence in a timely fashion. By doing so, you are showing the Examiner that you are on the ball and he or she may be more willing to give you the benefit of the doubt should you need it.

5. **Keep a calendar.** The application process for intent-to-use applicants involves a number of deadlines. If you miss them, you will have to start over again. For example, you have six months from the date you are issued a Notice of Allowance to file an Allegation of Use. Calendar it so you won't forget. Calendar all deadlines that arise during the prosecution of your application, including the deadlines for responses to rejections (discussed in Chapters 9 and 10).

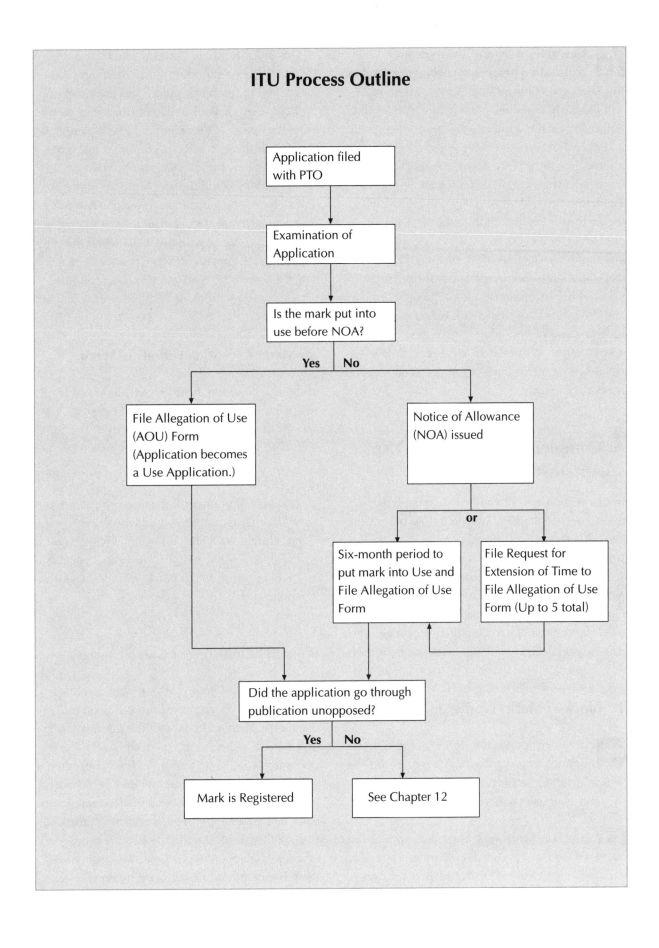

ITU Process Outline

Application filed with PTO

↓

Examination of Application

↓

Is the mark put into use before NOA?

Yes | **No**

Yes → File Allegation of Use (AOU) Form (Application becomes a Use Application.)

No → Notice of Allowance (NOA) issued

↓

or

Six-month period to put mark into Use and File Allegation of Use Form

File Request for Extension of Time to File Allegation of Use Form (Up to 5 total)

↓

Did the application go through publication unopposed?

Yes | **No**

Yes → Mark is Registered

No → See Chapter 12

⚠ New rules governing the trademark registration process are being proposed as this book goes to print (May 1999). These rules will likely affect the most basic trademark application requirements including signature, specimen and drawing requirements. The good news is that it looks like the PTO is poised to relax some of its more strict rules regarding trademark applications. The bad news is that we really don't know what the final rules will be until sometime between now and October 30, 1999. If you are using this book after October 30, 1999, please visit Nolo's website at http://www.nolo.com/ for the most updated information about the PTO's new rules and how they affect trademark registrations. To receive email notification of when these changes go into effect, subscribe to *NoloBriefs*, Nolo's email newsletter, at http://www.nolo.com/newsletter/join.cfm.

A. Completing the Intent-to-Use Application

In this section we tell you how to complete your registration application. As you follow our instructions, keep one point firmly in mind: Consistency is key. The mark that you describe and show with your drawing on the application must be the same mark that you eventually use. If your mark evolves into something different than the drawing you submit with your application, then your registration may be opposed by the PTO's trademark attorneys.

1. Block 1: Mark (Words and/or Design)

➡ If your mark consists entirely of words (no designs or graphics) and the letters are not stylized, skip to subsection a, below, and follow the brief instructions there.

▣ If you are creating a non-office application based on our sample in Chapter 2, use all caps and bold type to set your mark apart from the rest of the text in your application.

This block is where you describe your mark. Marks may be composed of many different elements: words, graphics, colors and combinations of these items. If your mark is made up of words only, the space in Block 1 should be big enough. But if your mark includes a graphic image, your description may be too long for the space. If this occurs, simply begin the identification in the box and state "continued on attachment." Then follow the instructions in the sidebar "Using Continuation Pages" below to prepare the attachment. But carefully note Strategy #1, above, about keeping it simple. Remember, you can always expand the appearance of your mark with future registrations.

a. Marks Consisting Entirely of Words

The mark should be typed exactly as you want it to appear. Use all capital letters unless you specifically want it to be case sensitive (always appear in specific upper and lower case letters).

> EXAMPLE:
> **Text only:** if your mark includes no distinctive style or design, then you may describe it in the application by typing it in capital letters. For example, if your mark is "Dynomat," you simply type in "DYNOMAT" in Block 1 of the application.

b. Marks Consisting of Graphic Images

If you are sure of your mark's design and know that it will not be altered before it is used in commerce, then proceed with the information in this section. However, if you are not sure that your mark is in its final form and won't be altered before it is actually used, then heed the advice given in Strategy #1 for successful ITU applications, above. In general, try to stick with word marks if you are filing an ITU application. Marks consisting of unique graphic designs don't necessarily need the advance protection afforded by an ITU application.

Trademark/Service Mark Application (Page 1)

TRADEMARK/SERVICE MARK APPLICATION, PRINCIPAL REGISTER, WITH DECLARATION	MARK (Word(s) and/or Design)	CLASS NO. (If known)

TO THE ASSISTANT COMMISSIONER FOR TRADEMARKS:

APPLICANT'S NAME:

APPLICANT'S MAILING ADDRESS:

(Display address exactly as it should appear on registration)

_____
_____
_____

APPLICANT'S ENTITY TYPE: (**Check one** and supply requested information)

	Individual - Citizen of (Country)
	Partnership - State where organized (Country, if appropriate):_____ Names and Citizenship (Country) of General Partners:_____
	Corporation - State (Country, if appropriate) of Incorporation:
	Other (Specify Nature of Entity and Domicile):

GOODS AND/OR SERVICES:

Applicant requests registration of the trademark/service mark shown in the accompanying drawing in the United States Patent and Trademark Office on the Principal Register established by the Act of July 5, 1946 (15 U.S.C. 1051 et. seq., as amended) for the following goods/services (SPECIFIC GOODS AND/OR SERVICES MUST BE INSERTED HERE) :

_____
_____
_____
_____
_____

BASIS FOR APPLICATION: (Check boxes which apply, **but never both the first AND second boxes,** and supply requested information related to each box checked in.)

[ ]	Applicant is using the mark in commerce on or in connection with the above identified goods/services. (15 U.S.C. 1051(a), as amended.) Three specimens showing the mark as used in commerce are submitted with this application. • Date of first use of the mark in commerce which the U.S. Congress may regulate (for example, interstate or between the U.S. and a foreign country):_____ • Specify the type of commerce:_____ (for example, interstate or between the U.S. and a specified foreign country) • Date of first use anywhere (the same as or before use in commerce date):_____ • Specify manner or mode of use of mark on or in connection with the goods/services:_____ (for example, trademark is applied to labels, service mark is used in advertisements)
[ ]	Applicant has a bona fide intention to use the mark in commerce on or in connection with the above identified goods/services (15 U.S.C. 1051(b), as amended.) • Specify intended manner or mode of use of mark on or in connection with the goods/services:_____ (for example, trademark will be applied to labels, service mark will be used in advertisements)
[ ]	Applicant has a bona fide intention to use the mark in commerce on or in connection with the above identified goods/services, and asserts a claim of priority based upon a foreign application in accordance with 15 U.S.C. 1126(d), as amended. • Country of foreign filing:_____ • Date of foreign filing:_____
[ ]	Applicant has a bona fide intention to use the mark in commerce on or in connection with the above identified goods/services and, accompanying this application, submits a certification or certified copy of a foreign registration in accordance with 15 U.S.C 1126(e), as amended. • Country of registration:_____ • Registration number:_____

NOTE: Declaration, on Reverse Side, MUST be Signed

PTO Form 1478 (REV 6/96)   U.S. DEPARTMENT OF COMMERCE/Patent and Trademark Office
OMB No. 0651-0009 (Exp. 06/30/98) There is no requirement to respond to this collection of information unless a currently valid OMB Number is displayed.

If all or part of the mark is a design or graphic image, do not draw it in this space (the drawing, described in Chapter 6, will show the PTO what the mark looks like). Instead, use words to describe the mark as accurately as you can. Don't agonize about your description; the PTO will suggest a different one if they don't like yours. If you disagree with theirs, discuss the matter with the Examiner at that time and an acceptable description will probably emerge. Following are examples of some common types of marks and their descriptions.

EXAMPLES:

Text with graphics: The mark below, which is owned by the Walt Disney Company, could be described as "Walt Disney World, with a mouse head inside the D."

Stylized text: If your mark consists of text with stylized letters, your description can be fairly simple. For example, using the ABA mark as shown below, the description would be as follows, "The stylized letters ABA."

Graphics only: One of the most famous graphic marks is owned by The Quaker Oats Company. It could be described as "The face of a smiling, white-haired older man wearing a hat of a type common in America in the early 17th Century."

Graphics only with color: The New York Statue of Liberty Celebration Foundation developed the mark shown below, lined for the colors red and blue. This mark would be described as follows, "A circle generally containing the outline of the upper portion of the Statue of Liberty, the mark including the colors red and blue." For more on describing colors, see Chapter 6, Section C.

Marks presented in the context in which they appear: Sometimes, a mark appears on and is an integral part of the product it represents. Your drawing and specimens will show the mark as it appears on the product and you will describe the mark in its context. For example, the stripes on the shoe shown below would be described as follows, "Two bands having a color contrasting with the color of the shoe, the bands being applied diagonally from the instep of the upper edge of the shoe, the lower extremity of the bands being closest to the front of the shoe."

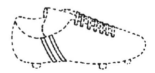

Using Continuation Pages

You can always use a blank piece of paper as a continuation page if you don't have enough room on the form. The top of each continuation page should have the following information in case it gets separated from your application:

- Applicant's complete name.
- Applicant's mailing address.
- Mark (use the words or description of your mark that you have developed here in this section).
- Goods or services with which mark is used.
- Which answer you are continuing.

EXAMPLE:

APPLICANT NAME: Quick-Byte, Inc.

APPLICANT BUSINESS ADDRESS: 1001 Badger Rd., Badger, VT, 98765

MARK: QUICK-BYTES

GOODS OR SERVICES: Computer consulting services

CONTINUATION OF APPLICATION

MARK, Continued: similar thick horizontal stripe, in golden yellow.

APPLICANT BUSINESS ADDRESS, Continued: Address in state of incorporation, 11 Pinkham Square, Denver, CO, 80100

2. Block 2: Class Number

Assign at least one class to the product or service for which you are using the mark. (Remember, each additional class will cost an extra $245.) If you aren't sure which class to use, call the PTO's Trademark Assistance Center at 703-308-9000 to get their opinion, or leave the block blank. The PTO will fill it in for you. Filling in the class yourself is better because you will have more control over what class is ultimately used.

3. Block 3: Applicant's Name

If you are seeking registration under your own name as a sole proprietor and owner of the mark and you know for certain that no one else is going to claim ownership over your mark, then simply insert your full, legal name in block three and go on to the next section. If you are a sole proprietor doing business under a fictitious business name, then simply insert your full, legal name followed by: "a sole proprietorship doing business as" (or "a sole proprietorship doing DBA"), and then your fictitious business name. You can also use "AKA" (also known as) or "TA" (trading as). Example: "James T. Smith, DBA Software Works."

The applicant is the person or business who owns the mark when the application is filed. Whether or not you own the mark you're seeking to register should not be an issue that overwhelms you at this point. As long as you, or the business you own, determines or controls the quality of the goods or services represented by the mark, then you should be fine to move ahead with your application.

For goods, this is usually the person or business identified on the specimens as the source of the goods. For example, the container for a pint of Ben & Jerry's ice cream contains the registered trademark "Ben & Jerry's," on the lid. The container itself gives information about the source of the ice cream, "Ben & Jerry's Homemade, Inc." To register the mark Ben & Jerry's, the applicant name would be Ben & Jerry's Homemade, Inc.

Following are the general rules that apply to different types of entities and examples of how different business entities would list their names in the Applicant Name box. Sole proprietors are discussed in the Fast Track box above. Partnerships, corporations, limited liability companies and joint ventures are discussed below.

a. Partnerships

If the partnership doesn't have a fictitious business name—that is, it does business using the partners' legal names—these names should be listed in the order they normally appear.

> EXAMPLE:
> APPLICANT NAME: Kim Bunch, Gloria Grant & Nancie Valle.

If the partnership uses a fictitious business name, then the partners' full legal names should be listed, followed by "a partnership doing business as," and then the fictitious business name. You can also use "AKA" (also known as) or "TA" (trading as).

> EXAMPLE:
> APPLICANT NAME: Kim Bunch, Gloria Grant & Nancie Valle, a partnership doing business as AB Company.

Another way to fill out this blank as a partnership using a fictitious name is to list the fictitious name first, followed by the legal names of the partners.

> EXAMPLE:
> APPLICANT NAME: AB Company, a partnership composed of Kim Bunch, Gloria Grant & Nancie Valle.

b. Corporations

The official name of the corporation should be listed in the Applicant Name box. Officers of the corporation should not be listed here, but an officer will have to sign the application at the end.

> EXAMPLE:
> APPLICANT NAME: Quick-Byte, Incorporated.

Divisions of corporations should not be listed here. Instead, list the parent corporation. If the mark is used only by a division, that may be stated in the second part of Block 7 (Basis for Application) or in a cover letter submitted with the application. For example, M&M/Mars distributes M&M chocolate candies and is a division of Mars, Inc. "M&M" is a registered trademark for the candies, but is not owned by the division, M&M/Mars. Rather, it is owned by the corporation, Mars, Inc. Therefore, Mars, Inc., would be the applicant for the trademark registration of "M&M."

c. Limited Liability Companies

Limited liability companies should state their official business name, whether it be a fictitious name or the names of the company's owners.

> EXAMPLE:
> APPLICANT NAME: Bridgeworks Design.

d. Joint Ventures

A joint venture is a single business entity and its official business name should go in the Applicant Name box.

> EXAMPLE:
> APPLICANT NAME: The Shacter/Alberts Company.

4. Block 4: Applicant's Mailing Address

Use an address at which mail is received, whether a physical location or a post office or private mail box service (the PTO prefers a street address). (If you need more room, continue on an extra page. See "Using Continuation Pages" in the sidebar, above.) If your mailing address changes at any time during the application process, you must send a written request to the PTO to have your correspondence address changed. The PTO will not change it over the phone.

For applicants applying as individuals: List both a home and a business address. They may both be the same.

If you are filing your own non-office application, you can add this information after the identification of the applicant. For example, "James Bonner, an individual and a citizen of the United States of America, whose business address is 2435 Marina Circle, Berkeley, CA 94712, and whose residence address is 5712 Adeline Ave., Berkeley, CA 94721," or "whose business and residence addresses are 5712 Adeline Ave., Berkeley, CA 94721."

For joint applicants: list the business addresses for all parties involved, specifying which address belongs to which applicant.

If you are filing your own non-office application, your statement would look something like, "Alice Kamamoto and Anthony Phillips, joint owners, both citizens of the United States of America. Alice Kamamoto's business address is 79 Jones Street, San Francisco, CA 94118, and Anthony Phillips's business address is 7689 Park Village Avenue, San Diego, CA 92129."

For sole proprietorships, partnerships, limited liability companies, corporations, joint ventures and associations: list the business address. If the corporation also has an address in its state of incorporation (different from its business address), list both.

If you're filing your own non-office application, your statement would look similar to the following example, "MindSet, Inc., a corporation of the State of California, whose corporate address is 2345 West End Blvd., Los Angeles, CA 90061, and whose business address is 45 Tailor Street, Virginia Beach, VA 23454."

5. Block 5: Applicant's Entity

Check the appropriate box (only one) and fill in the information requested.

- Individual applicants: Give your country of citizenship.
- Partnerships: Give the state and country under which the partnership was formed. Then list the names and countries of citizenship of the general partners. Silent, limited or inactive partners need not be listed.
- Corporations: Give the state (or country if outside the U.S.A.) of incorporation.
- Other: If the applicant is not an individual, partnership or corporation, check this box. For example, you would check this box if the applicant(s) was a sole proprietorship, an association, joint applicants, a limited liability company or a joint venture.

If a sole proprietorship, specify the national citizenship of the applicant.

EXAMPLE:
"Other: (Specify Nature of Entity and Domicile) Sole Proprietorship of the state of California. Leslie Ganes is the individual owner and a citizen of the United States."

If an association, specify the state or country where the association is organized or existing.

EXAMPLE:
"Other: (Specify Nature of Entity and Domicile) Association of the state of Texas."

If joint applicants, specify the national citizenship of each joint applicant.

EXAMPLE:

"Other: (Specify Nature of Entity and Domicile) Joint Applicants composed of Alice Abrams and Betty Bertrand, both citizens of the United States.

If a Limited Liability Company (LLC), specify the state or country where the LLC is organized or existing.

EXAMPLE:

"Other: (Specify Nature of Entity and Domicile) Limited Liability Company of the state of Michigan.

If a joint venture, specify the state or country where the joint venture is organized and list the members by name.

EXAMPLE:

"Other: (Specify Nature of Entity and Domicile) Joint Venture domiciled in Ohio, composed of Sabreen Hurt, Marn Reich and Sonja Eriksson."

Use the precise legal description of your business form. If you're not sure, call the local Small Business Administration office (check in your phone book). They may be able to provide some guidance. Whatever you do, don't simply use the word "firm" or "company" to describe your legal entity. These words are not specific enough for the PTO and could cause a delay in processing your application.

6. Block 6: Goods and/or Services

In this portion of the application, you are asked to identify the goods and/or services with which you will be using the mark in commerce. Describe the goods or services as clearly and succinctly as possible. Use ordinary English and be as accurate as you can. Here are some important guidelines to use when describing your goods or services.

a. Make Your Description Appropriately Inclusive

Subject to the other hints offered in this section, it is important to make your initial description broad enough to include all the goods or services for which you will want your mark to be protected. This is because of a PTO rule that, for the most part, doesn't permit the expansion of a description to include additional products or services once the application has been filed.

For example, assume you're a citrus fruit grower and your initial description lists "grapefruit, oranges, lemons, and limes." If you later realize that you should have included kumquats in this list, the chances are pretty good the Examiner won't let you amend your application to include them. Instead, you will probably be required to file another application—and pay another application fee—to extend your registration to the additional goods or services.

Beware of using labels, stationery, menus, signs and containers. If you are planning to describe your goods or services by reference to a label, menu, sign, stationery or container because that is where you think your mark will appear, then stop. You must not describe the mode or method by which you are using the mark in this section. The mode or method of use means the manner in which you affix the mark to the goods you are describing or in association with the services you are describing (for example, placing the mark on labels, signs, stationery, etc.). The labels, signs, stationery, etc., are not the goods or services themselves, and that is what you are being asked to describe here. Section 7 below explains where to place information about the manner or mode of use. If you mistakenly identify the goods or services as a label, stationery, menu, sign or container here, you will not be allowed to amend the application later to specify the actual goods or services. This means you will have to file another application and pay another fee.

b. Avoid an Overly Broad Description

In the previous section, we discussed how to make your description broad enough to include the goods and/or services under which you want your mark to be protected. The flip side of making your description broad enough is avoiding a description that is so broad, it actually encompasses more than the classes you intended. For example, for acrylic paints, you should use the specific phrase "artists' paints" rather than "artists' materials" ("materials" could mean paint brushes, canvasses, easels, etc., all of which could be listed in different classes).

A good rule of thumb is that the goods and services covered by your description should fall within the number of classes for which you want to pay. (Remember from Chapter 2 that you must pay $245 for each class under which you wish to register.) If the Examiner thinks that your description is too broad, he or she will give you an opportunity to amend it. (See "Calling the Patent and Trademark Office" and "Amending Your Application" below.) Remember, however, that if you amend your description to reduce the number of goods or services included in it, you won't later be able to add those goods or services back in if you change your mind.

If you find yourself using indefinite terms, such as "accessories," "components," "devices," "equipment," "food," "materials," "parts," "systems" or "products," then try using the words "namely" or "consisting of" afterwards and then list the goods or services by their more common commercial names. This will keep your description from inadvertently falling into an unintended class. For example, "Computer equipment, namely computer keyboards, computer monitors and modems."

> EXAMPLE: You produce a desk set that includes pens, pencils and scissors, and your trademark budget dictates that you register under only one class. Since scissors are in a different class than pens and pencils, your description should be "a desk set with pens and pencils" (Class 16), or, "a desk set with scissors" (Class 8), but not "a desk set with pens, pencils and scissors." If you inadvertently describe goods and/or services in more than one class, the trademark attorney examining your application at the PTO will likely allow you to amend your application to narrow your description so that it encompasses only one class, as intended.

c. Avoid Using Open-Ended and Indefinite Terms

Don't use open-ended, indefinite terms such as "including," "and the like," "such as," "and so on" or "for example."

- Unacceptable: Office supplies (pens, pencils and the like).
- Acceptable: Office supplies consisting of pens and pencils.
- Unacceptable: Typing paper including copy machine paper.
- Acceptable: Paper, namely that suitable for use in offices for typing and copy machines.

Indefinite phrases are not acceptable because they are not specific and could lead to the types of classification problems mentioned above in subsection b. For example, suppose you are applying for a mark which is to appear on a line of goods falling under Class 16, which includes Office Requisites. You wrote in Class 16 on your application and then described the goods as "pens, pencils and the like." The Examiner may decide the description is unacceptable because "pens, pencils and the like" could include items in more than one class (Class 16 for pens and pencils, Class 8 for scissors). If that were the case, you would have to pay double the filing fee, one for each class. When descriptions of goods and services are specifically defined or stated, the Examiner feels more certain that the proper class has been designated and the proper filing fee has been paid.

d. If You're Still Having Trouble

The PTO understands that, in our rapidly changing world, the number of possible goods and services (and descriptions of them) is limitless. Often when a good or service is first created it is difficult to describe it with common language. For example, when Ford first began making cars, the words "motor car" and "automobile" had not yet become common language. Similarly, in the mid-1970s there was no common language for describing consulting services in the field of personal computers (since personal computers had not existed before that time).

Fortunately, the PTO will help answer your questions about how to word the description of your goods or services. To speak with the Managing or Senior Attorney handling the class you plan to register under, call 703-308-9101 and follow the instructions on the recording. For example, if your mark is used in connection with mailbox rental services (Class 39, transportation and storage services), follow the instructions to get to the PTO office which handles Class 39 applications. Explain that you need help wording a description for your goods or services. The lawyer will give you some suggestions based on your description of the good or service involved. Don't feel bound by the Examiner's first suggestion, especially if it would reduce the number of goods and services included in your description or change the class you will register under. It is usually possible to discuss the goods or services and make counter-suggestions until a description that satisfies you and the Examiner is found.

Another way you can get help from the PTO is by reading this section, consulting the resources discussed in the sidebar below and putting your own description on your application. If the PTO finds your description unacceptable, they will call or write you and suggest another description, sometimes after they get more information about your goods or services. Be aware, however, that this may cause some delay in getting your registration accomplished.

Resources to Help You Describe Your Goods or Services

There are a number of resources available to help you decide how to describe your goods or services. Probably the best source is the list of approved descriptions the PTO has prepared for its Examiners to use when reviewing applications, called the *U.S. Patent & Trademark Office Acceptable Identification of Goods and Services Manual.* You may recall from Chapter 2 that this manual is also an excellent resource for choosing the appropriate class for your goods or services. Besides class information, this manual contains a list of descriptions the PTO deems acceptable.

You can search the manual for free at the PTO's website (http://www.uspto.gov) or you can order it for $40 plus shipping costs from the International Trademark Association, New York, N.Y. (212-986-5880). You can also find a copy at your nearest Patent and Trademark Depository Library (see Appendix for a listing). It is not available in hard copy from the PTO. This manual has over 13,000 listings, and if you are only planning to prepare one application, it's probably not worth purchasing it.

For a complete explanation of how to search the hard copy manual and the online manual, see Chapter 2, Section C3 which explains search techniques for choosing a class. The same techniques will help your search for acceptable descriptions of your goods and/or services.

You can also use the International List of Classes for Goods and Services to find more terms to describe your goods or services. You will find this list in the Appendix. The International Classification of Products and Services (under the Nice Agreement, 7th Edition) is helpful for the same purpose. You will find it published on the World Intellectual Property Organization's (WIPO) website at http://www.wipo.org/eng/clssfctn/nice/enmn01.htm.

One final suggestion: If you have access to the federal trademark database (on the web or at the nearest PTDL), you can search for marks used by competitors and then examine the goods and services description used for those marks. See Chapter 2, Section C3, for more information on how to do this.

This block also mentions an "accompanying drawing" being submitted with the application. Drawings are explained in Chapter 6.

7. Block 7: Basis for Application

In this block you indicate the basis for your application. Since you are reading this chapter, chances are you'll check the second box, "Applicant has a bona fide intention to use the mark in commerce on or in connection with the above identified goods/services." "Bona fide" is Latin for good faith.

You must also indicate how you intend to use your mark ("manner or mode of use") with your goods or services. Describe at least one way your mark will be used. You need not describe all the ways it will be used.

Examples of how marks are used to identify goods:

- If your mark will be employed on items such as books, jeans, hats or other goods on which the mark might appear, your manner or mode of use may be: "The mark will be placed directly on the goods and used in other ways customary to the trade."
- If your mark will be used in connection with items such as window glass, jewelry or other goods on which it is impractical to place the mark directly, try this or similar wording: "The mark will be used on labels attached to the goods and on packaging."
- If your mark will be used in connection with services, you may state something like: "The mark will be used in letters, advertisements and signs used to promote the services."

If you choose to file a non-office application, use the samples in the Appendix which demonstrate what the appropriate language is to designate the basis for your application as an intent-to-use application. The disk contains a template for the intent-to-use application with the appropriate language establishing the basis for the application included.

8. Block 8: Declaration (Back Side of the Application)

By signing the Declaration, you are stating under oath that you:

- understand that willful false statements are punishable by fine, imprisonment or both under federal law, and that such willful false statements may jeopardize the validity of the application or any resulting registration;
- are authorized to "execute" (sign) the application on behalf of the applicant (if the applicant is a business entity);
- believe the applicant is the owner of the mark for which registration is sought;
- believe no other person, firm, corporation or association has the right to use the mark or a mark so similar that consumers could be confused or deceived; and
- know all statements in the application are true or that you have been informed and believe that they are true.

This declaration is mostly to warn you that you had better be telling the truth. The PTO rarely, if ever, takes the time to figure out if people are lying or to prosecute them for making false statements. However, if you ever get into a dispute, any lies you make in your application may come to light and cause you to lose. The bottom line is that you should not file an application if any of the following is true:

- You are not sure whether you are the owner of the mark. (See Section 3, above, regarding who can apply for registration.)

- You know of a clear conflict with a mark used by someone else. (See Chapter 1, Section D.)
- You are making some other statement in the application that you believe is not true.

Be consistent. Make sure your signature (and title) is consistent with information you entered in Block 3.

If you are filing as an individual, simply sign your name, print your name, give the date and provide a phone number where you can be reached. If you are filing as another entity, skip to the appropriate section below and follow those instructions.

The rules for who should sign the declaration are as follows:

Individuals: If the applicant is an individual, sign here. If a wife and husband, or any other individuals, are applying together as separate individuals rather than as a partnership, each must sign as joint owners (see below).

Sole Proprietorships: If you are the sole owner of a business you must sign the application. On the line below, print your name and show your position as "sole proprietor."

Partnerships: Any partner of a general (as opposed to a limited) partnership may sign. You need not provide proof that the signer is a general partner with power to make business decisions binding the partnership, but such proof should be available in case the Examiner requests it.

Joint Ventures: Any principal member of the joint venture may sign.

Limited Liability Companies: Any officer of the limited liability company may sign. The following titles are acceptable: president, vice-president, secretary, treasurer, CEO, CFO (or controller or comptroller). Modifications such as VP of Sales or Executive VP are also acceptable.

Corporations (profit and nonprofit) and unincorporated associations (such as labor unions and community groups): The following corporate titles are acceptable: president, vice-president, secretary, treasurer, CEO, CFO (or controller or comptroller). Clerk is acceptable for mass corporations. Also acceptable are chairman or chairman of the board of directors (but not a director). Modifications such as VP of Sales or Executive VP are also acceptable. If you decide to use someone with another title not typically considered to be a corporate officer, you must provide proof that the person is in fact an officer. For example, if you decide to have the corporate general counsel sign the application, you should provide a declaration (statement under penalty of perjury) explaining that the person is an officer, and attach a copy of the corporate minutes in which the person was made a corporate officer. A corporate employee such as an executive director, publisher or managing director may not sign unless she is also a corporate officer.

Put the date on the line to the left of the signature line. The application must be filed with the PTO within a reasonable time after it is signed and dated. Eight weeks or less is considered reasonable by the PTO, but we recommend that the application be filed as soon as possible. Remember to add your phone number and printed name. Following is an example of how to complete the Declaration block of the application.

December 7, 1998	*Ken Andres*
Date	Signature

510-441-9100	Ken Andres, Treasurer
Telephone Number	Print or Type Name and Position

B. What's Next?

You have completed your trademark application. But you are not finished yet! You still need to prepare your drawing before you can file your application. Chapters 6 and 7 will take you through preparing the drawing and the filing process. And to get your mark actually registered,

Trademark/Service Mark Application (Page 2)

DECLARATION

The undersigned being hereby warned that willful false statements and the like so made are punishable by fine or imprisonment, or both, under 18 U.S.C. 1001, and that such willful false statements may jeopardize the validity of the application or any resulting registration, declares that he/she is properly authorized to execute this application on behalf of the applicant; he/she believes the applicant to be the owner of the trademark/service mark sought to be registered, or if the application is being filed under 15 U.S.C. 1051(b), he/she believes the applicant to be entitled to use such mark in commerce; to the best of his/her knowledge and belief no other person, firm, corporation, or association has the right to use the above identified mark in commerce, either in the identical form thereof or in such near resemblance thereto as to be likely, when used on or in connection with the goods/services of such other person, to cause confusion, or to cause mistake, or to deceive; and that all statements made of his/her own knowledge are true and that all statements made on information and belief are believed to be true.

_____   _____
DATE   SIGNATURE

_____   _____
TELEPHONE NUMBER   PRINT OR TYPE NAME AND POSITION

INSTRUCTIONS AND INFORMATION FOR APPLICANT

TO RECEIVE A FILING DATE, THE APPLICATION MUST BE COMPLETED AND SIGNED BY THE APPLICANT AND SUBMITTED ALONG WITH:

1. The prescribed **FEE ($245.00)** for each class of goods/services listed in the application;
2. A **DRAWING PAGE** displaying the mark in conformance with 37 CFR 2.52;
3. If the application is based on use of the mark in commerce, **THREE (3) SPECIMENS** (evidence) of the mark as used in commerce for each class of goods/services listed in the application. All three specimens may be the same. Examples of good specimens include: (a) labels showing the mark which are placed on the goods; (b) photographs of the mark as it appears on the goods, (c) brochures or advertisements showing the mark as used in connection with the services.
4. An **APPLICATION WITH DECLARATION** (this form) - The application must be signed in order for the application to receive a filing date. Only the following persons may sign the declaration, depending on the applicant's legal entity: (a) the individual applicant; (b) an officer of the corporate applicant; (c) one general partner of a partnership applicant; (d) all joint applicants.

SEND APPLICATION FORM, DRAWING PAGE, FEE, AND SPECIMENS (IF APPROPRIATE) TO:

**Assistant Commissioner for Trademarks
Box New App/Fee
2900 Crystal Drive
Arlington, VA 22202-3513**

Additional information concerning the requirements for filing an application is available in a booklet entitled **Basic Facts About Registering a Trademark,** which may be obtained by writing to the above address or by calling: (703) 308-HELP.

you will need to put your mark into actual use
and file an Allegation of Use along with specimens.
Chapter 11 will guide you through the important
final steps to achieving registration. ■

Drawings

After completing your application for registration, it is time to turn your attention to the drawing. All trademark applicants, both use and intent-to-use, must include a trademark drawing with their applications. This drawing will be the basis for the publication of your mark in the *Official Gazette*, a PTO periodical that notifies the public of marks for which registration is being sought.

What is a trademark drawing? You might think that a trademark drawing consists of a fancy artist's drawing of your mark on special paper. In reality, it's just a specially sized version of your mark in black and white on a letter-sized piece of paper. If your mark is a simple word mark (you're just trying to register a name), the actual "drawing" would consist of the name typed in the center of the drawing page. But there are other requirements you need to understand, which we'll discuss below.

There are three main requirements to remember when it comes to your trademark drawing:

- The drawing page must use a specific format and include a heading.
- The drawing itself must conform to certain technical requirements.
- The drawing must be nearly identical to the mark as it is represented on the specimens you submit to the PTO.

Let's look at these requirements in more detail.

A. Format Requirements for Drawing Page

The PTO has a number of technical rules for the drawing page. All drawings must be on pure white, durable, non-shiny paper 8½ inches (21.6 cm) wide and 11 inches (27.9 cm) long. Bond paper may be used but no watermark may be obvious. There must be a heading (described below) at the top of the page. There must be at least a 1-inch (2.54 cm) margin on the sides, top and bottom of the page and at least 1 inch between the heading and the drawing of the mark.

The drawing itself must be in black, either typed or drawn in ink, and may not be larger than 4" by 4" (see Section B below). The following sample shows the format specifications you'll need to use.

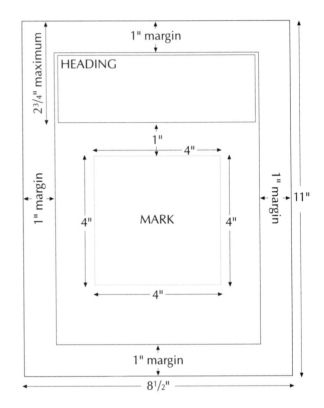

The heading must provide the following information from your application, each on a separate line:

- applicant's complete name
- applicant's mailing address
- date of first use of the mark (for use applications)
- date of first use of the mark in commerce (for use applications), and
- the goods or services the mark is (or will be) used to identify.

In addition, if your mark is a graphic design or symbol, a description of the essential features of the mark should be added as the last item of the heading. The idea is to depict and describe the mark in enough detail so it can be easily and accurately reproduced. Do your best; if the

Examiner thinks your description needs revision, he or she will contact you. Your main goal should be to make your drawing as accurate a depiction of the mark you intend to use as possible.

If any of the items in the heading is very long, continue it on a continuation page (see Chapter 4, Section A1, or Chapter 5, Section A1, for how to make a continuation page), so that the heading does not extend below the top one-quarter of the page (including the 1" margin at the top).

```
       ↕ 1"

Applicant: Linton & Company
Applicant Address: 123 Choice Rd.,
Twinsburg, OH 44087
Date of first use: June 25, 1991
Date of first use in commerce:
June 29, 1991
Goods or services: Computerized
sign design services

       ↕ 1"

SIGN DESIGNS
```

B. The Drawing Itself

Drawings fall into two categories: typewritten drawings, which include marks containing only words, numbers and/or certain typographical symbols in no particular color, type style or size; and special-form drawings (sometimes called ink drawings), which include all other marks. Each type has its own detailed requirements.

1. Typewritten Drawings

If your mark is made of only words or numbers, and the color, type style and size are not integral factors, simply type or print out your mark in all

capital letters in the center of the page. Despite the term "typewritten" drawing, printing the mark in all caps is acceptable. Use India ink or something similar so the black lines are solid. Ballpoint and felt pens may not be used. No white-out or other correction fluids or tape may be used. You must use all capital letters or your application will be returned. The drawing may not be larger than 4" by 4".

If you do type your mark with a typewriter, use one with a standard font. If you use a special typewriter or a computer (where you have many fonts to choose from), use the same size and style as that on a standard typewriter. The Courier font is a good example of a standard typewriter-style font:

```
SIGN DESIGNS
```

There is no need to bold, italicize or underline your mark.

In addition to numbers and letters, the following symbols (but no others) may be used in a typewritten (or printed out) drawing:

```
. ? " - ; ( % $ @ +
, ! ' : / ) & # * =
```

Typewritten drawings may be folded if absolutely necessary, but the mark on the drawing may not be creased by the fold; the drawing will be rejected if it has crease marks.

2. Special-Form (Ink) Drawings

If your mark includes a graphic design or symbol, your drawing should be an accurate rendering of that mark in ink. You must use flexible, smooth, non-shiny white paper. Bond paper may be used but no watermark may be obvious. Use India ink or something similar so the black lines are solid. You may not use ballpoint or felt-tip pens, or any correction fluids or tape. Again, the mark should be placed at least one inch below the heading and must not exceed 4" x 4".

Drawings (such as an artist's rendition) may be pasted to the drawing page, as long as they are flat and well-attached, and meet the requirements mentioned above (flexible, smooth, non-shiny white paper; no ballpoint or felt-tip pens or correction fluids or tape; correct placement on page).

💡 If you are not familiar with graphic arts or drafting, consider paying an artist to prepare your drawing. See "How to an Artist" below.

Ink drawings should never be folded, even if the fold does not go through the drawing itself. You should protect the drawing with cardboard or something similar to prevent bending or creasing during the mail.

How to Find an Artist

You can find an artist by looking in the phone book of your metropolitan area under "Artists—Commercial." Ask whether they have experience doing trademark application drawings. Hiring a freelance commercial or graphic artist can be expensive; expect to pay from $40 to $80 per hour for the work (which usually takes an hour or less). Local arts organizations are another good source of referrals to freelance artists. You could also use a student from an art school, but make sure she has the skills you need and that you give clear instructions (based on the information set out below).

For more information about how to make precise drawings and how to use a CAD program to make your own drawing, see *The Patent Drawing Book,* by Jack Lo (Nolo).

C. Additional Requirements

In addition to these basic requirements for marks in general, the PTO has additional rules for certain types of marks and elements within them.

1. Marks With Color As an Element

The PTO uses a number of different patterns to represent colors in trademark drawings. If you want to claim a certain color as part of your mark, you need to identify it with this pattern system. Don't use colors or gray shading in the drawing, only the PTO-approved patterns. Remember, however, that if you claim one or more colors as part of your mark, the specimens you submit must show the mark in those colors. If you don't color-code your drawing, the specimens may use any colors or none (just black and white). The PTO uses the following color/pattern system:

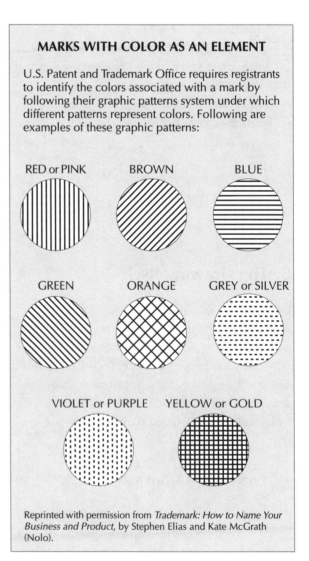

MARKS WITH COLOR AS AN ELEMENT

U.S. Patent and Trademark Office requires registrants to identify the colors associated with a mark by following their graphic patterns system under which different patterns represent colors. Following are examples of these graphic patterns:

RED or PINK   BROWN   BLUE

GREEN   ORANGE   GREY or SILVER

VIOLET or PURPLE   YELLOW or GOLD

Reprinted with permission from *Trademark: How to Name Your Business and Product,* by Stephen Elias and Kate McGrath (Nolo).

The appropriate lining should occur in the area of the mark where it would normally appear, as in the following example:

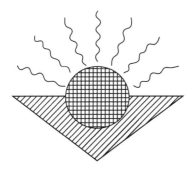

If your drawing is lined for color, you need to include a statement to that effect in the heading. If the mark is a particular shade of color, indicate that as well. For example:

(Heading)

APPLICANT'S NAME: Ground Zero, Inc.

APPLICANT'S ADDRESS: 250 Market Street, San Francisco, CA 94102

GOODS AND SERVICES: Specialty blend coffee

FIRST USE: December 30, 1997

FIRST USE IN COMMERCE: December 30, 1997

DESIGN: A steaming, harvest moon

LINING: The mark is lined for the colors maize yellow and chocolate brown

---

2. Marks on Three-Dimensional Objects

If your mark is positioned on a three-dimensional object (such as the placement of a label on a container) and its position is an important element of the mark, then the drawing must show the mark and its position in perspective in one view. Do this by showing the mark with solid lines and the rest of the drawing with broken lines so the Examiner can easily tell the mark from the product.

For example, some athletic goods companies place their marks consisting of stripes on their shoes in particular places. The stripes would be shown in solid lines and the shoe in broken lines.

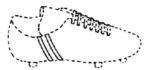

Again, consistency is essential. If your drawing shows one illustration of your mark, and you submit a specimen with even a slightly different appearance, your application could be jeopardized. Make sure the use matches the drawing so the specimens you submit (or will submit later as an ITU applicant) are consistent with the drawing.

D. Your Drawing and Specimens Must Match

Finally, it's crucial to remember that if you file a use application, your drawing must match—in spelling, style and appearance—the mark as it appears on the specimens you plan to submit. Before you decide exactly how to compose your drawing, make sure you have specimens that accurately depict it. If the person examining your application decides that your specimens and drawings don't match, he'll require that you change one or the other to achieve consistency.

If it is the drawing that you have to change, you may be forced to file a new application (and new filing fee) if the amended drawing is considered a "material alteration." A material alteration is any change that alters the essence of the original drawing—and therefore the mark that you were trying to register.

For example, assume that you originally submitted a mark which included words and a design that was integral to the mark as a whole. Later you were asked to amend the drawing because it did not match your specimens. You amend the drawing and take out the design aspect of the mark, which is now only a word mark. This amendment will not be accepted by the trademark attorney because you have materially altered the essence of the mark, which included a design element that was integral to the mark as a whole. To continue with your registration, you would have to file a new application.

Let's look at a real life example of how the material alteration concept works. In a case decided in 1974, the Richards-Wilcox Manufacturing Co. (the trademark applicant) sought to overturn a decision made by their trademark Examiner over an amendment to the mark proposed by Richards-Wilcox. In the amendment, Richards-Wilcox requested the mark be amended from the mark you see below (a diamond design within which the words "FYER-WALL" appear, with the R and W enclosed in an inverted channel bracket design) to "FYER-WALL" in plain, block letters.

The trademark Examiner rejected the amendment, and the Commissioner of Patents agreed with the Examiner, because changing the mark from the design shown above to plain, block letters was a material alteration of the mark. The Commissioner found that because the R and W were so greatly emphasized in the original mark (both by their greater size and by being surrounded by the inverted bracket), this portrayal effectively made the mark "RW FYER-WALL," and not just "FYER-WALL." ("RW" being the initials of Richards-Wilcox.) The Commissioner found the inverted bracket and the emphasized letters R and W to be integral parts of the mark, and that removing them changed the overall appearance of the mark and eliminated a prominent feature, constituting a material alteration.

So think about your mark carefully before submitting your application to the PTO. If you'd like to read the Richards-Wilcox case for yourself, you will find it in Volume 181 of the U.S. Patent Quarterly, page 735. You can find the U.S. Patent Quarterly at your local law library (see Chapter 14, Help Beyond This Book). ■

Filing Your Application

Once your application is complete and the drawing and specimens are ready, it's time to file the application. Just to make sure you are ready, here's a checklist for the steps you should have completed:

- The trademark application is complete (Chapter 4 or Chapter 5):
  - ☐ The mark has been described in Block 1.
  - ☐ A class number (or numbers) has been inserted in Block 2.
  - ☐ The applicant's name is stated in Block 3.
  - ☐ The applicant's mailing address is given in Block 4.
  - ☐ The applicant's entity status is indicated in Block 5, along with the applicant's state or country of citizenship or domicile.
  - ☐ The goods and/or services to which the mark is attached are described in Block 6.
  - ☐ The basis for the application is indicated in Block 7; the dates of first use anywhere and first use in commerce are filled in for use applicants; and the manner and mode of use is stated for both use and intent-to-use applicants.
  - ☐ The applicant has confirmed that all information in the application is true to the applicant's knowledge.
  - ☐ The applicant has confirmed that he or she has the authority to sign the application and the applicant's signature is present in Block 8.
- You have completed the drawing (Chapter 6):
  - ☐ The drawing page has a heading.
  - ☐ The drawing itself conforms to the requirements of either a typewritten drawing or a special form drawing ("ink" drawing).
  - ☐ The drawing is virtually identical to the mark as it is represented on the specimens.
  - ☐ The drawing is not larger than 4" by 4".
  - ☐ The drawing is appropriately placed in the center of the drawing sheet.

- You have gathered the necessary specimens (use applicants only; Chapter 3):
  - ☐ There are three specimens for each class you listed in Block 2.
  - ☐ The three specimens show the same mark as described in the application.
  - ☐ At least one of the specimens reflects a product or service that is consistent with the description of goods and services on the application.
  - ☐ The specimens are consistent with the description of the manner or mode of use of the mark. For instance, if the mark is being used on a label, at least one of the specimens should be a label.

Have you checked off all of the items above? Congratulations! You are now ready to file your trademark application.

Organization Is Key

If you haven't set up a good filing system for your trademark application, now is the time to do so. Use at least two file folders—one for correspondence with the PTO and one for copies of the documents you submit—and, if necessary, an accordion folder to keep all trademark-related documents together.

A. The Importance of Filing Promptly

For a number of reasons, it is a very good idea to file your application as soon as it's completed so that you obtain the earliest possible filing date. Your filing date is important because it determines priority in case more than one applicant submits an identical mark to the PTO. This section describes how a filing date is determined and how it may affect your rights to your mark.

⚠️ **Delay reduces the effectiveness of your trademark search.** For those who have invested time and money in a trademark search, remember that you're losing the value of that search every day that you wait to file your application. The longer you wait, the more chance there is that someone else has started using your mark or that someone else has already filed their application.

1. Filing Dates and Mail Services

It's important to realize that the way you mail your application to the PTO affects its filing date. If you use United States Post Office Express Mail with an Express Mail Certificate, the filing date is the date you mailed the application. For all other mail services—including Federal Express overnight, UPS, or regular U.S. mail—the filing date is the date your application is received by the PTO. For this reason, we recommend sending the application via Express Mail to get the earliest possible filing date.

There are two types of Express Mail: "Post Office to Post Office," and "Post Office to Addressee." A different mailing form is used for each. For your filing date to be the date you mailed the application, you must use the Post Office to Addressee type of Express Mail. If you use Post Office to Post Office, your filing date will be the date the application is received by the PTO.

Finally, to have your mailing date count as your filing date, you must include an Express Mail Certificate with your application. The Express Mail Certificate is simply a statement that the application was sent by Express Mail, and it must be signed by the person who handles the transaction with the Post Office or prepares the package for shipping. The Express Mail Certificate for the mark "Quick-Bytes," for example, would look like this:

Sample Express Mail Certificate

Applicant: Etta Linton
Mark: Quick-Bytes
Express Mail label No.: 77770
Date of Deposit: January 25, 1999

I hereby certify that this paper and fee is being deposited with the United States Postal Service "Express Mail Post Office to Addressee" service under 37 CFR 1.10 on the date shown above and is addressed to the Assistant Commissioner for Trademarks, Box New App/Fee, 2900 Crystal Dr., Arlington, VA 22202-3513.

Etta Linton
Etta Linton

2. Why Filing Dates Matter

Your filing date may prove to be critical in the event of a conflict with another filer who wants to register the same mark as yours. While it's impossible to say whether a particular filing date will make a difference in your particular situation, yours might be the one case in a thousand where a day's difference in the filing date will mean that your rights are superior—or inferior—to another filer's.

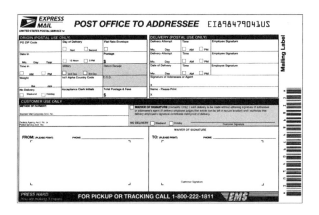

a. Priority Between Conflicting Marks

If two or more applications for the same mark are received by the PTO, the PTO will examine and publish for opposition the one with the earliest filing date. All conflicting applications will wait in line until the outcome of the first application is known. This means that if someone else with the same mark gets their application in first, their application will have priority over yours. If their application is approved, you will lose your mark.

> EXAMPLE: Mark sends his trademark application to the PTO via Express Mail on December 1, 1998. Because he sent his application via Express Mail, his filing date will be the date he sent the application (December 1, 1998) instead of the date the PTO actually received the application. Jane sends in her trademark application for a mark that is identical to Mark's via regular ground U.S. mail on November 29, 1998 and the PTO receives her application on December 2. Jane's filing date will be the date the PTO actually received her application (December 2, 1998). Since Mark's filing date is earlier than Jane's, his application will receive priority over hers, even though she mailed her application first. If Mark's mark is successfully registered, Jane will lose her mark.

b. Date of First Use

For intent-to-use applicants, your filing date will also serve as the date you first used the mark as long as you complete the registration process by putting the mark into actual use within the prescribed time period, filing an Allegation of Use with the PTO, and getting your mark placed on the federal trademark register. (See Chapter 5 on intent-to-use applications.) Again, if your mark conflicts with another filer's, your filing date may make (or break) your application.

c. International Rights

If you register your mark abroad, most countries will adopt your U.S. filing date if you file your international application within six months of your U.S. filing date. See *Trademark: Legal Care for Your Business Name and Product* by Stephen Elias and Kate McGrath (Nolo) for more information on registering your trademark internationally.

d. Re-execution of Application

It is common practice at the PTO to require re-execution of any application that was signed more than six months before being filed with the PTO. While it is ultimately up to the trademark Examiner's discretion either to accept the application or require re-execution, it's best just to file right away. Keep in mind, however, that re-execution of the application will not affect your filing date. Your filing date will still be the date the PTO actually received your original application, or, if you sent it via Express Mail, the date you sent the application.

B. Assembling the Package

Gather together all the documents you'll be sending to the PTO. These include:
- the main application form
- the drawing
- the check for the fees
- three specimens of use (for actual use applications)
- a self-addressed, stamped post card
- the Express Mail mailing certificate (if you use this method to file your application—see Section A1, above).

Use an envelope large enough to accommodate all your forms without folding them. This is especially crucial for the drawing. As stated in

Chapter 6, ink drawings can't be folded at all, and typed drawings should not be folded if the fold would put a crease through the drawing itself.

1. Filing Fees

As of the date of this book, the filing fee for your registration application is $245, regardless of the basis for your filing—use or intent-to-use. Still, it is always a good idea to check for updated fee information to make sure the fee you send is the correct one. (See "Application Fee Updates" below.) You may pay by check or money order made out to the Commissioner of Patents and Trademarks. *Don't send cash.* Note that if you send a check and it bounces, the filing of the application will be revoked and you will be notified by the PTO. This will require you to re-file, making your filing date later than it would have been had the check gone through.

Application Fee Updates

To obtain the most current information on trademark application fees, try any one of the following sources:
- The PTO's website at http://www. uspto.gov/. From the home page, choose "PTO Fees" from the menu on the left side of the home page. Click on "Trademark Processing Fees" and locate the fee for the Application for Registration.
- Call the Trademark Assistance Center at 703-308-9000 (office hours are 8:30 a.m. to 5:00 p.m., Monday through Friday, except federal holidays) or the PTO's automated information system for Patents and Trademarks (operating 24 hours a day, seven days a week, including holidays) at 703-557-INFO.

2. Self-Addressed Stamped Postcard

Normally the PTO will send you a filing receipt with a serial number about six to eight weeks after receiving your application. This serial number is the way the PTO keeps track of your application. If you want earlier notice that your application reached the PTO and the serial number they assigned to it, you can include with your application a self-addressed, postage-paid post card with your mark printed upon it clearly. The PTO will stamp the card with the date the application was received and your serial number, and return it to you. You should receive it within two weeks after you mailed the application. Keep the card in a safe place, as you may need to refer to your serial number frequently during the process.

Sample Post Card Front

Date: Serial No.:

Applicant Name:
Applicant Address

Mark: [In All Caps]

Sample Post Card Back

[SENDER'S NAME]
[Sender's Street Address]
[Sender's City, State and Zip]

3. Make Copies

Make photocopies of all the documents you will be sending to the PTO. Very often, you will need to refer to these documents when corresponding with the PTO, as described below.

C. Mailing Your Trademark Application

Mark the outside of your envelope "Trademark Application." For both actual use and intent-to-use applications, send it to the following address:

> The Assistant Commissioner for Trademarks
> Box NEW APP/FEE
> 2900 Crystal Drive
> Arlington, VA 22202-3513

Documents sent to the PTO after your initial application go to a different address, which we'll provide when we discuss these other documents you may be filing.

As discussed above in Section A1, we recommend sending your application via the United States Post Office Express Mail, Post Office to Addressee service, to get the earliest possible filing date. Applications sent via Federal Express, UPS or other overnight mail services, or Express Mail sent via the Post Office to Post Office will not qualify as filed when sent. They are only considered filed when received by the PTO.

D. Receiving the PTO Filing Receipt

About six to eight weeks after mailing your application, you should receive the PTO's filing receipt. (If you want earlier notice, include a self-addressed stamped post card with your application, as discussed above.) The current form is an 8½" by 11" white form titled "Filing Receipt for Trademark Application."

The filing receipt includes your application serial number, the date of filing, the mark, the applicant's name and address and other information. The information on the receipt should be checked carefully. If there is a mistake, you should send a correcting letter to the PTO immediately. See Chapter 8, Section D, on corresponding with the PTO.

The PTO filing receipt will explain that you should not expect to hear anything about your application for approximately three months. If you have not heard anything in three and a half months, it is wise to call and inquire as to the status of your application. There are two ways to do this:

- TRAM automated system: TRAM stands for Trademark Reporting and Monitoring. From any touch-tone phone, Monday through Friday from 6:30 a.m. to midnight Eastern time, dial 703-305-8747. After the welcome message and tone, enter your mark's eight-digit serial number and the pound sign. You should hear the current status of your mark along with the effective date of the status.

- If you want additional information or would prefer talking with a human, call the Trademark Assistance Center at 703-308-9400 and request a status check (office hours are Monday through Friday from 8:30 a.m. to 5:00 p.m., eastern time, except federal holidays). ∎

PART 2

Handling Problems With Your Application

Dealing With the PTO After You've Filed Your Application

After you file your trademark application, it will be processed through the PTO mail room, the Office of Finance and eventually assigned to a Legal Instruments Examiner. The Legal Instruments Examiner (not to be confused with the trademark attorney/Examiner, discussed below) will check to see if there is any major piece of information missing from your application such as the drawing or your name or address. If all of the major pieces of the application are present, your application will be checked by the Classification Team to make sure the class you chose fits the goods and/or services listed on your application. Next it will be recorded by the Data Unit for the PTO's records, at which point a filing receipt will be issued to you confirming the information in your application. Finally, the application will be assigned to a trademark attorney at the PTO (we call this person the Examiner). The Examiner will look closely at your application to see if there is any incorrect information or any other problem that may delay or prohibit the registration of your mark.

At a number of different points in this process, the PTO may communicate to you that a problem of some sort exists with your application. This chapter helps you understand:

- the basic types of correspondence the PTO is likely to send you and what your options are for responding to the PTO
- the correct formats for your correspondence with the PTO, and
- the human side of trademark Examiners— the people you'll be communicating with at the PTO—and how to communicate effectively with them.

Chapters 9 and 10 address in more detail the particular problems that are commonly raised by the PTO—such as drawing mistakes and rejections based on descriptiveness or likelihood of confusion—and how you should respond to each one. The information in this chapter will direct you to the appropriate discussion in one of those chapters for detailed information for your particular circumstances.

Keep in mind while you read this chapter that it is your responsibility to make sure your application gets through the examination process. You are in the driver's seat and are required to be diligent in pursuing your application. If you are expecting some action from the PTO and more than six months have elapsed since you've heard from them, call the PTO Status Line (703-308-HELP). If you discover a problem, call your Examiner immediately to discuss it.

Procedures at the PTO are in flux. The PTO has a huge backlog of applications that need action and is confronted with an increasing number of new applications every year. Because of the large number of applications, the PTO is currently undergoing changes in its procedures to help process them faster. While these are the standard procedures used by the PTO at the printing of this book, you may encounter different procedures if the PTO has changed them. We will do our best to keep you updated as to new procedures on Nolo's website at http://www.nolo.com. For the most part, however, you should be able to use the information we provide here and a little common sense to help you through.

A. Handling Simple Problems With Your Application

This section outlines the common problems with trademark applications that have relatively simple remedies. More complicated problems—ones that typically result in action letters from the PTO—are covered in detail later in this chapter in Section B, and in the following two chapters.

1. Remedying Incorrect Information on Your Filing Receipt

As mentioned above, once your application has been received by the PTO mail room, it will eventually end up at the Data Unit of the Application

Branch at the PTO. There, your application will be entered into the PTO's records and a document called Filing Receipt for Trademark Application will be issued. You should receive the filing receipt within six to eight weeks from the time you filed your application. If you have not received your filing receipt within that time frame, call the Trademark Assistance Center at 703-308-9000.

Occasionally, a filing receipt is sent with incorrect information on it. If the filing receipt contains incorrect information, you must write a letter to the PTO requesting a correction. An example of that letter appears in Section D2.

2. Notice of Incomplete Trademark Application

If anything is missing from your application that causes the PTO to return it to you along with your application fee, you will receive a Notice of Incomplete Trademark Application. Missing drawings, for example, are a common cause of an application being returned. If you receive such a notice and believe it was wrongfully sent to you, you may call the Legal Instruments Examiner, whose name and phone number will be listed at the bottom of the notice. Otherwise, take note of the reasons for the deficiency listed on the notice and send the corrected application and fee back to the PTO. You may want to refer back to Chapters 3 through 7 for information on how to correctly fill out your application and provide the specimens and the drawing.

B. Dealing With Action Letters

The Examiner reviewing your application will send you what's called an action letter if he or she has come across one or more problems with your mark or your application that warrant rejection. You'll know it's an action letter if it has an action number on it and the words "Office Action" on the front page. The action letter details each problem and explains why the Examiner believes the items are reasonable grounds for rejecting your application.

When you see the word "rejection," you may think that it's all over. However, action letters can refer to minor problems as well as major problems, so it's important that you not panic. Most action letters raise issues that can be fixed, and if the action letter you received is concerned with those types of issues, the Examiner will continue reviewing your application until all problems have been resolved. This section will help you evaluate the information in any action letter you might receive and decide how to proceed.

1. Rejection Isn't the Last Word

When an application has a problem which keeps it from moving forward in the process, the Examiner is required to reject it. The application is then officially rejected until the problem is fixed.

If the problem is fixed, the Examiner will reconsider the application in light of the amendments and continue with the examination process. (But remember that your application is in a state of rejection until you fix the problem.) Thus, a rejection, unless it is a final rejection, doesn't mean that it's all over.

If, however, the problem is never fixed, the Examiner will issue a final rejection, which means you've run out of options for keeping the application alive and your chances for achieving registration are over, absent entering the appeals process (which would, in most cases, require an attorney). Chapter 10, Section C, discusses final rejections.

2. Two Types of Rejections

There are essentially two types of rejections (besides final rejections) an Examiner can make. These are:

Notice of Incomplete Trademark Application (Page 1)

Assistant Commissioner for Trademarks   Date:
2900 Crystal Drive   Mark:
Arlington, VA 22202-3513   Misassigned Serial No: 75/
                                                     Applicant's Name:

NOTICE OF INCOMPLETE TRADEMARK APPLICATION

Correspondent's Name:
Correspondent's Address:

The Patent and Trademark Office (PTO) is returning the attached papers received on   , because they do not meet the minimum requirements for receiving a filing date (see below for further explanation). 37 C.F.R. §2.21. **To re-file your application papers, resubmit the entire application package, with any necessary modifications, including: 1) the written application with signed declaration; 2) the drawing page; 3) specimens, only if required; 4) certified copy of a foreign registration, only if required; and 5) the filing fee of at least $245 to Assistant Commissioner for Trademarks, Box New App/Fee, 2900 Crystal Drive, Arlington, VA 22202-3513.**

☐ **You will receive a full refund of the application fee. Note: The refund will not accompany this letter. Refunds made by mail should be received within 4 weeks. Payments made to a deposit account will be credited the appropriate amount.**
                                              -OR-
☐ **The check which accompanied your application is enclosed herewith.**

This letter is designed to address the minimum requirements an application must satisfy to receive a legal filing date. For further information about the application process, please contact the **Trademark Assistance Center** (TAC) at **(703) 308-9000.**

EXPLANATION FOR RETURN OF APPLICATION PAPERS: (Continued on Next Page)

The federal registration of trademarks is governed by the Trademark Act of 1946, 15 U.S.C. §1051 *et seq., as amended,* and the Trademark Rules of Practice, 37 C.F.R. Part 2. "TMEP" refers to the *Trademark Manual of Examining Procedure* (2nd edition 1993).

1.   Filing Fee. An application filing fee of $245.00 per class is required. 37 C.F.R. §2.6(a)(1) and §2.21(a)(7).
☐ **a.** No fee is included with the application papers.
☐ **b.** The fee received $, is insufficient to cover the application fee.
☐ **c.** The Deposit Account No.   has insufficient funds. 37 C.F.R. §1.25(a).
☐ **d.** The check received is in foreign currency. Only U.S. currency is acceptable.
☐ **e.** The check was not made payable to the Assistant Commissioner for Trademarks or the Commissioner for Patents and Trademarks.
☐ **f.** The check was returned to the PTO unpaid. (Please Note: A processing charge of $50 is charged for handling a returned check. If you re-apply, you must include payment of the $50 processing charge in addition to the application filing fee together with a copy of this notice.)
2.   Drawing of the Mark.
☐ **a.** No drawing of the mark was included with the application papers. 37 C.F.R. §2.21(a)(3).
☐ **b.** No mark appears on the drawing page. 37 C.F.R. §2.21(a)(3).
☐ **c.** There is more than one mark in the application. Only one representation of a mark on a drawing page is permitted per application.
☐ **d.** Color appears on the drawing of the mark. A mark must be depicted in black and white only. No shading or color is permitted. No pencil drawings are permitted. 37 C.F.R. §2.52(a).
☐ **e.** No heading appears on the top of the drawing page. 37 C.F.R. §2.52(d).
☐ **f.** The proposed drawing page merely states "no drawing" or sets forth only a written description of the mark for a color mark. 37 C.F.R. §2.21(a)(3); TMEP §1202.04(e)(i).

Notice of Incomplete Trademark Application (Page 2)

3.   Legal Basis for Application.

☐ **a. No legal basis** has been identified for registration of the mark (e.g. actual use, intent-to-use, foreign registration, etc.) 37 C.F.R. §2.21(a)(5).

☐ **b.** The application fails to state a **date of first use of the mark in commerce**. Note: This date must be at least as early as the date on which the application declaration was signed. 37 C.F.R. §2.21(a)(5)(i).

☐ **c.** The applicant fails to state that **"applicant has a *bona fide* intention to use the mark in commerce."** An application based on Section 1(b) [intent-to-use], Section 44(d) and/or Section 44(e) of the Trademark Act must include this statement. 37 C.F.R. §2.21(a)(5)(ii), (a)(5)(iii) and (a)(5)(iv).

☐ **d. A claim of benefit** of a prior filed application in a foreign country [Section 44(d)] was not included in the application papers. 15 U.S.C. §1126(d); 37 C.F.R. §2.21(a)(5)(iii).

☐ **e.** The application was **not filed within 6 months** from the date of the foreign application [Section 44(d)]. 15 U.S.C. §1126(d)(1); 37 C.F.R. §2.21(a)(5)(iii).

☐ **f. A certification or certified copy of the foreign registration** [Section 44(e)] was not included with this application. 15 U.S.C. §1126(e); 37 C.F.R. §2.21(a)(5)(ii).

☐ **g.** An application for registration on the Supplemental Register, based on an intent-to-use the mark in commerce, is not permitted. 37 C.F.R. §2.47(c); TMEP §1114.02.

☐ **h.** A concurrent use application based on an intent-to-use the mark in commerce is not permitted. 37 C.F.R. §2.99(g); TMEP §1207.04(b).

4.   Specimen.

☐ **a.** A specimen showing **actual use** of the mark in the goods or in connection with the services has been omitted. At least one specimen showing how the mark is being used in commerce is required for all applications filed under Section 1(a) of the Trademark Act. 15 U.S.C. §1051(a)(1)(c); 37 C.F.R. §2.21(a)(5)(i). Note: Reproductions of the drawing are not acceptable specimens. 37 C.F.R. §2.57(b).

5.   Identification of Goods and Services.

☐ **a.** The application fails to identify *recognizable* goods or services. TMEP §804.02. Language such as the name of the trademark, "Miscellaneous Goods or Services" or "Business" is not acceptable. 37 C.F.R. §2.21(a)(4).

☐ **b.** The identification of goods and/or services was omitted from the application. 37 C.F.R. §2.21(a)(4).

6.   Signature and Declaration.

☐ **a.** The application is unsigned. The applicant must sign the application.

☐ **b.** The application neither is verified (i.e. notarized) nor does it contain a properly worded declaration in accordance with 37 C.F.R. §2.20.

7.   Applicant's Name.

☐ **a.** The applicant's name was omitted.

☐ **b.** An address with which to correspondence was omitted.

8.   Application

☐ **a.** A trademark/servicemark application for registration is missing.

9.   Instructions for applications returned in error: If you believe that this application was returned to you in error, please resubmit: (1) the application papers (including the drawing page, any specimens and/or certificate of registration) as originally filed, (2) the application filing fee of $245 and (3) a copy of this Notice of Incomplete Trademark Application, to the Office of the Assistant Commissioner for Trademarks, 2900 Crystal Drive, Arlington, VA 22202, Attention Filing Date. **With your submission,** please request that the earlier filing date be restored and provide proof that you complied with the minimum filing date requirements on the original filing date. If you have a deposit account, you may fax your written request to restore the earlier filing date, the application papers and Notice of Incomplete Trademark Application, together with a written authorization to debit your deposit account for the filing fee, to (703) 308-9395 Attn: Filing Date. Any issue that must be considered on petition to the Commissioner must be filed with the Office of the Assistant Commissioner for Trademarks within sixty (60) days of this Notice. 37 C.F.R. 2.146.

10.   Other Remarks:

Name of Legal Instruments Examiner

(Rev. 11/3/98)

- formal rejections (less serious), and
- substantive rejections (more serious).

a. Formal Rejections

Formal rejections relate to defects in the form of the application (for example, the entity of the applicant is not correctly stated or the application is signed by an individual on behalf of a corporation, without specifying that the individual was signing as an officer of the corporation). Formal rejections are generally less serious than substantive rejections.

When the Examiner issues a formal rejection, the applicant is typically required to amend the application to fix the problem. The various reasons for formal rejections and ways to amend the application are topics covered in more detail in Chapter 9. For each problem the Examiner finds, you may either:

- receive an action letter explaining the problem and notifying you that you may receive a call from the Examiner to resolve the problem over the phone. (If the problem is resolved in that manner, you will likely later receive a confirmation of the amendment or you can send a confirmation letter, as described below.) Or,
- receive an action letter explaining the problem and requiring some communication from you in response. See Section D below for information about communicating with the PTO.

b. Substantive Rejections

Substantive rejections relate to more serious defects in the application—for example, the mark itself is too descriptive to be registered on the Principal Register, or is superseded by another mark that is already registered. When the Examiner issues a substantive rejection, it is basically a refusal to register the mark because registration appears to be prohibited by federal law.

Typically, substantive rejections cannot be fixed by an amendment. If you wish to move forward with your application, you most likely will have to convince the Examiner that the Examiner's assessment of your mark's eligibility for registration was wrong. This involves advocacy of a type that is usually best delivered by an experienced trademark attorney. See Chapter 10 for more on Substantive Rejections and Chapter 14 for tips on finding a trademark attorney.

Now that we've discussed the types of rejections you may have encountered, let's move on to an overview of the possible types of responses you might deliver.

3. Possible Responses to a Rejection

Later in this chapter, and in Chapters 9 and 10, we give detailed information on how to respond to specific rejections from the PTO. For now, here is a brief overview of the different types of responses you can make to various PTO rejections.

If you have received a formal type of rejection, there are two options. You can either amend your application (change one or more pieces of information to conform to the PTO's requirements) or you can put forth a credible argument that the Examiner is wrong and your application is okay as is.

If you wish to amend your application, you send the PTO a specific type of letter called an amendment. You will likely need to file another document called a declaration along with your amendment. A declaration is simply a statement of facts that, by your signature, you declare to be true. A sample amendment and a sample declaration are given after subsection c, below.

If you wish to argue that the Examiner is mistaken and your application is fine as it stands, then you will need to file a different type of letter called a formal response. A sample formal response is given after subsection c, below. So you won't be confused, we use the term "formal response," even though the PTO refers to them simply as "responses."

With substantive rejections, it also possible to amend your application or file a formal response. There is another option, however, that may make sense for this type of rejection, but not for a formal rejection, and that is abandonment. If your mark presents such great legal difficulty that it is best to cut losses and drop the application altogether, then abandonment is certainly a viable option.

Before we move on to look at a sample amendment, sample declaration and sample formal response, it's appropriate here to make some brief remarks on the anatomy of these documents. First, whether you are preparing an amendment, declaration or formal response, you must use the same heading we use in the samples below. The heading is the part of the document and looks like this:

In the header for your response, you will fill in the spots for Applicant, Mark, Serial No., Filed (meaning date of filing), Trademark Law Office number and Trademark Attorney name. You will find this information in the header of the action letter.

The next line of your response will indicate the type of document you are presenting, either an amendment, declaration or response (meaning a formal response).

The next section of your response is the body itself. The body will contain a few paragraphs or more and will contain specific information, depending on which type of response it is. For the appropriate type, you should enter the following information:

Amendments: The body of an amendment contains: 1) a request for an amendment, explaining what is to be changed and the exact wording for the new information on the application; 2) a "remarks" section where you restate the Examiner's reasons for rejection and how you have solved

Sample Heading

TRADEMARK
UNITED STATES DEPARTMENT OF COMMERCE
Patent and Trademark Office

Applicant:) Trademark Law

Mark:) Office _____

Serial No. (1)   ) Trademark Attorney

Filed:) _____

those problems. For example, "The Trademark Attorney has indicated that the mark is more properly registered in Class 9. This problem has been resolved by the amendment requested." And 3) a statement indicating that it is your belief that the application is now fit for publication and registration.

Declarations: The body of a declaration simply consists of a series of numbered statements and a paragraph in which the declarant (the person signing the declaration, typically—this may or may not be you) attests to the truth of the statements.

Formal Responses: The body of a formal response contains: 1) an opening paragraph requesting reconsideration of the application for registration; 2) the arguments for why the application is fit for registration; and 3) a statement indicating that it is your belief that the application is now fit for publication and registration.

The final section of your document contains the date signed, the signature line and, for amendments and formal responses, your telephone number.

Now that you understand the standard, basic structure of these documents, let's look at each one individually.

a. Amendment of a Trademark/Service Mark Application

The majority of rejections can be corrected by sending the PTO an amendment. An amendment of a trademark/service mark application is simply a response from the applicant to the Examiner asking for a change in the applicant's original application information. The sample below demonstrates how an amendment to the description of goods in an application might be worded.

b. Declaration

Declarations are often used to establish facts which support your response to the Examiner (either an amendment or a formal response). In a declaration, you basically state important facts regarding the trademark application or the circumstances surrounding the mark for which registration is sought. Part of the declaration is a statement which certifies that the facts in the declaration are true to the best of the declarant's knowledge, and the facts must be presented in a form showing that the declarant has first-hand knowledge of them. The declaration must be signed. A sample appears below.

c. Formal Response to a PTO Rejection

A formal response is essentially a letter in which you explain why you believe your mark is entitled to registration despite the PTO's rejection. Formal responses are appropriate for either formal rejections (depending on the type of formal rejection you receive) or substantive rejections. It just depends on what your situation is and how you wish to proceed after you receive the action letter from the PTO. More details on when a formal response is an option are given in Chapter 9 for formal rejections and Chapter 10 for substantive rejections. A sample formal response is given below.

Sample Amendment

TRADEMARK
UNITED STATES DEPARTMENT OF COMMERCE
Patent and Trademark Office

Applicant:) Trademark Law
Mark:) Office _____
Serial No. (1)   ) Trademark Attorney
Filed:) _____

BOX RESPONSES
NO FEE

Assistant Commissioner for Trademarks
2900 Crystal Drive
Arlington, VA 22202-3513

AMENDMENT

Sir:

In response to a communication from the Trademark Attorney dated _____, please amend the application identified above as follows:

Please change the description of goods given in the application to read as follows: "Clothing namely t-shirts, shirts, caps and jackets in International Class 25."

REMARKS

Reconsideration of the application as amended respectfully is requested.

The Trademark Attorney has asserted that the present identification of goods is indefinite for purposes of registration and has submitted an alternative description. That alternative description is acceptable to the applicant and the applicant requests amending the application to substitute the original description with the Trademark Attorney's suggested description. Such amendment is requested above.

For the foregoing reasons, it is submitted that the present application is in condition for publication and registration, and such action is requested.

Dated: _____

Respectfully,

_____
Applicant

Telephone Number: _____

Sample Declaration

TRADEMARK
UNITED STATES DEPARTMENT OF COMMERCE
Patent and Trademark Office

Applicant:) Trademark Law
Mark:) Office _____
Serial No. (1)   ) Trademark Attorney
Filed:) _____

DECLARATION

I, _____ *[insert full name of declarant]* _____ , do hereby declare that:

1. I am an officer of the corporation named as the applicant in the trademark application identified above.

2. Attached to this response are five (5) specimens of the mark sought to be registered in this application. These specimens were in use by the applicant on and prior to October 1, 1998 (the filing date of the application) and are still in such use.

I further declare that all statements made herein of my own knowledge are true and that all statements made on information and belief are believed to be true; and further that these statements are made with the knowledge that willful false statements and the like so made are punishable by fine or imprisonment, or both, under Section 1001 of Title 18 of the United States Code, and that such willful false statements may jeopardize the validity of the application and any registration resulting therefrom.

Dated:_____

_____ *[signature of declarant]* _____

_____ *[print name of declarant]* _____

Sample Formal Response

TRADEMARK
UNITED STATES DEPARTMENT OF COMMERCE
Patent and Trademark Office

Applicant:	) Trademark Law
Mark:	) Office _____
Serial No. (1)	) Trademark Attorney
Filed:	) _____

BOX RESPONSES
NO FEE

Assistant Commissioner for Trademarks
2900 Crystal Drive
Arlington, VA 22202-3513

RESPONSE

Sir:

In response to a communication from the Trademark Attorney dated _____,
reconsideration of the application identified above is requested for the reasons stated in the
following paragraphs.

The trademark attorney has stated that the mark "FOREVER YOUNG BEAUTY SALON," for
which registration is sought, is deceptively misdescriptive of the goods (or services) provided in the application for registration. The applicant asserts that the mark is not deceptively misdescriptive because no reasonable consumer would likely believe that a beauty
salon would provide any service that would keep a person young forever.

For the foregoing reasons, it is submitted that the present application is in condition for
publication and registration, and such action is requested.

Dated: _____

Respectfully,

_____
Applicant

Telephone Number: _____

C. What Type of Rejection Do You Have?

In order to analyze the action letter and determine the appropriate response, you'll probably need to look at a copy of your application to confirm that it says what the Examiner says it says. Most deficiencies are minor, and even if there are several, they can probably be cleared up with one phone call and one letter.

The top of the first page of the action letter shows its mailing date and the information necessary to identify your application. The remainder of the letter will probably be form paragraphs. Read them carefully.

Below is a checklist of common formal and substantive rejections issued by the PTO. Use the checklist to identify which type of rejection you've received. Each item in the list contains a sample of the language the PTO uses to notify you that a problem exists, and directs you to a specific section of either Chapter 9 or Chapter 10. There, you will find detailed information on how to respond to the specific rejection you've received. Chapter 9 deals with formal rejections and Chapter 10 with substantive rejections. Before you read the section that pertains to your particular rejection, it's important that you read the introduction to the chapter (either Chapter 9 or 10) first.

Formal Rejections

• **Identifying the mark:**
"The mark sought to be registered does not correspond to the mark shown in the specimen. Amendment is required." (See Chapter 9, Section A1.)

• **Class-related problems:**
"Applicant's _____ (goods or services) are properly classified in International Class ___, rather than in International Class ___. Amendment is required."

or

"Combined applications are permitted under Section 30 of the Trademark Act, provided a filing fee is paid for each Class in which the goods and/or services are Classified. Applicant may elect to restrict the goods and/or services herein to a single Class, or pay the additional fee." (See Chapter 9, Section A2.)

• **Applicant's citizenship:**
"The application fails to state the applicant's citizenship. Appropriate amendment is required." (See Chapter 9, Section A3.)

• Applicant's address:
"The application fails to include the applicant's address (or to include a complete address for the applicant in an appropriate form). Appropriate correction is required."

• **Drawing:**
"NOTICE OF INCOMPLETE TRADEMARK APPLICATION: The Patent and Trademark Office (PTO) is returning papers received on _____, because they do not meet the minimum requirements for receiving a filing date (see below for further explanation).

☐ No drawing of the mark was included with the application papers;

☐ No mark appears on the drawing page;

☐ Color appears on the drawing of the mark. A mark must be depicted in black and white only. No shading is permitted. No pencil drawings are permitted.

☐ No heading appears on the top of the drawing page."

or

"The mark _____ shown on the drawing does not agree with the mark _____ actually used, as evidenced by the specimens of record. Either the drawing should be amended so that the mark thereon agrees with the mark as actually used, or specimens showing use of the mark presented in the drawing should be submitted.

Sample Written Office Action (First Page)

UNITED STATES DEPARTMENT OF COMMERCE
Patent and Trademark Office

	PAPER NO.
SAMPLE WRITTEN OFFICE ACTION	ADDRESS: **Assistant Commissioner for Trademarks 2900 Crystal Drive Arlington, VA 22202-3513** If no fees are enclosed, the address should include the words "Box Responses - No Fee." Please provide in all correspondence: 1. Filing Date, serial number, mark and Applicant's name. 2. Mailing date of this Office action. 3. Examining Attorney's name and Law Office number. 4. Your telephone number and ZIP code.

A PROPER RESPONSE TO THIS OFFICE ACTION MUST BE RECEIVED WITHIN 6 MONTHS FROM THE DATE OF THIS ACTION IN ORDER TO AVOID *ABANDONMENT*. *For your convenience and to ensure proper handling of your response, a label has been enclosed. Please attach it to the upper right corner of your response. If the label is not enclosed, print or type the* Trademark Law Office No., Serial No., *and* Mark *in the upper right corner of your response.*

RE: Serial Number: 74/123456 HIGH THERE

The assigned examining attorney has reviewed the referenced application and determined the following.

LIKELIHOOD OF CONFUSION - SECTION 2(d)

The examining attorney refuses registration under Trademark Act Section 2(d), 15 U.S.C. Section 1052(d), because the applicant's mark, when used on or in connection with the identified goods, so resembles the mark in U.S. Registration No. XXXXXXX as to be likely to cause confusion, to cause mistake, or to deceive. TMEP section 1207. See the enclosed registration.

The examining attorney must analyze each case in two steps to determine whether there is a likelihood of confusion. First, the examining attorney must look at the marks themselves for similarities in appearance, sound, connotation and commercial impression. *In re E. I. DuPont de Nemours & Co.*, 476 F.2d 1357, 177 USPQ 563 (CCPA 1973). Second, the examining attorney must compare the goods or services to determine if they are related or if the activities surrounding their marketing are such that confusion as to origin is likely. *In re August Storck KG*, 218 USPQ 823 (TTAB 1983); *In re International Telephone and Telegraph Corp.*, 197 USPQ 910 (TTAB 1978); *Guardian Products Co., v. Scott Paper Co.*, 200 USPQ 738 (TTAB 1978).

"In the latter event, the use of the substitute specimens as of a date at least as early as the filing date of the application must be supported either by an affidavit or by a declaration in accordance with 37 C.F.R. § 2.20." (See Chapter 9, Section A4.)

• **Goods/services identification:**
"The present identification of goods/services is indefinite for purposes of registration. The following identification is suggested, and should be adopted, if accurate: _____ [the Examiner will give his or her suggested description of goods/services]." (See Chapter 9, Section A5.)

• **Date of first use and type of commerce:**
"Applicant's choice of the term 'foreign commerce with the United States' is unacceptable. It is suggested that the applicant substitute the following, if accurate:
    'Commerce between _____ and the United States.'" (See Chapter 9, Section A6.)

• **Specimens:**
"The specimens do not show use of the mark on any goods/services identified in the application. Five specimens showing use of the mark for the goods/services identified in the application should be submitted. If the specimens are of a type other than those originally filed, the use of additional specimens as of a date at least as early as the filing date of the application must be supported either by an affidavit or by a declaration in accordance with Trademark Rule 2.20, Trademark Rule 2.87, TMEP §§ 808.01(b) and 1113.01." (See Chapter 9, Section A7, for this type of notice, or any other use of the term "specimens" in the notice.)

• **Prior registrations:**
"If applicant is the owner of registration no(s). _____, _____ and _____, a claim of ownership of said registration(s) should be

made of record. Trademark Rule 2.36." (See Chapter 9, Section A8.)

• **Consent to register surname:**
"The name (or individual) shown in the mark on the drawing should be identified. If it is the name (or a picture) of a particular living individual, written consent from said individual to the use and registration of the name (or photograph) must be filed. If said name is merely fanciful and does not identify a particular individual, this fact should be indicated." (See Chapter 9, Section A9.)

• **Incorrect filing fee:**
"Combined applications are permitted under Section 30 of the Trademark Act, provided a filing fee is paid for each Class in which the goods and/or services are classified. Applicant may elect to restrict the goods and/or services herein to one Class or pay the additional fee." (See Chapter 9, Section A10.)

• **Delay in filing:**
"The present application was not filed in the Patent and Trademark Office within a reasonable time after the date on which the application papers were signed. Eight weeks (plus mailing time to this Office) for domestic applicants or twelve weeks (plus mailing time to this Office) for foreign applicants is considered a reasonable time. For this reason, a statement that the mark is still in use must be submitted. Such statement must be supported by an affidavit or by a declaration in accordance with Trademark Rule 2.20." (See Chapter 9, Section A11.)

Substantive Rejections

• **Descriptiveness:**
"Registration is refused on the Principal Register because the mark, when applied to the goods and/or services, is considered to be merely descriptive (or geographically descriptive,

deceptively misdescriptive or primarily merely a surname) thereof. Section 2(e) of the Trademark Act." (See Chapter 10, Section A.)

- **Likelihood of Confusion:**

"The examining attorney refuses registration under Trademark Act Section 2(d), 15 U.S.C. Section 1052 (d), because the applicant's mark, when used on the identified goods, is likely to be confused with the registered mark in U.S. Registration Nos. _[conflicting mark's registration number or numbers]_ . TMEP section 1207. See the enclosed registration(s)."

or

"Registration is refused because the mark, when applied to the goods and/or services of the applicant, so resembles the mark(s) cited below as to be likely to cause confusion, or to cause mistake, or to deceive. Section 2(d) of the Trademark Act; TMEP § 1205. (See attached copies.) Reg. No(s). _[conflicting mark's registration number or numbers given here.]_ (See Chapter 10, Section B.)

D. How to Communicate With Examiners

Learning how to communicate effectively with PTO Examiners and how to follow the PTO's procedures will help you deal with any difficulties regarding your application. This section discusses general guidelines to use when corresponding with the PTO.

1. Corresponding by Mail

After your application is filed, all correspondence with the PTO must include:

- applicant name,
- your application's serial number,
- class number,
- date of filing, and

- your mark (an actual depiction or a description).

See the sample letter below which demonstrates how to change incorrect information that shows up in your filing receipt from the PTO. (For example, an incorrectly spelled name or the wrong address.)

If you are responding to an action letter, also include:

- the mailing date of the action letter,
- your telephone number,
- your Zip code and
- the PTO examining attorney's name and office number.

See the example headers in Section B3, above. Always keep copies of your correspondence; if the Examiner calls, you will be in a better position to discuss the letter if you are looking at a copy.

2. Where to Send Your Correspondence

Whether you are sending a letter to change incorrect information on your filing receipt from the PTO or responding in some way to an action letter (with a formal response or an amendment, for example), your correspondence will be sent to:

BOX RESPONSES, NO FEE
Assistant Commissioner for Trademarks
2900 Crystal Drive, Arlington, VA 22202-3513

For example, letters sent to change information in your filing receipt from the PTO, as described earlier, should look something like this for an actual use application:

Applicant: Don Re
Serial No.: 73/123456
Class: 9
Date Filed: 3/25/99
Mark: REMARKABLE

BOX RESPONSES
NO FEE

Assistant Commissioner for Trademarks
2900 Crystal Drive
Arlington, VA 22202-3513

Attention: OATPA Data Base Maintenance Staff

Re: Request for Correction of Filing Receipt for Trademark Application

Sir:

Please change the file in this application to reflect my correct mailing address of 9595 Virginia Way, Tulare, California 93274. A copy of the filing receipt is enclosed for your convenience.

Also, please correct the spelling of my last name from Rey to Re.

Feel free to contact me if you have any questions.

Sincerely,

Don Re
Don Re
Phone: 209-555-5555

Use Express Mail if a deadline is near. When you are responding to a PTO action letter, you will be given a deadline within which to respond, usually six months. Your application will not proceed until you respond, and your application will be rejected if you don't respond within the period stated. It is therefore best to respond as soon as possible. Keep in mind that if the deadline is upon you, you can use the U.S. Postal Service Express Mail with Express Mail certificate, as described in Chapter 7, Section A1, to have your response considered received on the date you mailed it. You should have the serial number and filing date of the application by then, so that information should be included in the Express Mail certificate.

It is best to deposit your correspondence directly with an employee of the U.S. Postal Service to ensure that he or she receives a legible copy of the Express Mail mailing label with the "date-in" box clearly filled in. If the PTO receives the Express Mail package without a properly filled in "date-in" box (the date is not legible or not there at all), the PTO will deem the correspondence filed on the date received, not the deposit date.

3. Communicating by Phone

In the course of dealing with the Examiner, you may end up on the telephone on one or more occasions. Sometimes the call will be initiated by you while other times the Examiner will be the one calling. Here are some basic tips for when and how to conduct these conversations, keeping in mind our earlier advice to respect the Examiner's time constraints and to be as efficient as possible.

Don't call the Examiner the Examiner. We use the term "Examiner" in this book because it is short and easy. When you correspond with your Examiner or speak to him or her on the phone, however, don't refer to him or her as the "Examiner." While conversing on the phone, you may use Mr. or Ms., or many prefer to be called by their first names (or so we're told).

• **Respond to each correspondence.** It is always a good idea and good form to call the Examiner each and every time you receive correspondence from him or her to confirm that you received their letter. This is a matter of courtesy. If you prefer, a brief letter will also suffice.

• **Use the phone for formal rejections.** If the action letter you receive from the Examiner is primarily a formal rejection (the type of rejection that can most easily be fixed—see Section B), you can usually call the Examiner (if he or she has not already called you) to resolve the issues over the phone. See Chapter 9 for information about responding to formal rejections by phone and in writing.

- **Check your application's status.** If a great deal of time has passed since you last heard from your Examiner and the ball was in his or her court, then you may call to ask about the status of your application. As mentioned above, you can also call the PTO Status Line (the TRAM Automated System, described in Chapter 7, Section D) for information about the status of your application.

- **Prepare in advance.** The best way to utilize your time on the phone with the Examiner is to prepare, in advance, the issues you want to discuss and the points you wish to make. Next to each issue, list the goal for that issue.

For example, suppose you receive an action letter from the Examiner. The action letter states that the identification of goods is unacceptable as indefinite. The Examiner suggests an alternative wording for your identification of goods, but after some thought you decide to try to negotiate an identification that is somewhere between what you want and what the Examiner wants.

The issue is "Identification of Goods/Services." Next to this issue list the reasons why you think your suggested compromise is appropriate. Then list the goal as negotiating an identification of goods that is closer to your compromise position. Making a list of issues and goals and sticking to your list during your phone conversation with the Examiner will make the conversation more productive for you and more efficient for the Examiner, who will appreciate how organized you are.

Examiner's Amendments: When the Examiner Calls You

If the Examiner has a brief question, she will likely call you, resolve the question and then issue and mail you an Examiner's amendment. This is a form on which the Examiner records in handwriting a phone conversation or meeting with the applicant. Read the amendment carefully to make sure it matches your understanding of the conversation. If you disagree, or don't understand the amendment, first call the Examiner, and then, if necessary, write her a letter with your concerns, explaining your point of view on the communication.

One common example of an Examiner's amendment is one that asks you to disclaim words as part of your mark that don't qualify for registration. The Examiner will ask you to formally state in writing that you are not claiming the word or words in question as part of your trademark, and therefore not seeking trademark protection for them. Then, although the mark will be registered in its entirety, you will only have the exclusive right to use the portion not disclaimed.

EXAMPLE: The Exotic Perfume Company manufactures a line of fragrances named for various wildflowers. One of these is called California Snapdragon. If Exotic wants to register this mark, it will have to disclaim the "California" part of it, since California is a geographic term and thus not registrable. If Exotic refuses to disclaim "California," the Patent and Trademark Office will probably refuse registration. If disclaimer is made, however, the entire mark can be registered. But, only the "snapdragon" portion will qualify for protection, and only in relation to perfume or related goods. Then, if a competing fragrance company comes out with California Wild Rose fragrance, there will be no infringement. On the other hand, if the competitor produces Oregon Snapdragon fragrance, it is likely that a court will find infringement.

• **Document all telephone correspondence.**
When you communicate with the PTO over the telephone, keep notes of the date and time of your call, and names of everyone you speak with. Most people are easier to talk to if you call them by name. You may also need to talk to that person again, or to remind them of an agreement you made about how to prepare or change your application. Keeping notes of your conversations is especially important when you call the Examiner and discuss changes she has suggested in your application.

Before the call ends, repeat your understanding of any agreements reached to clear up any possible misunderstandings. If the agreement is about something significant, confirm the agreement in a letter which includes the date of your call.

EXAMPLE: Suppose Frieda claimed her mark was used in connection with buying services for nonprofit institutions and organizations, and submitted specimens showing advertisements of food products aimed at schools. That description would be found to be too indefinite, and the Examiner might suggest "buying services for nonprofit organizations and institutions in the field of food products." If Frieda's services extended beyond food products to include items such as medical and automotive supplies, she probably wouldn't want to agree to the Examiner's suggestion. However, after talking with the Examiner she should be able to arrive at a description inclusive enough for her, yet definite enough for the Examiner. In this instance, perhaps, this would be "buying services for nonprofit institutions and organizations in the fields of food products, medical supplies and automotive parts."

Following our advice to confirm all agreements in writing, Frieda would send the following letter to the Examiner:

Applicant: Frieda R. Willington
Serial Number: 75/316535
Class: 42
Date of Filing: April 30, 1997
Mark: AccuBuy

BOX RESPONSES
NO FEE

Assistant Commissioner for Trademarks
2900 Crystal Drive
Arlington, VA 22202-3513

September 15, 1998

Dear Ms. Jensen:

This letter is to confirm the understanding we reached on the following matters pertaining to my trademark application during our phone conversation on September 15, 1998:

Goods And/Or Services

We agreed that the Goods and/or Services section of my application would be amended to read, "Buying services for nonprofit institutions and organizations in the fields of food products, medical supplies and automotive parts."

With this amendment, my application should be ready for publication and registration and I respectfully request that such action be taken.

If you have any other issues you need to discuss or if this letter does not reflect what you believe to be the current status of my application, please contact me at the above address and/or phone number.

Respectfully,

Frieda R. Willington
Frieda R. Willington
Applicant

4. Tips for Dealing With Trademark Examiners

One of the keys to success when dealing with the PTO is to maintain good relations with the PTO employee responsible for your application. This section provides some information about how to communicate effectively with him or her.

- **Try to understand the Examiner.** When speaking to an Examiner, remember that Examiners are people too. They are graded each day on their ability to handle as many cases as possible. It therefore almost always benefits them to receive an application with as few problems as possible. When they receive an application with problems, they may not be very happy about it. If an Examiner calls you to discuss an issue, and you are argumentative or needlessly keep the Examiner on the phone for too long, he or she may become especially unhappy with you. From the Examiner's perspective, you are keeping him or her from meeting his or her job performance goal for the day. Keep this in mind before you call the Examiner to discuss a problem. While it may seem like you shouldn't have to worry about the Examiner's job status, the more understanding and empathy you project, the better results you're likely to get.

- **Some Examiners may be more difficult than others.** Despite the pressures on them to work in a quick and efficient manner, most Examiners are helpful and want to see the application succeed. But sometimes, for whatever reason, an applicant will be assigned an Examiner who seems rude and out to see that the application fails, or who doesn't follow the PTO's own rules. Difficult people can be found in every profession and in all walks of life.

  If you think you have such an Examiner overseeing your application, you should do your best to be cooperative. It's best not to raise your voice or make accusations at the Examiner. Stick to the facts of your situation and to the rules that you think weigh in your favor. Maintain a professional demeanor.

  If you still think you're in the right but are not being heard, get the supervising/managing Examiner's name and contact that person. Explain your situation. Don't personally attack the Examiner and try not to lay blame. Again, stick to the facts. Before initiating the call to the managing Examiner, prepare an outline of the reasons why you think you're in the right, along with references to the PTO's own rules and the law that you think is in your favor. This will help you to remain calm and focus on the facts instead of the Examiner's shortcomings. ■

Correcting Minor Problems With Your Application

As discussed in Chapter 8, there are two categories of responses Examiners may give:

- formal rejections, and
- substantive rejections.

This chapter explains how to deal with formal rejections, which are rejections primarily relating to the technicalities of your application. Substantive rejections are covered in the next chapter.

⚠ **Substantive rejections are more serious and sometimes can't be cured.** If you receive a substantive rejection and want to fight it, you may need the help of a trademark attorney. See Chapter 14 for information on attorneys and other trademark resources.

Understanding the reason for the Examiner's rejection is the first step in preparing your response, whether it be a verbal response over the phone, or a written response sent to the Examiner. Read the Examiner's action letter very carefully. If the Examiner has identified more than one problem with your application, he or she will keep his or her discussion of the individual problems separated by headings (see the sample office action in Chapter 8, Section C). You may recall from the previous chapter that the type of response you should make depends on the type of rejection you receive.

This chapter explains which type of response is appropriate for particular rejections. Find the section in this chapter which addresses your particular situation and you will be on your way to preparing a response. Formal rejections are usually easily dealt with without the help of a lawyer, so unless otherwise noted you should be able to respond on your own.

💡 **Common reasons for rejection.** The two most common formal rejections are based on problems relating to:

- the drawing submitted with your application, and

- the identification of goods and services you submitted in your application.

If the Examiner had a problem with your drawing, skip down to Section A4, below. If the Examiner had a problem with the way you identified your goods and/or services, skip down to Section A5, below.

Whatever the reason for the rejection and however you respond, we want to stress that you should respond appropriately and diligently to every issue raised by the Examiner. Failing to do so may cause the Examiner to label your response incomplete and your application abandoned ("abandoned" here means that you are no longer pursuing the application).

A. Responding to Formal Rejections

This section discusses 11 common formal rejections and how you should respond to each. Throughout this section, you will find many references to Section B. Section B contains the models you will use for drafting your own written amendment or formal response. (Consult Chapter 8, Section B, if you need to review the topics of amendments and formal responses. Review Chapter 8, Section B3, for the anatomy of amendments, declarations and formal responses. Remember from that section that you will need to use the same header for all documents.) Review Chapter 8 for detailed information about sending your amendment or response to the PTO.

1. Identifying the Mark

In an application based on actual use of the mark (see Chapter 4), the specimens are key in helping the Examiner determine what your mark is and/or how it looks. Your mark as represented in the drawing accompanying your use application must

Beware of Material Alteration

Amendments to drawings later in the examination process are sometimes allowed by the PTO's Examiners (and sometimes requested by them), but are not acceptable if the amended drawing turns out to be very different from the original drawing. This concept is known as "material alteration." If your amended drawing alters (changes) the essence of the original drawing, then you have materially altered the original mark and it will not be accepted by the Examiner.

For example, assume that you originally submitted a mark which included words and a design that was integral to (a very important part of) the mark as a whole. Later you were asked to amend the drawing because it did not match your specimens. You amend the drawing and take out the design aspect of the mark, which is now only a word mark. This amendment will not be accepted by the Examiner because you have materially altered the essence of the mark, which included a design element that was integral to the mark as a whole.

Let's look at a real life example of how the "material alteration" concept works. This example involves a real case. In this case, Richards-Wilcox Manufacturing Co. (the trademark applicant) sought to overturn a decision made by their trademark Examiner over an amendment to the mark proposed by Richards-Wilcox. In the amendment, Richards-Wilcox requested the mark be amended from the mark you see directly below (a diamond design within which the words "FYER-WALL" appear, with the R and W enclosed in an inverted channel bracket design) to "FYER-WALL" in plain, block letters.

The Examiner rejected the amendment, and the Commissioner of Patents agreed with the Examiner, because changing the mark from the design shown above to plain, block letters was a material alteration of the mark and is not allowed. Why was it a material alteration? The Commissioner found that because the R and W were so greatly emphasized in the original mark (both by their greater size and by being surrounded by the inverted bracket), this portrayal effectively made the mark "RW FYER-WALL," and not just "FYER-WALL." ("RW" being the initials of Richards-Wilcox.) Taking out the emphasis on the R and W changed the overall appearance of the mark and eliminated a prominent feature, which constitutes a material alteration. As part of the decision, the Commissioner found the inverted bracket and the emphasized letters, R and W, to be integral parts of the mark, which cannot be removed without being considered a material alteration.

match the mark shown on your specimens. If they do not match, you will be told:

"The mark sought to be registered does not correspond to the mark shown in the specimen. Amendment is required."

With this type of rejection, your options are the following:

- provide a new drawing that matches the specimens you originally filed,
- provide different specimens which match the drawing you originally filed, or
- argue that the drawing accompanying the application does sufficiently correspond to the specimens you submitted.

If you decide to provide a new drawing, make sure it does not materially alter the mark as originally shown. See "Beware of Material Alteration" above.

If you decide to provide different specimens, you will have to prepare and send in a declaration with your new specimens stating that the specimens were in use before the application was filed. See the discussion about declarations in Chapter 8, Section B3, and a full sample declaration for your needs in Section B, below.

If either of the first two options listed above are available to you, then we recommend that you resolve this problem using one of them. Arguing that the drawing does in fact match the specimen (the third, above) is a more complicated undertaking. If you have no other option, however, you should be prepared to show why the Examiner is mistaken—that is, how the mark on the specimens matches the mark on the application. (If you find yourself in this situation, the advice of a lawyer may be needed. Consult Chapter 14, Help Beyond This Book, for information about how to find a lawyer.) Use the sample Amendment of a Trademark/Service Mark Application in Section B, below, as the format for your response, regardless of which option you choose.

2. Class-Related Problems

Remember way back to those days when you were filling out your application and you were encouraged to choose a class (or classes) for your goods and/or services? If those days have come back to haunt you, here is some information to help you sort through these class-related issues. There are essentially two types of class-related problems that might be identified by the Examiner: 1) Identifying the Class and 2) Adding Classes.

a. Identifying the Class

You might remember from Chapter 2 that you did not need to include a class in your application. If you did not include a class, one will be chosen for you. However, if you did provide a class but the class or classes you chose were deemed inappropriate by the Examiner, then the Examiner's comment to you will look something like the following:

"Applicant's _____ (goods or services) are properly classified in International Class ___, rather than in International Class ___. Amendment is required."

Possible responses to this problem are discussed below.

If you agree with the Examiner's opinion that you've misclassified your mark, prepare a response modeled after the sample Amendment, below. Under the "Amendment" section, state as follows: "Please change the Class for which registration is sought from International Class ___ to International Class ___."

Sample Amendment to Change Classes

AMENDMENT

In response to a communication from the Trademark Attorney dated _____, please amend the application identified above as follows:

Please change the Class for which registration is sought from International Class 9 to International Class 42.

REMARKS

Reconsideration of the application as amended is respectfully requested.

The Trademark Attorney has asserted that the proper Class for applicant's services is Class 42, and not Class 9. Applicant has respectfully requested the amendment above to change the classification of applicant's mark from Class 9 to Class 42.

For the foregoing reasons, it is submitted that the present application is in condition for publication and registration, and such action is requested.

Dated: _____

Respectfully,

_____
Applicant

Telephone Number: _____

tion in Chapter 8, Section B3, and the sample amendment in Section B, below, substituting your own language in the body of the amendment. The language you use for the body will mirror the agreement you reached with the Examiner over the phone. Clarify with the Examiner before you get off the phone which method will be used to confirm the amendment.

If you are not able to arrange a telephone interview with the Examiner, prepare the amendment from the sample below. State, under the "Amendment" section, what you consider to be a sufficient revised class designation. Under the "Remarks" section of the amendment, give the reasons why you think your revised class designation is more appropriate than the one suggested by the Examiner (or supplied by the Examiner if you didn't provide one to begin with).

If you disagree with the Examiner, or if the Examiner provided a class and you disagree with that, try to schedule a telephone interview with the Examiner to resolve the disagreement. If an agreement is reached, either the Examiner will send you a confirmation of the amendment or you can send an amendment using the informa-

**Sample Amendment
to Revise the Class Designation**

AMENDMENT

In response to a communication from the Trademark Attorney dated January 10, 1999, please amend the application identified above as follows:

Please change the Class for which registration is sought from International Class 9 to International Class 42.

REMARKS

Reconsideration of the application as amended is respectfully requested.

The Trademark Attorney has asserted that the services stated in the application referred to in the heading above were incorrectly classified in Class 9. The Trademark Attorney recommended Class 35, which represents services. But the Trademark Attorney mistakenly perceived applicant's services as advertising services. Applicant's services are actually computer consulting services. As such, Applicant is requesting the above amendment to Class 42 as the correct Class for Applicant's services.

For the foregoing reasons, it is submitted that the present application is in condition for publication and registration, and such action is requested.

Dated: _____

Respectfully,

_____

Applicant

Telephone Number: _____

If you believe your class designation is appropriate as it was originally presented in your application, and you were not able to come to an agreement with the Examiner over the telephone, you may need a lawyer to prepare a formal response for you if you wish to pursue your original classification. A sample formal response is provided in Section C, below. Suggestions for how to find a lawyer are given in Chapter 14, Help Beyond This Book.

b. Adding Classes

If the goods and/or services described in your application fall into more classes than the one or ones you listed, the Examiner will tell you so. The notice you get will look something like the following:

"Combined applications are permitted under Section 30 of the Trademark Act, provided a filing fee is paid for each Class in which the goods and/or services are Classified. Applicant may elect to restrict the goods and/or services herein to a single Class, or pay the additional fee."

If you choose to pay the additional fee (or fees) to apply for two or more classes under the same original application, you will be changing your original application to a multiple class application—a strategy we do not recommend. (See Chapter 2, Section C4 for the reasons why multiple class applications are not recommended.) Instead, you should submit a new application for each new class recommended by the Examiner. To review the information about preparing and filing trademark applications, see Chapters 2 through 7.

3. Applicant's Citizenship

Your trademark application must state your citizenship. If it does not, the Examiner will notify you of this deficiency and ask that you amend your application to correct the problem. The Examiner's notice will look something like the following:

"The application fails to state the applicant's citizenship. Appropriate amendment is required."

You can authorize the amendment to state your citizenship by telephone or in a written amendment to the Examiner. If you wish to authorize the amendment via telephone, call the Examiner indicated at the end of the action letter you received using the phone number listed under the Examiner's name. Indicate your application's serial number and tell the Examiner you'd like to amend the application to indicate your citizenship (or the domicile of your business). If an amendment is agreed to during the telephone interview, either the Examiner will send you a confirmation of the amendment or you can send an amendment using the sample described here. Clarify with the Examiner before you get off the phone which method will be used to confirm the amendment.

If you wish to send a written amendment yourself, use the sample in Section B, below. Under the Amendment section, here is a sample of an appropriate statement to amend: "Please amend the application to add, after the identification of the applicant, the following statement—a citizen of _____."

Sample Amendment to State Citizenship

AMENDMENT

In response to a communication from the Trademark Attorney dated January 10, 1999, please amend the application identified above as follows:

Please amend the application to add, after the identification of the applicant, the following statement—a citizen of the United States.

REMARKS

Reconsideration of the application as amended is respectfully requested.

The Trademark Attorney has asserted that the application referenced in the heading above fails to state the applicant's citizenship. Applicant has respectfully requested in the amendment above that the application be amended to state the applicant's citizenship as the United States.

For the foregoing reasons, it is submitted that the present application is in condition for publication and registration, and such action is requested.

Dated: _____

Respectfully,

_____
Applicant

Telephone Number: _____

For information about how to correctly indicate citizenship or domicile, see Chapter 4, Section A5 (for use applicants) or Chapter 5, Section A5 (for intent-to-use applicants). If you do not amend your application or respond to the Examiner within the time indicated on your letter, your application may be deemed abandoned (after which you can no longer pursue it).

4. Drawing

All federal trademark applications must include a drawing. There are many possible problems that could arise with the drawing that is submitted with the application for registration. To review all of the drawing requirements (and there are many), go back to Chapter 6, Drawings. In fact, the drawing seems to cause the most problems for applicants. The most common errors found by Examiners at the PTO include the failure even to submit a drawing, the failure to put the drawing on the drawing page and the failure to include a heading at the top of the drawing page. If you committed an error like this, you likely received your application and filing fee check back in the mail. This means you did not receive a filing date and you have to start all over again. These mistakes (and the mistakes listed as 1 through 6, below) are easily corrected by reviewing Chapter 6 and resubmitting your application, a correct drawing page, the specimens and the filing fee to the PTO.

Other common drawing problems are:
1. the drawing is off-center,
2. the drawing is not the correct size,
3. the drawing is in color or shades of gray (it needs to be in black and white),
4. the drawing does not use the PTO's lining and stipling codes for color,
5. the drawing is in pencil, and
6. the drawing does not match the specimens submitted with the application.

A more complicated problem arises when your drawing does not match the specimens you submitted with your application. If the Examiner doesn't think they match, you will likely get the following notice from him or her:

"The mark _____ shown on the drawing does not agree with the mark _____ actually used, as evidenced by the specimens of record. Either the drawing should be amended so that the mark thereon agrees with the mark as actually used, or specimens showing use of the mark presented in the drawing should be submitted.

"In the latter event, the use of the substitute specimens as of a date at least as early as the filing date of the application must be supported either by an affidavit or by a declaration in accordance with 37 C.F.R. § 2.20."

According to this notice, you have two options:
- If you want to register the mark shown in your drawing, you need to submit new specimens showing the mark as it appears in your drawing.
- If you are not fixed on using the mark as shown in your drawing and you do not want to submit new specimens, then your second option is to amend the drawing so that it matches the specimens you originally submitted.

a. Submit New Specimens

If you choose to keep the mark as it is represented in your drawing, then you will need to submit new specimens. The mark on the specimens must match the drawing. Along with the new specimens, you will need to submit an amendment (much like the sample in Section B, below; also see the sample amendment language below) and a declaration (see Section B and the sample declaration below, and Chapter 8, Section B3) stating that the new specimens were being used at least as early as the filing date of your application.

To summarize, the documents you need to send to the Examiner if you decide to submit new specimens are the following:
- three new specimens showing a mark that conforms to the drawing
- an amendment, and
- a declaration.

For information about how to send documents to the Examiner, see Chapter 8, Section D.

Sample Amendment to Submit New Specimens

AMENDMENT

In response to a communication from the Trademark Attorney dated January 10, 1999, please amend the application identified above as follows:

Please substitute the three specimens attached to the accompanying declaration for those originally presented.

REMARKS

Reconsideration of the application as amended is respectfully requested.

In the Trademark Attorney's communication, dated January 10, 1999, the Trademark Attorney noted the discrepancy between the drawing submitted with the trademark application (whose serial number appears above) and the specimens also submitted with that application. In that letter, the Trademark Attorney gave two options for fixing this problem: either substitute new specimens or amend the drawing. The applicant has chosen to substitute new specimens, which are attached, along with the required declaration stating that the specimens were in use on or before the application's filing date.

For the foregoing reasons, it is submitted that the present application is in condition for publication and registration, and such action is requested.

Sample Declaration to Submit New Specimens

I, Denise Lewis, do hereby declare that:

1. I am the applicant in the application identified above.

2. Attached hereto are the three specimens which show the mark as applied to multimedia design services for others and software development services for others.

These specimens were in use by the applicant on and prior to October 1, 1998 (the filing date of the application), and are still in such use.

I further declare that all statements made herein of my own knowledge are true and that all statements made on information and belief are believed to be true; and further that these statements are made with the knowledge that willful false statements and the like so made are punishable by fine or imprisonment, or both, under Section 1001 of Title 18 of the United States Code, and that such willful false statements may jeopardize the validity of the application and any registration resulting therefrom.

b. Amend the Drawing

If you decide that you'd rather amend the original drawing so that it conforms to the specimens you originally submitted, then you have two options. You can either prepare a new drawing or use a bonded draftsman to correct the original drawing. Either way, you should call the Examiner (his or her phone number is listed below their name on the action letter they sent to you). Before you spend time and money preparing or amending the drawing, be sure you understand how the Examiner views the mark. Discuss the details of the mark at length and the commercial impression that is intended. Once you've come to an agreement on the mark, then you can prepare a drawing that matches what both you and the Examiner believe to be the mark that is represented on the specimens.

If you decide to prepare a new drawing, be sure to review the guidelines for preparing a drawing in Chapter 6. You must also be very careful not to materially alter the mark in your new or amended drawing. See "Beware of Material Alteration" in Section 1, above, which explains in more detail the concept of material alteration.

Along with the new or amended drawing, you will need to submit an amendment (see Section B, below). A sample amendment follows:

5. Goods/Services Identification

If the Examiner finds that your application does not properly specify your goods and/or services, he or she will send you a notice similar to the following:

"The present identification of goods/services is indefinite for purposes of registration. The following identification is suggested, and should be adopted, if accurate: *[the Examiner will give his or her suggested description of goods/services]*."

Usually, the Examiner's recommendation will be acceptable. If you agree with the suggested description, prepare an amendment modeled after the one in Section B, below (a sample amendment follows).

Sample Amendment to Amend the Drawing

AMENDMENT

In response to a communication from the Trademark Attorney dated January 10, 1999, please amend the application identified above as follows:

Please substitute the attached drawing for the drawing originally submitted.

REMARKS

Reconsideration of the application as amended is respectfully requested.

The Trademark Attorney has asserted that the mark shown on the drawing does not agree with the mark actually used on the submitted specimens. By the foregoing amendment, substitution of the attached drawing for that originally submitted is requested. The attached drawing presents the mark as shown on the specimens of record.

For the foregoing reasons, it is submitted that the present application is in condition for publication and registration, and such action is requested.

Sample Amendment

AMENDMENT

In response to a communication from the Trademark Attorney dated January 10, 1999, please amend the application identified above as follows:

Please change the description of goods given in the application to read as follows: "Clothing, namely t-shirts, shirts, caps and jackets in International Class 25."

REMARKS

Reconsideration of the application as amended is respectfully requested.

The Trademark Attorney has asserted that the description of goods given in the application is too indefinite for registration purposes. It is therefore requested that the foregoing amended description be substituted for the description originally submitted.

For the foregoing reasons, it is submitted that the present application is in condition for publication and registration, and such action is requested.

If you do not agree with the Examiner's suggested description, it is best to call the Examiner to discuss the description and to ultimately come up with a description you can both agree upon. His or her phone number is listed below their name on the letter you received. Once you have come to an agreement, you can prepare an amendment, much like the one above, and send it to the Examiner. You should briefly describe the telephone conversation you had with the Examiner in the "Remarks" section of the amendment, giving the date of the call and the agreement you came to.

Also, be aware of how the amended description affects the existing Class or list of Classes under which you are filing. If the amended description now includes items under more than one class, you will have to submit additional specimens and pay more fees to maintain the application. Also be aware of how the amendment affects dates of use.

6. Date of First Use and Type of Commerce

Your application sets forth the date the mark was first used in commerce and the date the mark was first used anywhere. If this portion of your application is worded as we directed in either Chapter 4 or 5, then you should not be subject to any problems in this area. If you encounter a problem with the way the dates are worded, the notice the Examiner sends you may look similar to the following example:

"Applicant's choice of the term 'foreign commerce with the United States' is unacceptable. It is suggested that the applicant substitute the following, if accurate:

'Commerce between _____ and the United States.'"

If you agree with the Examiner's suggested language, prepare an amendment following the sample in Section B, below and the sample amendment directly below.

Sample Amendment to Change First-Use Wording

AMENDMENT

In response to a communication from the Trademark Attorney dated January 10, 1999, please amend the application identified above as follows:

Please amend the type of use set forth in the application to read, "Commerce between Canada and the United States."

REMARKS

Reconsideration of the application as amended is respectfully requested.

The Trademark Attorney has asserted that the term, "foreign commerce with the United States," was unacceptable. It is therefore requested that the foregoing amended specification for the type of use be substituted for the type of use originally submitted.

For the foregoing reasons, it is submitted that the present application is in condition for publication and registration, and such action is requested.

If, for some reason, you do not agree with the Examiner's suggested change, call the Examiner using the telephone number listed below the Examiner's name on the letter you received. After you've come to an agreement about the language for the type of use, prepare an amendment using the example above. In the "Remarks" section, add a description of the telephone conversation you had with the Examiner, including the date of the call and the outcome of the call.

7. Specimens

If the Examiner sends you a notice regarding a deficiency in the specimens you submitted with your application, it is probably because one or more of the following problems were found:

1. The specimens do not show the mark.
2. The specimens do not show the mark separate and distinct from anything else.
3. The specimens show an entity that is different from the applicant but that appears to represent the source of the goods or services.
4. The specimens do not show use of the mark on or in connection with the goods or services listed on the application.
5. The specimens are not a size that can fit in the PTO files.
6. The specimens do not show compliance with applicable federal regulations (such as FDA labeling requirements, etc.).
7. The specimens include objectionable material (for example, an ® symbol—see Chapter 1, Section E for an explanation as to why using the ® symbol is objectionable).

A typical notice from an Examiner who detects a problem with your specimens like that in #4, above, would look something like the following:

"The specimens do not show use of the mark on any goods/services identified in the application. Five specimens showing use of the mark for the goods/services identified in the application should be submitted. If the specimens are of a type other than those originally filed, the use of additional specimens as of a date at least as early as the filing date of the application must be supported either by an affidavit or by a declaration in accordance with Trademark Rule 2.20, Trademark Rule 2.87, TMEP §§ 808.01(b) and 1113.01."

To respond to the Examiner's notice above, you can either submit new specimens along with a declaration or convince the Examiner that the specimens originally submitted do, in fact, show use of the mark in connection with the goods or services described in your application. Note that you will need to submit a total of five specimens this time (instead of the three specimens required with your application for registration). If you are sending new specimens (that is, these specimens are not the specimens you sent with your application), then you must also send a declaration which states you were using these specimens on or before your application's filing date. See the sample declaration in Section B, below.

If you receive a notice alerting you to a different type of specimen problem, follow the same routine as we discussed above. Read the notice carefully to identify the problem. If you think a discussion with the Examiner would be helpful to clarify issues for you, follow the guidelines we give in Chapter 8 for when and how to communicate with the PTO by phone. If you decide to submit new specimens, follow the instructions in the notice you received, paying particular attention to how many specimens are required and whether or not a declaration, such as that in Section B below, is also required.

8. Prior Registrations

If you own other registered trademarks, the Examiner will likely find them and require you to include this fact on your application. Why? To establish common ownership of all the marks. Establishing common ownership here avoids claims of likelihood of confusion that really don't apply where the similar marks are owned by the same people.

If the Examiner finds your prior registrations, he or she will require you to include them in your application by a notice similar to the following:

"If applicant is the owner of registration no(s). _____, _____ and _____, a claim of ownership of said registration(s) should be made of record. Trademark Rule 2.36."

If you own all the registrations stated in the notice, then you will respond with a request that the application be amended to include a claim of ownership. You will prepare an amendment modeled after the amendment in Section B, below. Following is an example of the language you would use:

Sample Amendment to Claim Ownership

AMENDMENT

In response to a communication from the Trademark Attorney dated January 10, 1999, please amend the application identified above as follows:

Please amend the application to include the following statement—the applicant is the owner of registration no(s). _____, _____, and _____.

REMARKS

Reconsideration of the application as amended is respectfully requested.

The Trademark Attorney has asserted that if applicant is the owner of registration no(s). _____, _____, and _____, then the applicant is required to claim such ownership in the application. It is therefore requested that the foregoing claim of ownership be added to the application.

For the foregoing reasons, it is submitted that the present application is in condition for publication and registration, and such action is requested.

If you do not own any of the registrations listed on the Examiner's notice, then you should report this fact to him or her. You can expect,

however, that the Examiner will then reject your application as seeking a registration that is likely be confused with the mark or marks that were cited by the Examiner and not owned by you. Because rejection based on likelihood of confusion is possible, you should address the reasons why you don't think there is a likelihood of confusion in your response if, in fact, you wish to continue pursuing registration. For more information about likelihood of confusion rejections, see Chapter 10.

TIFFANY & CO.

9. Consent to Register a Surname

If your mark contains a surname (your family name is an example of a surname) or otherwise identifies an individual (by a photograph or drawing of that individual), then the Examiner will require permission from that individual to use their name or likeness. The Examiner's notice to you will look something like the following:

"The name (or individual) shown in the mark on the drawing should be identified. If it is the name (or a picture) of a particular living individual, written consent from said individual to the use and registration of the name (or photograph) must be filed. If said name is merely fanciful and does not identify a particular individual, this fact should be indicated."

If the name or likeness included in the mark is not of a specific person (it is a stylized representation of no particular person), or if it is of a particular person, but that individual is no longer living, then prepare a response modeled after the response in Section B, below. The language in the body of such a response should follow one of the following examples:

Sample Responses

Sir:

In response to a communication from the Trademark Attorney dated January 10, 1999, reconsideration of the application identified above is requested for the reasons stated in the following paragraphs.

The name (or photograph) shown in the mark is merely fanciful and does not identify a particular individual.

For the foregoing reasons, it is submitted that the present application is in condition for publication and registration, and such action is requested.

Sir:

In response to a communication from the Trademark Attorney dated January 10, 1999, reconsideration of the application identified above is requested for the reasons stated in the following paragraphs.

The name (or photograph) shown in the mark is of a particular individual, but that individual is no longer living.

For the foregoing reasons, it is submitted that the present application is in condition for publication and registration, and such action is requested.

Sir:

In response to a communication from the Trademark Attorney dated January 10, 1999, reconsideration of the application identified above is requested for the reasons stated in the following paragraphs.

The name (or photograph) shown in the mark is of a particular living individual. That individual signed the present application, which is deemed to constitute consent.

For the foregoing reasons, it is submitted that the present application is in condition for publication and registration, and such action is requested.

Sir:

In response to a communication from the Trademark Attorney dated January 10, 1999, reconsideration of the application identified above is requested for the reasons stated in the following paragraphs.

The name (or photograph) shown in the mark is of a particular living individual. Accompanying this response is a document signed by that individual (or their guardian) and confirming the individual's consent to the applicant's use and registration of the name (or photograph).

For the foregoing reasons, it is submitted that the present application is in condition for publication and registration, and such action is requested.

If your mark contains a name or likeness of a living person who has not signed your application, then you should use the last example above for your response. You should include, with your response, a consent form, signed by the person whose name or likeness you used. The consent should be in the form of a declaration and modeled after the following example:

Sample Declaration

I, Louise Brown, do hereby declare that:

1. I am aware that federal registration of my name (or photograph) is sought by the applicant in the application identified in the heading of this document.

2. I hereby confirm my consent to the use of my name (or photograph) by that applicant and to its registration by that applicant.

I further declare that all statements made herein of my own knowledge are true and that all statements made on information and belief are believed to be true; and further that these statements are made with the knowledge that willful false statements and the like so made are punishable by fine or imprisonment, or both, under Section 1001 of Title 18 of the United States Code, and that such willful false statements may jeopardize the validity of the application and any registration resulting therefrom.

Dated:_____

_[Signature of Declarant]_____

_[Printed name of Declarant]_____

If the person who is identified in the mark is a minor, then a guardian will have to sign a consent on the minor's behalf. The first paragraph of the Declaration should state that the person signing the declaration is a guardian of the minor and is signing the consent on behalf of the minor. All the other paragraphs should be modified to reflect the guardian's point of view. For example, paragraph two would read, "The minor and guardian are aware that federal registration of the minor's name is sought by the applicant in the application identified in the heading of this document."

When Your Mark Consists Primarily of a Surname

A mark which contains a surname will sometimes be rejected because marks that are merely surnames are too descriptive to be registered, and registration of the surname might work to preclude other people with that name from using it for their own businesses—which they have an inherent right to do. If you receive a rejection based on this problem, see Chapter 10, Section A, for a more in-depth discussion.

10. Incorrect Filing Fee

You must send the filing fee for at least one class with your application in order to receive a filing date. If you are seeking registration of a mark in more than one class, or if you have described the goods and/or services in your application such that the description falls into more than one class, then you will likely receive a notice from the Examiner that is similar to the following if you did not send in the correct filing fee with your application:

"Combined applications are permitted under Section 30 of the Trademark Act, provided a filing fee is paid for each Class in which the goods and/ or services are classified. Applicant may elect to restrict the goods and/or services herein to one Class or pay the additional fee."

If you received a notice similar to the one above, you have two options: 1) amend your application to limit the goods and/or services to one class, making your initial filing fee adequate; or 2) seek registration in more than one class by preparing and sending an amendment (see discussion below) along with the appropriate fees.

If you choose to amend your application to limit the goods and/or services described in it, it might be best to call the Examiner first and discuss an appropriate limitation. For example, if your application was for the following goods: coffee stirrers (Class 16), coffee filters (Class 21) and coffee cups (Class 21), you might call the Examiner to discuss limiting the goods to the two Class 21 products (coffee filters and cups), rather than paying an additional $245 to add Class 16 for coffee stirrers. You will find the Examiner's phone number listed below his or her name on the letter you received.

After you have come to an agreement regarding the description of the goods and/or services, be sure to clarify who will be sending confirmation of the agreement. Will you be sending a written amendment to the Examiner after your telephone interview, or will the Examiner send you a written confirmation? If you need to send a written amendment to the Examiner, you can do so by preparing an amendment modeled after the amendment sample in Section B, below. Follow the instructions for preparing an amendment to the description of goods and/or services in Section 5, above.

If you decide to amend the application to add one or more classes, prepare an amendment modeled after the sample amendment in Section B, below. Following is an example of how the body of that amendment might look:

Sample Amendment to Add Classes

AMENDMENT

In response to a communication from the Trademark Attorney dated January 10, 1999, please amend the application identified above as follows:

Please register the mark (as given in the trademark application whose serial number is provided in the heading above) for the goods and services in the following International Classes: Class 9 and Class 42.

REMARKS

Reconsideration of the application as amended is respectfully requested.

The present application now seeks registration of the mark in more than one Class. Attached to this document is a check in payment of the additional filing fee now required.

For the foregoing reasons, it is submitted that the present application is in condition for publication and registration, and such action is requested.

The correct filing fee should be included with your amendment. For example, if you paid the filing fee equivalent for registration under one class when you filed your application ($245) and you seek registration in one more class, then you will need to send an additional fee of $245 for that additional class. As with your original application fee, make checks payable to Commissioner of Patents and Trademarks.

For instructions on how to send documents to the PTO, see Chapter 8.

11. Delay in Filing

If you signed and dated your application, but then did not send it in to the PTO until much later, then the Examiner may give you a serial number and filing date, but send you a notice much like the following:

"The present application was not filed in the Patent and Trademark Office within a reasonable time after the date on which the application papers were signed. Eight weeks (plus mailing time to this Office) for domestic applicants or twelve weeks (plus mailing time to this Office) for foreign applicants is considered a reasonable time. For this reason, a statement that the mark is still in use must be submitted. Such statement must be supported by an affidavit or by a declaration in accordance with Trademark Rule 2.20."

If, in fact, the time between the date you signed your application and the date you sent it to the PTO falls outside the eight weeks allowed for domestic (within the U.S.) applicants or outside the twelve weeks allowed for foreign applicants, then you will need to file a formal response modeled after the sample response in Section B, below. In addition to the formal response, you will need to file a declaration stating that the mark is still in use. Following are examples of the substantive paragraphs for the response and the declaration:

Sample Response to Correct Timing Problem

RESPONSE

Sir:

In response to a communication from the Trademark Attorney dated January 10, 1999, reconsideration of the application identified above is requested for the reasons stated in the following paragraphs.

The Trademark Attorney has asserted that the present application was not filed in the Patent and Trademark Office within a reasonable time after the date on which the application papers were signed. The Trademark Attorney has required that a statement, supported by a declaration, be submitted confirming that the mark was in use on the application's filing date and is still in use. Such statement and declaration is attached to this response.

For the foregoing reasons, it is submitted that the present application is in condition for publication and registration, and such action is requested.

Sample Declaration

DECLARATION

I, Joseph Lopez, the applicant in the application
identified in the heading of this document (or
having been duly authorized by the applicant
identified in the heading of this document) state
that the mark sought to be registered by the
present application was in use on September 1,
1997 (the filing date of the application), and is
still in use by the applicant.

I further declare that all statements made herein
of my own knowledge are true and that all
statements made on information and belief are
believed to be true; and further that these statements are made with the knowledge that willful
false statements and the like so made are punishable by fine or imprisonment, or both, under
Section 1001 of Title 18 of the United States
Code, and that such willful false statements
may jeopardize the validity of the application
and any registration resulting therefrom.

B. Using the Correct Format for Your Response

This section provides an overview of three
different types of documents you can send to the
PTO in response to a PTO rejection. Although we

discussed these documents in Chapter 8, we provide a full sample for each document type here.

1. Amendment of a Trademark/Service Mark Application

An amendment of a trademark/service mark
application is simply a response from the applicant to the Examiner asking for a change in the
applicant's original application information.

2. Formal Response to the PTO

A formal response is generally a document prepared by the applicant to the Examiner detailing
all of the reasons why the applicant believes he
or she is entitled to registration despite the
Examiner's rejection of his or her application.

3. Declarations

A declaration in the trademark registration context
is a document which states important facts regarding the trademark application or the circumstances
surrounding the mark for which registration is
sought. These facts are spelled out in the declaration, along with a statement which certifies that
the facts in the declaration are true to the best of
the declarant's knowledge. The declarant must
then sign the declaration.

Sample Formal Response

TRADEMARK
UNITED STATES DEPARTMENT OF COMMERCE
Patent and Trademark Office

Applicant:) Trademark Law

Mark:) Office _____

Serial No. (1)   ) Trademark Attorney

Filed:) _____

RESPONSE

Sir:

In response to a communication from the Trademark Attorney dated _____,
reconsideration of the application identified above is requested for the reasons stated in the
following paragraphs.

*[Here discuss each requirement and objection, preferably in the order set forth in the
communication from the Trademark Attorney, pointing out that it has been complied
with, or the reasons for non-compliance.]*

For the foregoing reasons, it is submitted that the present application is in condition for
publication and registration, and such action is requested.

Dated: _____

Respectfully,

_____

Applicant

Telephone Number: _____

Sample Amendment

TRADEMARK
UNITED STATES DEPARTMENT OF COMMERCE
Patent and Trademark Office

Applicant:) Trademark Law
Mark:) Office _____
Serial No. (1)   ) Trademark Attorney
Filed:) _____

AMENDMENT

In response to a communication from the Trademark Attorney dated _____, please amend the application identified above as follows:

[Here in separate paragraphs describe each amendment to be made to the application, for example:]

Please change the description of goods given in the application to read as follows: "_____
_____."

Please enter the following disclaimer immediately after the dates of use given in the application: "Without waiving rights now existing or hereafter arising, the applicant disclaims the word _____ separate and apart from the mark as shown."

REMARKS

Reconsideration of the application as amended is respectfully requested.

[Here, discuss each requirement and objection, preferably in the order set forth in the communication from the Trademark Attorney, pointing out that it has been complied with, or the reasons for non-compliance.]

For the foregoing reasons, it is submitted that the present application is in condition for publication and registration, and such action is requested.

Dated: _____

Respectfully,

_____
Applicant

Telephone Number: _____

Sample Declaration

TRADEMARK
UNITED STATES DEPARTMENT OF COMMERCE
Patent and Trademark Office

Applicant:) Trademark Law
Mark:) Office _____
Serial No. (1)   ) Trademark Attorney
Filed:) _____

DECLARATION

I, _____ *[insert full name of declarant]* _____ , do hereby declare that:

1. *[Identify declarant here and state the declarant's relationship to the applicant. For example:]*

I am an officer of the corporation named as the applicant in the trademark application identified above.

2. *[In this and subsequent paragraphs, present the facts as stated by the declarant. Each paragraph may be numbered. No paragraph need be more than a sentence long if the fact presented is brief and to the point. The facts must be presented in a form showing that the declarant has first-hand knowledge of the fact. For example:]*

Attached to this response are five (5) specimens of the mark sought to be registered in this application. These specimens were in use by the applicant on and prior to October 1, 1998 (the filing date of the application), and are still in such use.

I further declare that all statements made herein of my own knowledge are true and that all statements made on information and belief are believed to be true; and further that these statements are made with the knowledge that willful false statements and the like so made are punishable by fine or imprisonment, or both, under Section 1001 of Title 18 of the United States Code, and that such willful false statements may jeopardize the validity of the application and any registration resulting therefrom.

Dated: _____

_____ *[signature of declarant]* _____

_____ *[print name of declarant]* _____

C. Responding to Final Rejections

A "final" rejection will not arrive until after you have received, and, we hope, responded to, at least one action letter with some sort of rejection. Most formal rejections are relatively easy to resolve with your Examiner and should not result in a final rejection. If, however, you do receive a final rejection concerning a formal rejection, you have several options once the final rejection is received. You can:

- write again and ask the Examiner to reconsider your application and previous responses.
- talk with the Examiner by phone or in person to get a better idea of what, if anything, can be done to fix the application.

- file an appeal (if the grounds for rejection are appealable) asking the Trademark Trial and Appeal Board to consider your application. Any substantive dispute is appealable. This includes any judgment made by the Examiner (such as when he or she believes you should disclaim one or more words).
- request suspension of the application (if allowed this could give you more time to prepare a response or request for reconsideration).

By the time your application has received a final rejection, the Examiner's boss has reviewed the whole file and approved the rejection. It is therefore very unlikely that you will obtain registration after receiving a final rejection. ■

Descriptive and Confusion Rejections

Before embarking on this chapter, we hope you have read Chapter 8, which explains the different types of rejections you may encounter after submitting a trademark application, and further explains how to identify the type or types of rejections you have received. This chapter focuses on descriptive and confusion rejections and explains to you, in general terms, what descriptive and confusion rejections are and what your options are if you've received one. They include:

- responding formally to the rejection
- switching your application to a different register to make registration easier, or
- abandoning the application altogether.

Preparing a response to a descriptive or confusion rejection is not an easy task and we do not recommend you do it on your own. (We'll leave that topic to a future book!) We, instead, recommend that you read this chapter and decide upon a course of action that makes sense to you given your own individual business needs. If you receive a descriptive or confusion rejection, we recommend you seek the help of a lawyer, either to help you sort out why the Examiner has a problem with your mark or to help you draft a response to the Examiner's rejection. If you decide you need help, advice on choosing a lawyer is provided in Chapter 14, Help Beyond This Book.

A. Dealing With a Descriptive Rejection

A trademark may receive a descriptiveness rejection if it communicates in a descriptive or otherwise mundane way something about the product or service to which it is attached. If you've received an action letter rejecting your mark because it is descriptive, the rejection may look something like the following:

"Registration is refused on the Principal Register because the mark, when applied to the goods and/or services, is considered to be merely descriptive (or geographically descriptive, decep-tively misdescriptive or primarily merely a surname) thereof. Section 2(e) of the Trademark Act."

Descriptive marks are usually not registrable on the Principal Register for two reasons:

- Consumers are so used to commercial hype that descriptive terms don't make the kind of impact on them that would help them to effectively distinguish one product or service from another. For example, the name Canine Clipping Center doesn't by itself clearly differentiate that pet care shop from any other.
- Descriptive terms need to remain freely available for everyone's commercial or everyday use. Trademark law only protects terms that are unique to a particular product or service brand and that aren't, therefore, necessary for another business to use if it wishes to describe or hype its business in advertising or marketing copy.

For a more thorough discussion of what makes a mark strong or weak, including its distinctiveness or descriptiveness, see Chapter 1, Section C.

If you receive a descriptive rejection, you have a few options: fight, convert your application or abandon it altogether. Which option you choose will depend on:

- how much money and/or other resources you have to throw at the problem
- how important registration is to your business plan
- whether or not you think you have a good argument that the mark isn't descriptive, and
- whether or not you've been using the mark continuously for a long period of time (secondary meaning). We explain each of these options in more detail below.

1. Fighting the Rejection

Your fighting tools in this situation are your wits, a good lawyer who knows the ropes and a little bit of luck. You'd choose to fight if you believed that you had a winning chance of convincing the Examiner that your mark is either not descriptive *or* that because you've been using the mark continuously for five years straight, it has now "acquired distinctiveness" such that it is still registrable, even though it is admittedly descriptive.

Another prerequisite to fighting it out is money. You need to have the money to hire an attorney, if for no other reason than to help you draft that important document known as a response. How much money you will need depends on how much the attorney charges per hour, how long the attorney's work will take and how complex your response is. Get that estimate up front before hiring your attorney.

The response is the key to success or failure here. It is a formal document which explains, in detail, all of the reasons why you think your mark is registrable. A response can be a simple matter, or it can be complicated, depending on your individual circumstances. And the first response may not be enough. If the Examiner does not agree with the arguments laid out in your first response, you may need to file a second one.

The first task in laying out a response to your descriptiveness rejection is to evaluate the strengths and/or weaknesses of the Examiner's comments. Why does the Examiner believe your mark is descriptive? Are his or her arguments credible? Do you have good reasons to believe your mark is not descriptive? Is there a chance that simply amending (changing) the mark in some way will solve the problem? All of these issues should be discussed with your lawyer. The Sample Response to a Merely Descriptive Mark Rejection is given below to give you a basic idea of what such a response should look like.

Occasionally a descriptive rejection can be handled by amending your application to claim that the mark has become distinctive under the secondary meaning rule. Even descriptive names can become legally strong enough to get full trademark protection through the secondary meaning rule. That's when a trademark becomes so closely identified with a specific product or

service that the public no longer thinks first of the original ordinary meaning of the words. Then the mark is said to have taken on a new "secondary"—and distinctive—meaning, and rivals can no longer use it to identify their products or services. For example, usually the word ivory means a color or animal tusk. However, to many people, in the context of soap it has a secondary meaning and identifies a specific product. Another term for secondary meaning is "acquired distinctiveness." This concept is covered in § 2(f) of the Trademark Act (15 U.S.C. § 1052(f)).

To claim acquired distinctiveness under the secondary meaning rule, you usually have to prove you have continuously and exclusively used the mark for five years (before the application was filed), and offer various facts showing that consumers know the mark refers to your goods or services. You will need to discuss whether or not your situation lends itself well to an amendment claiming secondary meaning with your lawyer.

The Sample Response to a Descriptive Mark/ Secondary Meaning Rule Rejection, shown below, shows you how you might respond to a refusal based on descriptiveness using the secondary meaning rule (acquired distinctiveness) as the basis for reconsideration of the mark and ultimate registration of the mark.

If the secondary meaning argument doesn't work, you should ask if the Examiner will let you amend your application to apply to the Supplemental Register. See the next section for information about how to convert your application to register on the Supplemental Register.

Sample Response to Merely Descriptive Mark Rejection

UNITED STATES PATENT AND TRADEMARK OFFICE
TRADEMARK EXAMINING OPERATION

In re Application of:)
DMX, Inc.) Trademark Law Office IV
Serial No.: 75/382915)
Filed: December 10, 1998) Attorney: Jim Lyone
Mark: TRIPHASE)

BOX RESPONSES
NO FEE

Assistant Commissioner for Trademarks
2900 Crystal Drive
Arlington, VA 22202-3513

RESPONSE TO OFFICE ACTION PURSUANT TO 37 C.F.R. § 2.62

Sir:

In response to a communication from the Trademark Attorney dated January 10, 1999, reconsideration of the application identified above is requested for the reasons stated in the following paragraphs.

The trademark attorney has stated that the mark "TRIPHASE," for which registration is sought, is descriptive of the goods provided in the application for registration. The applicant concedes that its goods have three separate but related uses: degreaser, cleaner and brightener. If applicant were seeking registration of the marks TRI-USE or TRI-PURPOSE, it is conceded that there are good arguments to support the decision that these marks would be too descriptive or at least highly suggestive. However, the word "phase" is not synonymous with "use" or "purpose." The trademark attorney's attention is invited to any dictionary for the definition of "phase." "Phase" is a word with many meanings, but in all those meanings, there are none which imply "use" or "purpose."

Applicant's mark TRIPHASE may be slightly suggestive of a product with three uses. However, applicant's product is a homogenous alkaline liquid concentrate and doesn't exist in three physical phases. Therefore, applicant's mark should not be refused registration on the ground of descriptiveness.

For the foregoing reasons, it is submitted that the present application is in condition for publication and registration, and such action is requested.

Respectfully submitted,
Brian Jones
Brian Jones, President
DMX, Inc.
18 Market Street
San Diego, CA 92110
(619) 123-4567

Date: June 10, 1999

Sample Response to a Descriptive Mark/Secondary Meaning Rule Rejection

UNITED STATES PATENT AND TRADEMARK OFFICE
TRADEMARK EXAMINING OPERATION

In re Application of:	)
Charing Corporation	) Trademark Law Office IV
Serial No.: 74/487965	)
Filed: August 10, 1998	) Attorney: Martha Sims, Esq.
Mark: SPRAY IT OFF	)

BOX RESPONSES
NO FEE

Assistant Commissioner for Trademarks
2900 Crystal Drive
Arlington, VA 22202-3513

AMENDMENT AND RESPONSE UNDER 37 C.F.R. § 2.62

Sir:

In response to the Office Action of January 10, 1999, kindly amend the above-identified application as follows:

Add the following statement to the application: "The mark has become distinctive of Applicant's goods as a result of substantially exclusive and continuous use of the mark by Applicant in commerce and for the five years preceding the date on which this claim of distinctiveness is made."

Applicant is seeking to register the above-indicated trademark for a "cleaning and stain-removing composition." The specimens submitted show use of the mark on a product dispensed from a spray container.

REMARKS

The Examiner has rejected this application on the ground that the mark sought to be registered is merely descriptive when applied to Applicant's goods. Applicant has enjoyed continuous and substantially exclusive use of this trademark for the five-year period preceding this claim of distinctiveness. Accordingly, the application has been amended to allege this fact and registration is now being sought under the provision of Section 2(f) of the Trademark Act of 1946, as amended (15 U.S.C. § 1052(f)).

Attached to this response is a Declaration of Ms. Gillian Small, filed under the provisions of Rule 41. This Declaration sets forth facts supporting Applicant's entitlement to the provisions of Section 2(f).

Sample Response—Descriptive Mark/Secondary Meaning Rule (continued)

It is noted that a search of the Patent and Trademark Office records fails to show that Applicant's mark so resembles any registered mark as to be likely to cause confusion, mistake or deception. In view of the foregoing Amendment, it is believed that this application is now in condition for prompt publication. Favorable action is therefore requested.

Respectfully Submitted,

Gillian Small

Gillian Small, CEO

Charing Corporation

2200 Market Street

San Francisco, CA 94107

(415) 123-4567

Date: March 10, 1999

2. Converting Your Application

If, in the end, the Examiner issues a final rejection (a final rejection is the end of the line—see Section C, If You Receive a Final Rejection, below) based on your mark's descriptiveness, you still have the option of converting your application from one seeking registration on the Principal Register to one seeking registration on the Supplemental Register. Although we refer to it as a conversion, what you are really doing is amending your application. For more information about the rights given to you on the Supplemental Register as opposed to the Principal Register, see Chapter 1, Section A.

You would prepare an amendment much like the Sample Amendment to Convert Application to Supplemental Register below.

3. Abandon Your Application

If you think the Examiner is right and/or you don't think registering the mark is worth the fight, then you can write the Examiner a letter informing him or her that you do not wish to pursue the matter and are abandoning the application. Or, doing nothing (i.e. not responding to the Examiner's action letter) will have the same effect as abandoning the application. By the way, abandoning the application will not prevent you from filing another application later on, even if it's for the same mark. This is because circumstances may change (even within a few weeks) and the problem you encountered with your earlier application may no longer exist. For example, you may develop a new good or service upon which to use your mark that doesn't conflict with a registered mark.

B. Dealing With a Confusion Rejection

You will know that the Examiner has issued a refusal based on a likelihood of confusion if the action letter contains a paragraph labeled "LIKELIHOOD OF CONFUSION—SECTION 2(d)" and the paragraph reads substantially as follows:

"The examining attorney refuses registration under Trademark Act Section 2(d), 15 U.S.C.

Section 1052 (d), because the applicant's mark, when used on the identified goods, is likely to be confused with the registered mark in U.S. Registration Nos. *[conflicting mark's registration number or numbers]*. TMEP section 1207. See the enclosed registration(s)."

or:

"Registration is refused because the mark, when applied to the goods and/or services of the applicant, so resembles the mark(s) cited below as to be likely to cause confusion, or to cause mistake, or to deceive. Section 2(d) of the Trademark Act; TMEP § 1205. (See attached copies.) Reg. No(s). *[conflicting mark's registration number or numbers given here.]*"

Since confusion rejections can involve fairly complex issues, let's take a step back to consider the "likelihood of customer confusion" standard in trademark law.

1. What "Confusion" Means in Trademark Law

A confusion rejection is based on § 2(d) of the Trademark Act (15 U.S.C. § 1052(d)), which says:

"No trademark by which the goods of the applicant may be distinguished from the goods of others shall be refused registration on the Principal Register on account of its nature unless it:

...

(d) Consists of or comprises a mark which so resembles a mark registered in the Patent and Trademark Office or a mark or trade name previously used in the United States by another and not abandoned, as to be likely, when applied to the goods of the applicant, to cause confusion, or to cause mistake, or to deceive."

The phrase "likelihood of confusion" is the key to most trademark conflicts, whether they occur before or after registration. Remember that the whole purpose of trademark law is to allow product or service providers the opportunity to claim exclusivity on marks that they use to identify the origins of their products or services.

Allowing such exclusivity ensures that consumers of products and services will ultimately be able to know where their favorite products and services come from and to easily repurchase those products or services again and again. Likewise, the laws are meant to keep competing businesses from palming off the efforts of the mark owner by using the same mark on the same goods or services to intentionally confuse consumers.

You can see that prohibiting the registration of marks that are likely to be confused with already-registered marks lies at the heart of trademark law. But how does one determine that one mark is likely to be confused with another?

Being able to assess whether customer confusion is likely in a particular situation is a skill that depends as much on experience and intuition as it does on any hard and fast principles. While we can and do explain how courts (and, ultimately, trademark Examiners) generally go about assessing the likelihood of confusion, each case is inevitably unique in some particular. Predicting the future outcome of any given case is definitely an art rather than a science. As we suggest throughout the book, if you are uncertain about the correct course of action after applying our guidelines to your situation, you will be wise to consult with an experienced trademark lawyer (see Chapter 14, Help Beyond This Book.)

A likelihood means that confusion is probable—not necessarily that it has happened, or that it will happen, but that it is more likely than not that a reasonable customer will be confused.

Confusion in this context can mean two different things. Most commonly, it means that the goods or services a customer buys are different from what the customer intended to buy. For instance, if a consumer wants to purchase the services of ABC Emergency Care on the basis of a friend's recommendation, but ends up going to ABD Emergency Room by mistake because of the similarity of the two names, you have an example of customer confusion between the two services.

Sample Amendment to Convert Application to Supplemental Register

UNITED STATES PATENT AND TRADEMARK OFFICE
TRADEMARK EXAMINING OPERATION

In re Application of:	)
Zelig Corporation	) Trademark Law Office IV
Serial No.: 75/497266	)
Filed: October 10, 1998	) Attorney: Ted Williams
Mark: SPRAY IT OFF	)

BOX RESPONSES
NO FEE

Assistant Commissioner for Trademarks
2900 Crystal Drive
Arlington, VA 22202-3513

AMENDMENT AND RESPONSE UNDER 37 C.F.R. § 2.62

Sir:

In response to the Office Action of March 10, 1999, kindly amend the above-identified application as follows:

Please change the application from one seeking registration of the mark on the Principal Register, to one seeking registration of the mark on the Supplemental Register.

Please cancel the paragraph of the application reciting the applicant's use of the mark, and substitute therefor: "The mark sought to be registered is in lawful use in interstate commerce in connection with the goods or services."

Applicant is seeking to register the above-indicated trademark for a "cleaning and stain-removing composition." The specimens submitted show use of the mark on a product dispensed from a spray container.

REMARKS

The Examiner has issued a final rejection for this application on the ground that the mark sought to be registered is merely descriptive when applied to Applicant's goods. Applicant now seeks to register the mark on the Supplemental Register and requests that the application for the foregoing mark be amended accordingly.

Respectfully Submitted,

Faye Manning
Faye Manning, CEO
Zelig Corporation
500 Branning Street
Detroit, MI
555-123-4567

Date: April 10, 1999

The other situation that creates customer confusion is where a misleading mark causes the customer to believe—wrongly—that a product or service is sponsored by, approved by, or somehow connected with a business she already frequents or knows about. In other words, the customer is confused about the source of the product or service. This would be the case, for example, if a customer took his or her TV to a repair shop called IBM Electronics because they thought that IBM somehow sponsored the business.

Court decisions have produced a number of criteria to determine when there's a likelihood of confusion between two marks. As would a judge, you (and your lawyer, if you choose to hire one) will want to ask the following questions regarding your mark and the registered marks in question:

Factor 1: Are the goods and services represented by the marks related—that is, are they sold in the same marketing channels to the same general group of customers?

Factor 2: Do the goods or services compete—that is, will the decision by customers to buy one business's product or service be made at the expense of the other business?

Factor 3: How similar are the marks in sound, appearance and meaning?

Factor 4: How strong is each mark? (Is the mark in question very distinctive when compared to a competing mark?)

Factor 5: How much do the underlying goods or services cost? (How carefully does the public usually decide whether to buy the goods or services offered by the two businesses?)

Factor 6: Do the two marks share the same customer base?

Factor 7: Does one owner use the mark on several different products or services, or is it likely to do so in the future?

These factors have not been placed in any particular order of importance because each one is considered equally along with all the others and any one of them may be the reason the Examiner decides your mark is confusingly similar to a registered mark. Nonetheless, Factors 1

through 3 bear taking a closer look because they represent some of the more common problems with confusingly similar marks.

A positive response to Factor 1 regarding the relatedness of the marks would tend to show that the marks are too confusingly similar. If similar marks are used on related goods or services and they are sold in the same marketing channels (sold in similar outlets, marketed in similar media, placed near each other in stores, for example), then the risk of confusion is high.

For example, you should determine if the same sorts of information sources (billboards, newspapers, magazines, radio) would carry ads bearing both marks. Would both marks appear in ads in the same trade journals? Might the products or services be displayed or sold in the same store/catalog, or under the same heading in a trade directory? Will they both target the same customer base? Do both marks appear in advertising on the World Wide Web? If the answer to most of these questions is yes, the marks are used in the same marketing channels. That increases the likelihood of customer confusion.

Beyond marketing channels, the Examiner might also look at the classes under which the marks are registered or under which registration is sought. If the same class is used by both marks, then it is evidence that they are too closely related, since they are within the same classification of goods or services.

Factor 2 goes to how closely the goods or services compete with each other. If the goods or services are in direct competition with each other, so that the consumer would likely encounter and make a purchasing decision on both, then the goods or services may be too closely related.

Factor 3 raises one of the most difficult questions, because the inquiry is very subjective. How similar are the marks in question? Do they sound or look alike, and if so, how much? Do they convey the same meaning? The closer two marks are in sight, sound and meaning, the more likely it is that a problem will arise.

In comparing marks, remember that variations in spelling or punctuation do not make marks different if they sound the same. Thus, Phansee-pants is functionally the same as Fancy Pants, and Duncan Doughnuts duplicates Dunkin Donuts. Even using foreign language equivalents can't make a mark different enough, if most of the public could tell they mean the same. So La Petite Boulangerie would infringe on "The Little Bakery," and El Sombrero Blanco probably infringes on "The White Hat."

Even marks with more substantial differences may be confusingly similar, in the same market. So courts have found Quirst is too close to Squirt, Sarnoff too much like Smirnoff, Lorraine too reminiscent of La Touraine. Each of these pairs of marks were used on nearly identical goods. Probably the use of such duplicate marks would have passed legal muster if they had been on products that weren't so similar. Again that's because the more competitive marks are in a class or market channels, the less similar the marks have to be to cause confusion.

2. What Are Your Options?

If you have received an action letter issuing a refusal based on a likelihood of confusion between your mark and another registered mark, you may be facing quite a difficult task if you wish to proceed with your application. There are a number of factors which make challenging this refusal difficult. First, remember that doubt is always resolved by the Examiner in favor of the senior user of the mark (not you). Second, the concept of likelihood of confusion and the law to which it is attached is convoluted and difficult to master, even for seasoned attorneys.

Depending on your situation, it is often best just to try to reach an agreement with the owner of the conflicting mark to see if you can either purchase the use of your mark from that owner or reach some agreement to negate any likelihood of confusion between the two marks. We discuss that option in subsection b, below. If you can't reach an agreement, it may be best simply to abandon your mark and choose another if, after giving it extensive thought, you think pursuing the application further is not worth the trouble and that choosing another mark will not set your business back too much. We discuss abandonment in subsection c, below.

Finally, if you don't want to give up and you want to fight to keep your application in the running, you will need to prepare yourself for the time and expense that responding to such a rejection inevitably entails. You will need a lawyer to help you sort out your best arguments for why your mark is not confusingly similar to the marks cited by the Examiner and to prepare your written response.

A written response is a formal document which explains, in detail, all of the reasons why you think your mark is registrable. A response can be a simple matter, or it can be complicated, depending on your individual circumstances. And the first response may not be enough. If the Examiner does not agree with the arguments laid out in your first response, you may need to file a second one.

If you decide to seek a lawyer, follow the guidelines we provide in Chapter 14, Help Beyond This Book. We discuss the "fight" option below.

a. Fighting the Rejection

The first task in evaluating the confusion rejection is gathering and assessing information about your mark and the mark which has been deemed similar enough to yours to cause a problem. Your lawyer may ask you to delve into the following resources to help show the Examiner that your mark is not likely to cause confusion.

- Your own records are your own best friend. Look through your files for press clips, prior registrations of the same mark or other marks that are related to the mark for which registration is sought, and sales records. Any of these items may establish a date of actual use, which may or may not show that your mark was in use before the mark in question.

- The Examiner will attach copies of the registration with which your mark is in conflict. But if for any reason you need to look up the registration record yourself, you can do so using a number of resources, including CASSIS (the PTO's database of registered marks and pending applications for marks, available for free on the Internet and in Patent and Trademark Depository libraries). To learn more about where to find and how to use this and other trademark search resources, consult *Trademark: Legal Care for Your Business & Product Name,* by Stephen Elias and Kate McGrath (Nolo). The registration record of the mark with which your mark is in conflict is important to have because it gives you useful information about that mark, such as the official rendition of the mark itself, the owner of the mark, the location of the owner, the dates of first use of that mark, the description of that mark's goods and/or services, and more. You and your attorney will be able to use that information to determine whether or not you have good arguments for why your mark is not confusingly similar to the competing mark.

- Trade journals may be useful for looking up articles about the competing mark's owner(s) or about the goods and/or services for which the mark is used. This information is helpful because it may show whether or not the competing marks are placed on goods or services that are in the same marketing channels. The information about the mark's owner(s) may reveal more information about the goods and/or services they provide.

A Sample Response to a Confusion Rejection is shown below.

b. Obtaining a Consent Agreement

When there is probable confusion, one relatively simple way around it is to secure the consent of the other mark's owner(s) for your registration. If you can get one, a consent agreement is always a good route to take in responding to a confusion rejection. The PTO takes them very seriously and you are more likely to have your application moved on to registration and the confusion rejection dropped if you have a consent in hand. Simply put, a consent agreement is an agreement between you and the competing mark holder that there is no conflict nor likelihood of confusion between your two (or more) marks, and that the competing mark holder consents (agrees) to the use and registration of your mark.

The time to secure a consent agreement is as soon after you receive your confusion rejection as possible. It may take time for you to get the agreement and you have less than six months before your response is due. Once you locate the competing mark's owner, you or your lawyer can send a letter explaining your situation and requesting consent to your registration. You can include two copies of the agreement with your letter. If the competing mark's owner agrees, he or she can sign both copies of the agreement, keep one for his or her records and send one copy back to you. You or your lawyer will then send a copy of that agreement to the Examiner, along with your official response (samples are shown below).

Since drawing up such an agreement can be daunting, we recommend you use a lawyer to draw one up for you. If you'd like to try drafting your own, you can use the sample consent agreement as a model.

Sample Response to a Confusion Rejection

UNITED STATES PATENT AND TRADEMARK OFFICE
TRADEMARK EXAMINING OPERATION

In re Application of:)
[applicant's name]   ) Trademark Law Office:
Serial No.: *[number]*   ) *[number]*
Filed: *[date]*   ) Attorney: *[name]*
Mark: SMART SCENTS   )

BOX RESPONSES
NO FEE

Assistant Commissioner for Trademarks
2900 Crystal Drive
Arlington, VA 22202-3513

RESPONSE TO OFFICE ACTION UNDER 37 C.F.R. § 2.62

Sir:

This is in response to Office Action No. 1 dated January 28, 1998.

The Examiner has refused registration of Applicant's trademark on the ground of confusing similarity to the trademark SMART-SCENTS, Registration No. 1,007,545, for "self-adhesive bathroom hardware." Reconsideration of this refusal to register is respectfully requested.

It is conceded that Applicant's trademark and the trademark shown on the cited registration are essentially identical. It is submitted, however, that the differences in the respective goods are such as to preclude any reasonable likelihood of confusion. Applicant's product is an air freshener, i.e., a room deodorant product. It comprises an absorbent substance impregnated with a deodorant. The substance is contained within a housing shaped somewhat like a flower. The housing consists of two sections, which can be separated by twisting. When the user separates the two parts, the absorbent material is exposed and the deodorant exudes. This product is not a permanent fixture. In time, depending largely upon how much of the absorbent material is exposed to the air and for how long, applicant's product loses its deodorizing properties and has to be replaced.

The goods in the cited reference are described as "self-adhesive bathroom hardware." The definition of the goods is somewhat vague, in that it conveys no information as to their function. Furthermore, Applicant and the undersigned attorney have not been able to obtain, from the Registrant, any information concerning the nature of the goods. It is noted that the goods are classified in Class 11 of the International Classification System, and it is therefore

Sample Response to a Confusion Rejection (continued)

believed that the goods are plumbing accessories such as, for example, faucets. (Non-plumbing metallic hardware such as, for example, toothbrush holders, would probably be classified in Class 6 of the International System.) As such, the goods of the cited registration are of a distinctly "permanent nature," and are not frequently replaced. This is an essential difference between Applicant's goods and those of the cited registration.

By no stretch of the imagination can Applicant's goods and those of the cited registration be regarded as having the same descriptive properties. It is admitted, of course, that the standard under Section 2(d) of the Trademark Act of 1946 is "likelihood of confusion," not "same descriptive properties." Nevertheless, the descriptive properties of the respective goods should be taken into consideration in an instance where, such as in the instant situation one would not expect manufacturers of hardware to be selling room deodorant products of a "temporary" nature. Under the circumstances, it is submitted that persons familiar with the goods of the cited registration would not expect Applicant's room deodorant to emanate from the same source. It is therefore urged that the Examiner withdraw his refusal to register Applicant's trademark.

In the Office Action, the Examiner requested that Applicant's mark be retyped so as to appear without the hyphen. This, however, has already been accomplished by means of a Preliminary Amendment filed on January 13, 1998.

In view of the foregoing remarks, it is believed that Applicant's trademark is in condition for prompt publication. Favorable action is therefore requested.

Respectfully Submitted,

_____

Applicant

[name, address and telephone no.]

Date _____

Sample Response Regarding Consent Agreement

UNITED STATES PATENT AND TRADEMARK OFFICE
TRADEMARK EXAMINING OPERATION

In re Application of:)
[applicant's name]   ) Trademark Law Office:
Serial No.: [number]   ) [number]
Filed: [date]   ) Attorney: [name]
Mark: ASEPTICALLY CLEAN   )

BOX RESPONSES
NO FEE

Assistant Commissioner for Trademarks
2900 Crystal Drive
Arlington, VA 22202-3513

RESPONSE UNDER 37 C.F.R. § 2.62

Sir:

This is in response to Office Action No. 1, dated May 10, 1999.

The Examiner has refused registration of Applicant's trademark on the ground that it is confusingly similar to the trademark ASEPTIC, Registration No. 1,083,455, for a monthly newsletter about patient care. Reconsideration of this refusal to register is respectfully requested. It is requested that the Examiner consider the attached consent agreement between Applicant and MEDTECH, INC., registrant for ASEPTIC, consenting to registration by Applicant of its trademark ASEPTICALLY CLEAN.

For the reasons given in the Letter of Consent, Applicant concurs with the conclusion of MEDTECH, INC. that there is no likelihood of confusion between the trademark ASEPTIC shown in cited registration No. 1,083,455 and the trademark ASEPTICALLY CLEAN which is the subject of the above-indicated application.

In view of the foregoing remarks, it is believed that Applicant's trademark is in condition for prompt publication. Favorable action is therefore requested.

Respectfully Submitted,

_____
Applicant (or Attorney for Applicant)
[Applicant's or Attorney's name, address and telephone number.]

Date:_____

Sample Consent Agreement

CONSENT AGREEMENT

This Agreement, made this 28th day of June, 1999, is by and between MEDTECH, INC., a Delaware Corporation, having its principal place of business at 1234 Main Street, Wilmington, DE 19810, and HEALTH PUBLISHERS, INC., a California Corporation, having its principal place of business at 45 Claremont Avenue, San Diego, CA 92117.

Whereas, MEDTECH, INC. is the owner of U.S. Registration No. 1,083,455 of the mark ASEPTIC for a monthly newsletter about patient care;

Whereas, HEALTH PUBLISHERS, INC., desires to use the mark ASEPTICALLY CLEAN for a magazine about disinfection techniques and standards in health care facilities; and

Whereas, HEALTH PUBLISHERS, INC., recognizes the validity of MEDTECH, INC.'s registered mark and wishes to avoid any conflict with it,

Now, therefore, in consideration of the sum of One Dollar and other good and valuable considerations, it is agreed as follows:

1. MEDTECH, INC., believes, there is no likelihood of confusion or conflict between the two trademarks described above;

2. MEDTECH, INC., consents to the use and registration by HEALTH PUBLISHERS, INC., of the trademark ASEPTICALLY CLEAN for a serial magazine dealing with subjects related to technical data and dialog concerning disinfection in health care facilities, as specified in HEALTH PUBLISHER's application Serial No. 234,455; and

3. MEDTECH, INC., will take no action to interfere with the use and registration of ASEPTICALLY CLEAN by HEALTH PUBLISHERS, INC.

In witness whereof, the parties hereto set their hands and seals hereto on the date first written above.

MEDTECH, INC.

By: _____
    Name & Title

[SEAL]

Attest:

_____
Secretary

HEALTH PUBLISHERS, INC.

By: _____
    Name & Title

[SEAL]

Attest:

_____
Secretary

c. Abandon Your Application

Even if you believe the Examiner's rejection of your application is wrong, unless you have plenty of money and care a great deal about registering that particular mark, you will probably want to pick another mark. The chances are you will spend countless hours preparing a response yourself or spend thousands of dollars in legal fees for a lawyer to prepare a response, and still not get your mark registered.

You can either write the Examiner a letter informing him or her that you do not wish to pursue the matter and are abandoning the application, or you can do nothing and doing nothing (i.e. not responding to the Examiner's action letter) will have the same effect as abandoning the application. We do not recommend using the mark after you abandon your application. Doing so may open you up for a lawsuit based on trademark infringement. To learn more about trademark conflicts, consult *Trademark: Legal Care for Your Business & Product Name*, by Stephen Elias and Kate McGrath (Nolo).

C. If You Receive a Final Rejection

A "final" rejection will not arrive until after you have received, and, we hope, responded to, at least one action letter. A final rejection typically looks like the following:

Sample Final Rejection

U.S. Department of Commerce
Patent and Trademark Office
Serial No. 74/468800

This letter responds to the applicant's communication filed on October 5, 1998.

Section 2(d)—Final Refusal to Register

Registration was refused under Trademark Act Section 2(d), 15 U.S.C. Section 1052(d), because the mark for which registration is sought so resembles the mark shown in U.S. Registration No. 1,930,589 as to be likely, when used on the identified goods, to cause confusion, or to cause mistake, or to deceive.

The examining attorney has considered the applicant's arguments carefully but has found them unpersuasive. For the reasons below, the refusal under Section 2(d) is maintained and made FINAL.

[The Action Letter goes on to explain the reasons for the final refusal.]

Your options once the final rejection is received are several. You can:
- write again and ask the Examiner to reconsider your application and previous responses.
- talk with the Examiner by phone or in person to get a better idea of what, if anything, can be done to fix the application.

- file an appeal (if the grounds for rejection are appealable) asking the Trademark Trial and Appeal Board to consider your application. Any substantive dispute is appealable. This includes any judgment made by the Examiner (such as when he feels your mark is confusingly similar to another mark, or believes you should disclaim one or more words).

- file a petition asking the Commissioner of Patents and Trademarks to consider your application (if the grounds for rejection are not appealable).

- request suspension of the application (if allowed this could give you more time to prepare a response or request for reconsideration).

- file an amendment asking for registration on the Supplemental rather than the Principal Register (described above in Section A2).

- abandon (give up) the application (described above in Sections A3 and B2c).

By the time your application has received a final rejection, the Examiner's boss has reviewed the whole file and approved the rejection. It is therefore very unlikely that you will obtain registration after receiving a final rejection. A discussion of trademark appeals and appealable grounds is beyond the scope of this book. (See Chapter 14, Help Beyond the Book.) ■

PART 3

Publication and Follow-Up

CHAPTER 11

Following Up Your Intent-to-Use Application

In Chapter 5 we explained that filing an intent-to-use application for registration requires some follow-up activity if you want the mark actually to be registered. In brief, you must:

- put the mark into actual use, and
- file a form known as an "Allegation of Use for Intent-to-Use Application, With Declaration."

This chapter explains what the PTO's requirements are for putting your mark into use, and how to file the Allegation of Use form.

A. Putting Your Mark Into Use

The first thing to understand about putting your mark into use is that to the PTO, not all uses qualify as "use." For a trademark to be officially in use, the PTO requires that it be "in use that Congress may regulate." (This is the same rule that applies to use applicants.) Technically speaking, this definition has two parts: the trademark must be "in use," plus the use must be "in commerce that Congress may regulate." If either of these elements is not true for your trademark, then it is not technically considered to be in use, and you may not proceed with filing an Allegation of Use form to finalize your registration.

1. "In Use"

As a general rule, "in use" means that the mark is being utilized in the marketplace to identify your goods or services. This doesn't mean that you need to have actually sold the product or service, just that the product or service associated with the mark is available for sale in the marketplace. The criteria used to determine whether a trademark is in use are different depending on whether the trademark is being used for a product or a service.

For products, your mark is in use if the mark appears on the goods (or on labels or tags attached to them) and the goods have either been shipped to a store for resale or use as a sample,

or are available for sale by mail or over the Internet. However, a token sale made only for the purpose of getting your mark "in use" doesn't count. The use has to be a true attempt (sometimes called a "bona fide" attempt) to identify and distinguish your goods or services in the marketplace.

EXAMPLE 1: The day Ben sent his first sample of pants to a department store potentially interested in selling them was the date of first use of his mark, No-Knees.

EXAMPLE 2: When Emily's earrings were shipped in a box carrying the label All Ears, for the legitimate purpose of resale by a local street vendor, that was the date of first use of her mark.

EXAMPLE 3: Peter developed a system for taking orders and processing credit card payments over the web, and launched the sale of his Bearware software online. He used the mark Bearware prominently on his website The first day the software was available for purchase online was the date of first use anywhere (and first use in interstate commerce, by the way—see Section 2, below).

For services, your mark is in use if the services are actually being marketed under the mark and you can legitimately deliver them to end users.

EXAMPLE 1: Toby purchased a 900-line for providing sports trivia under the name Sports R Us. The date he began his advertising was the date he first used the mark, as long as the line was up and running (it doesn't matter how long he waits for the first call).

EXAMPLE 2: Helen decided to call her housecleaning service Mrs. Clean. When she first advertised her services under that name on a bulletin board at a local market, that was the date of first use of her mark.

EXAMPLE 3: Alice started her own Internet service provider business under the mark CosmoNet. She set up her system and prepared all of the equipment she would need to offer her services. The day she first started advertising her services under her mark and with all of her systems in place and ready to go was the date of first use.

2. "Use That Congress May Regulate"

For the PTO's purposes, being in use isn't enough—federal registration is allowed only for marks that are being used in commerce that Congress may regulate. "Commerce that Congress may regulate" means a business or trade which the federal government, through the U.S. Congress, may control. Technically, Congress may control interstate commerce, territorial commerce and international commerce. In practice, this means that to qualify for federal trademark registration, your business must do one or more of the following:

1. Ship a product (upon which the mark is used):
   - across state lines
   - between a state and a territory or a territory and another territory, or
   - between a state or territory and another country.
2. Use the mark to advertise in other states services offered by your business in your state.
3. Use the mark in connection with or to advertise a service business that you conduct:
   - across state lines
   - in more than one state, or
   - across international or territorial borders.
4. Use the mark in connection with or to advertise a business that you operate catering to interstate or international travelers.

Examples of the activities listed above are provided in the chart below.

Once you have put your mark into use according to this technical definition, you can proceed to the next step of the registration process for intent-to-use applicants, filing the Allegation of Use form.

B. The Allegation of Use Form

Why do you have to file this form? The PTO wants you to follow up your intent-to-use application with this form because it wants you to show that you have actually started using your mark before it grants you a registration. One of the tricky things about the Allegation of Use form is that it's called different names depending on when you put your mark into use. Although there's only one form for you to worry about, it's helpful to understand why the PTO uses different terms for it. In the past, the PTO used two different forms called an Amendment to Allege Use, and a Statement of Use, which were used by intent-to-use applicants to notify the PTO that they had put their marks into use. If the applicant put the mark into use before the PTO had approved the mark for publication, they were supposed to use the Amendment to Allege Use form. If, on the other hand, the applicant put their mark into use after the PTO had approved it for publication, the applicant was required to use the Statement of Use form.

These days, the PTO has only one form. The title of this form is "Allegation of Use for Intent-to-Use Application, With Declaration (Amendment to Allege Use/Statement Use)." Even though there's only one form now, the PTO continues to call it different names depending on when you put your mark into use. The rules can be confusing, so here's all you need to know: Think about the date you put your mark into use (as explained in Section A, above). Was that date *before* the date of your notice of publication in the *Gazette*, or *after* the date of your notice of publication? If the date of first use was *before* the date of the notice, your follow-up filing will be called an Amendment to Allege Use. If the date of first use was *after* the notice, your filing will be

Types of Commerce That Congress May Regulate	
Commerce That Congress May Regulate	**Example**
Shipping across state lines	Shipping products from California to Virginia
Shipping between a state and a territory or a territory and another territory	Shipping products from New York to Puerto Rico or Puerto Rico to the Virgin Islands
Shipping between a state or territory and another country	Shipping products from California to Hong Kong or Puerto Rico to Cuba
Using the mark to advertise in other states services offered by your business in your state	Advertising in a national magazine a business that performs services in Illinois
Using the mark in connection with or to advertise a service business that you conduct across state lines	Advertising a business that performs services nationwide
Using the mark in connection with or to advertise a service business that you conduct in more than one state	Advertising a business that maintains several locations nationwide
Using the mark in connection with or to advertise a service business that you conduct across international or territorial borders	Advertising a business that performs services internationally
Using the mark in connection with or to advertise a business that you operate catering to interstate or international travelers	Advertising a business aimed at tourists from outside the U.S.

called a Statement of Use. But the bottom line is not to be confused, because it's the very same form. We'll generally refer to it as the Allegation of Use form.

The rest of this section will explain how and when to file the Allegation of Use form based on when you put your mark into use.

1. Marks Put Into Use Before Being Approved for Publication

You may recall from Chapter 5 that part of the process for all trademark applications is being approved for publication in the *Official Gazette*. If you have started using your mark but the PTO has not yet approved it for publication in the *Official Gazette*, you can file the Allegation of Use form anytime after you've put the mark into use. In this case, since the PTO hasn't yet approved the mark for publication, you will not receive a certificate of registration until after your mark has made it through the 30-day publication period without opposition. See Chapter 12 for more information about publication and opposition.

2. Marks Put Into Use After Being Approved for Publication

If you started using your mark after the date on which the PTO approved it for publication, you may file the Allegation of Use form—but, you may only do so *after* the PTO has sent you a Notice of Allowance. (Recall from Chapter 5 that a Notice of Allowance is the PTO's way of granting you the exclusive right to use the mark on the condition that you put it into use within a certain time period.) In other words, there is a blackout period between the time the PTO approves the mark for publication in the *Official Gazette* and the time that the PTO issues a Notice of Allowance, during which you may not file the Allegation of Use form. Typically this blackout period runs from three to six months. If you do file the Allegation of Use form during this period, the PTO will refuse to accept it.

Once you do receive the Notice of Allowance, you must file the Allegation of Use form within six months of the date of the Notice of Allowance. If you cannot meet this deadline, you can file for a six-month extension (see Section D, below). Since

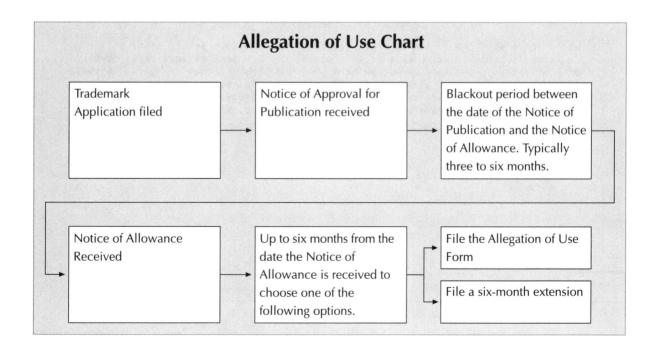

Sample Notice of Allowance

U.S. Patent and Trademark Office (PTO)
NOTICE OF ALLOWANCE

(NOTE: If any data on this notice is incorrect, please submit a written request for correction of the NOA to: Assistant Commissioner for Trademarks, Box ITU, 2900 Crystal Drive, Arlington, VA 22202-3513. Please include the serial number of your application on ALL correspondence with the PTO. 15 U.S.C. 1063(b)(2))

ISSUE DATE OF NOA:

TRADEMARK COUNSELORS OF AMERICA PC
915 BROADWAY 19TH FL
NEW YORK NY 10010

**ATTORNEY
REFERENCE NUMBER**

** IMPORTANT INFORMATION: 6 MONTH DEADLINE **

To avoid **ABANDONMENT** of this application, either a "Statement of Use" (a.k.a. " Allegation of Use") or a "Request for Extension of Time to File a Statement of Use" (a.k.a. "Extension Request") and the appropriate fee(s) must be received in the PTO within six months of the issue date of this Notice of Allowance (NDA). Failure to do so will result in the **ABANDONMENT** of this application.

Please note that both the "Statement of Use" and "Extension Request" have many legal requirements, including fees. These requirements are explained in the PTO booklet "Basic Facts About Trademarks", which can be obtained upon request at (703) 308-9000. In addition, there are printed forms contained in this booklet (for "Statement of Use" and "Extension Requests") for your use.

The following information should be reviewed for accuracy:

SERIAL NUMBER:
MARK:
OWNER:

GOODS/SERVICES BY INTERNATIONAL CLASS

042—retail store services featuring — sculptures of non—precious metal; posters; educational books; travel books; picture postcards; stationery; tote bags; novelty works of art in the nature of overpainted non—functional football helmets, footballs and soccerballs; ceramic plates, mugs and vases; sunglasses; watches; clothing, namely, T—shirts, baseball caps and ties sold boutique—style with etchings, overpaintings and graphic art; and ornamental novelty pins

ALL OF THE GOODS/SERVICES IN EACH CLASS ARE LISTED

TMFRF6(REV 07/97)

ADDITIONAL INFORMATION MAY BE PRESENT IN THE PTO RECORDS

the Allegation of Use may only be filed after your mark has already gone through the publication process unopposed (see Chapter 12), you should receive your certificate of registration once your Allegation of Use is accepted by the PTO.

The reason for the blackout period is simply a matter of administrative efficiency. The fact that you are temporarily prevented from filing the Allegation of Use form should not cause you any harm, provided that you do file the Allegation of Use form within six months after receiving the Notice of Allowance (or obtain a six-month extension).

C. Completing the Allegation of Use Form

This form requests some information already set out in your original ITU application, as well as some new information. Here, we provide instructions for filling in the form in the order in which the blanks appear. You'll find a copy of the form in the Appendix.

⚠ If you are filing the Allegation of Use after the PTO has issued a Notice of Allowance on your intent-to-use application, examine the Notice of Allowance carefully. If there are any mistakes, such as wrong spelling of the mark or wrong date of first use, notify the PTO immediately by phone or letter and request a corrected Notice of Allowance.

1. Identify the Mark

Fill in the same description of the mark as shown on your ITU application. Use identical wording.

2. Serial Number

If you included a postage-paid postcard with your application as we suggest in Chapter 5, you should have received the postcard back from the PTO with your application's serial number upon it, a week or two after you filed your application. Otherwise, the serial number should be on the filing receipt you received several weeks after sending out your application.

3. Applicant Name

Put in this blank the exact name that appears in the applicant box on your ITU application.

4. Description of Goods or Services

Check box (a) if your mark is being used in connection with all of the exact same product(s) and/or service(s) shown in your original application or on the Notice of Allowance received from the PTO.

Check box (b) if you are using the mark on some, but not all, of the goods or services identified in your original intent-to-use application and then describe the goods or services that don't contain the mark.

> EXAMPLE: When Etta prepared her ITU application she expected to market computer consulting services and computer programs under the mark Quick-Bytes and listed those goods and services in her application. However, it took her a year, and more money than she expected, to get her consulting business off the ground. She decides to build the consulting business and delay putting any effort into writing and marketing software. She uses this form to delete the computer programs from her application.

If you are unsure of how to complete this blank, call the PTO and ask an Examiner for assistance. As usual, keep records of the Examiner's name and what is said. At worst, the Examiner who is reviewing this document will contact you and ask you to fix the goods/services statement at that time.

Allegation of Use (Page 1)

<table>
<tr><td>ALLEGATION OF USE FOR INTENT-TO-USE APPLICATION, WITH DECLARATION
(Amendment To Allege Use/Statement Use)</td><td>MARK (Identify the mark)

SERIAL NO.</td></tr>
</table>

TO THE ASSISTANT COMMISSIONER FOR TRADEMARKS:

APPLICANT NAME:

Applicant requests registration of the above-identified trademark/service mark in the United States Patent and Trademark Office on the Principal Register established by the Act of July 5, 1946 (15 U.S.C. §1051 *et seq.*, as amended). Three specimens per class showing the mark as used in commerce and the prescribed fees are submitted with this statement.

Applicant is using the mark in commerce on or in connection with the following goods/services (CHECK ONLY ONE):

☐ (a) those in the application or Notice of Allowance; **OR**

☐ (b) those in the application or Notice of Allowance **except** (if goods/services are to be deleted, list the goods/services to be **deleted**): _____
_____
_____

Date of first use in commerce which the U.S. Congress may regulate:_____
Specify type of commerce: _____
                    (for example, interstate and/or commerce between the U.S. and a foreign country)
Date of first use anywhere: _____

Specify manner or mode of use of mark on or in connection with the goods/services: (for example, trademark is applied to labels, service mark is used in advertisements):_____
_____
_____

The undersigned, being hereby warned that willful false statements and the like so made are punishable by fine or imprisonment, or both, under 18 U.S.C. §1001, and that such willful false statements may jeopardize the validity of the application or any resulting registration, declares that he/she is properly authorized to execute this Amendment to Allege Use or Statement of Use on behalf of the applicant; he/she believes the applicant to be the owner of the trademark/service mark sought to be registered; the trademark /service mark is now in use in commerce; and all statements made of his/her own knowledge are true and all statements made on information and belief are believed to be true.

_____   _____
Date   Signature

_____   _____
Telephone Number   Type or Print Name and Position

☐   **Check here if Request to Divide is being submitted with this statement** (if Applicant wishes to proceed to publication or registration with certain goods/services on or in connection with which it has used the mark in commerce and retain an active application for any remaining goods/services, a divisional application and fee are required. 37 C.F.R. §2.87)

PLEASE SEE REVERSE FOR MORE INFORMATION

PTO Form 1553   U.S. Department of Commerce/Patent and Trademark Office
OMB No. 0651-000 (Exp. 06/30/98) There is no requirement to respond to this collection of information unless a currently valid OMB Number is displayed.

Be patient with the PTO. For a number of reasons having to do with funding and a radical turnover in top management staff, the trademark division of the PTO is in some disarray. This means that you may experience some delays and frustrations when you contact the PTO. See Chapter 8, where we offer some suggestions for how to deal with the PTO's trademark Examiners and attorneys. Now more than ever, you should take these suggestions to heart.

5. Dates of First Use of Mark

The next two blanks ask for two dates:
- when your mark was first actually used anywhere.
- when your mark was first used in commerce that Congress may regulate.

Once you have figured out the date of first use anywhere and the date of first use in commerce that Congress may regulate, enter the dates in the appropriate boxes. (For more information on the precise definitions of "use," see Section A, above.)

6. Type of Commerce

After you list the two dates of first use, indicate the type of commerce in which the mark was used for the date of first use in commerce. This will be one of the following:
- interstate commerce (between one state and one or more other states)
- territorial commerce (between a state and a territory, such as Florida and Puerto Rico, or between two territories, such as Puerto Rico and the Virgin Islands), or
- international commerce (between a state and a foreign country or between a territory and a foreign country).

For territorial or international commerce, name the state, territory or foreign country involved in the transactions.

If your first use (as discussed above) was in commerce which the U.S. Congress may regulate, both dates (the first two lines in block 7) will be the same. Even so, you still must fill in both blanks.

If you are claiming use for more than one good or service, you need only put the dates of first use and first use in commerce for any one of them (identify the good or service that the date of use pertains to). Remember, however, that you must be actually using (in commerce that Congress may regulate) all of the goods or services that you listed earlier, unless you described them after checking box b.

7. Specify Manner or Mode of Use of Mark

In Chapter 5, Sections A6 and A7, we discuss the different ways a mark may be used with goods and services and how to specify the manner or mode of use of the mark. In this blank you must again describe at least one such way your mark is being used. You need not describe all the ways it is used. It is best to stay with the description you used in your application. If there was some amendment related to the manner or mode of use after you filed your application, use the amended version.

Examples of How Marks Are Used to Identify Goods

- If your mark is employed on books, jeans, hats or other goods on which a mark might appear, your manner or mode of use may be: "The mark is placed directly on the goods and used in other ways customary to the trade."
- If your mark is used in connection with window glass, jewelry or other goods on which it is impractical to place the mark directly, try this or similar wording: "The mark is used on labels attached to the goods and on packaging."

Examples of How Marks Are Used to Identify Services

- If your mark is used in connection with accounting services, you may state something like: "The mark is used in letters, advertisements and signs used to promote the services."
- If your mark is used in connection with Internet services (such as providing Internet connections to the general public), you may state something like: "The mark is used on a website and in advertisements used to promote the services."

Consistency Reminder

In Chapter 1, Section E, we explained that you have to submit specimens of how your mark is being used as part of the trademark registration process. However, when you filed your ITU application, you didn't submit these since your mark was not yet in actual use. Now, however, you must submit specimens with your Allegation of Use form. We discuss this in Section 10 below.

When you describe the manner and mode of your use of the mark, you'll have to be careful that your description is consistent with the specimens you plan to submit. If it isn't, the PTO will ask for clarification. For instance, suppose you describe the manner or mode of use as follows: "The mark is used in newsletters used to promote the services." If the specimens you submit are copies of phone book advertisements rather than newsletters, the PTO will logically conclude that your specimens are inconsistent with the manner or mode of use you are claiming, and send your application back for clarification. For this reason, it is often best first to decide which specimens you plan to use (Chapter 3) and then fill in this box.

8. Declaration

This declaration is mostly to warn you that you had better be telling the truth. The PTO rarely, if ever, takes the time to figure out if people are lying or to prosecute them for making false statements. However, if you ever get into a dispute, any lies you make in your application may come to light and cause you to lose. The bottom line is that you should first read the declaration very carefully. If any part of it is not true, don't sign it and file it until all of the information is true. If you can confirm all of the information in the declaration, then date the form, sign it and provide your telephone number and printed name and position.

9. Request to Divide

Check the Request to Divide box if you wish to "divide" your ITU application into two applications. This would apply only if all of the following statements are true:

- Your original application designated your mark to apply to more than one good or service.
- You have used the mark in connection with one or some, but not all of those goods or services. And,
- You still intend to use the mark in connection with one or more additional good(s) or service(s).

If all these statements are true, you should consider dividing your application so that one application now claims usage for one or more of the goods or services while the other application remains on an intent to use (ITU) status in respect to the other goods or services.

EXAMPLE: Suppose Etta's ITU application claimed she was going to use Quick-Bytes in connection with computer consulting services and computer programs. If she began offering services two months after her application was filed, she may want to amend her application to claim use of Quick-Bytes in connection with the services. When she divides the application she will then have two applications: one, in which use has been alleged, for use of the mark for her services; and one in which she plans to use the mark for computer programs in the future.

The benefit of dividing an application, rather than waiting until the mark is in use for all goods or services originally contemplated, is that the mark in use can be placed on the federal register more quickly. The sooner your proposed mark is on the federal register, the sooner the world will have notice of it and the less likely someone else will try to use it.

The downside of dividing the application is that additional paperwork and fees are involved (a divisional application with a $100 fee and another Allegation of Use when the divided mark is put into actual use). If money is scarce, or you soon expect to have the mark in use with all the goods or services you claimed, it's probably best to not divide your application. Just wait until you are using the mark in all the ways you intend and then file one Allegation of Use.

EXAMPLE: Now suppose that Etta's ITU application claimed she was going to use Quick-Bytes in connection with computer consulting services and computer programs and she begins offering services two months after her application was filed. Instead of amending her application to claim use of Quick-Bytes in connection with the services, like the example above, Etta decides to wait until she begins to offer her programs before

she files her Allegation of Use form since she is short on cash and she plans to begin offering her programs soon. This strategy will save Etta $100, which would have been the fee for dividing the application.

We provide a form to be used for dividing an application in Appendix D. You may submit the completed form with your Allegation of Use. Remember that even if you are filing a Request to Divide, you must respond to any office actions on time or risk giving up your application.

10. Other Materials to Submit

In addition to the completed Allegation of Use form, you must submit three specimens per class showing the mark as it is being used in commerce and the correct fee.

- Specimens: You must submit three specimens of your use. Read Chapter 3 for advice on how to choose acceptable specimens. Remember to make your specimens consistent with your description of the goods or services, the manner and mode of the mark's use and the description of your mark.
- Fees: A filing fee ($100 for each class) must be submitted with your Allegation of Use form and specimens. See Chapter 2, Section C, for more on the trademark classification system.

11. Filing Your Allegation of Use

See Chapter 7 regarding mailing information to the PTO. Your Allegation of Use form, specimens and fees should be mailed to this address:
Assistant Commissioner for Trademarks
BOX AAU/SOU
2900 Crystal Drive
Arlington, Virginia 22202-3513

D. Getting a Six-Month Extension to File Your Allegation of Use Form

Assume that you've filed an ITU application and have received a Notice of Allowance, but still haven't put the mark in use yet. Now what? As long as you still intend to use your mark on at least one of the goods or services mentioned in your application, and are willing to pay $100 per class as a filing fee, you can request an extension and get an extra six months before you have to file your Allegation of Use form. As stated earlier, this request must be filed before your six months run out.

You can request up to five six-month extensions, as long as each is filed before the last extension runs out. However, after the first extension request (for which no reason need be given), you must convince the PTO that there is a good reason why your mark hasn't been used yet, as explained below. No extension of time will be granted beyond 36 months after the Notice of Allowance was issued.

You may be tempted to forego these extensions, abandon the application and file a new application when the mark is finally put into use in commerce. While this may save you money, you will lose your original filing date that you could otherwise claim if you are ultimately able to register your mark under your original application. Remember that your original filing date may turn out to be important because:

1. Assuming you complete the registration process under your original application, your original filing date will serve as your date of first use. That date can be very important in resolving disputes over trademark ownership.

2. Your application will have priority over other applications for a competing mark that are filed after your original filing date. This means that the subsequent applications will

have to wait until 1) your mark is registered (in which case the competing application will be denied) or 2) your registration is denied (and the competing application can move forward).

It is therefore best, if you can, to keep your earlier filing date, rather than settling for a later date—the filing date of your new application for registration if you abandon your original application.

1. Completing a Request for Extension of Time

The Request for Extension of Time form (PTO Form C-60) is in the Appendix. Here we will discuss each blank in that form.

a. Mark

The mark in this block should be exactly the same as the one in your original application.

b. Serial Number

This is the number the PTO stamped on your self-addressed postcard (if you included one with your original application). It also appears on your filing receipt and Notice of Allowance.

c. Applicant Name

Fill in this block exactly as you did for your original application.

d. Notice of Allowance Mailing Date

Get this date from your Notice of Allowance.

Request for Extension

REQUEST FOR EXTENSION OF TIME TO FILE A STATEMENT OF USE, WITH DECLARATION	MARK (Identify the mark)
	SERIAL NO.

TO THE ASSISTANT SECRETARY AND COMMISSIONER OF PATENTS AND TRADEMARKS:

APPLICANT NAME:

NOTICE OF ALLOWANCE MAILING DATE:

Applicant requests a six-month extension of time to file the Statement of Use under 37 CFR 2.89 in this application.

Applicant has a continued bona fide intention to use the mark in commerce on or in connection with the following goods/services: (Check One below)

☐ Those goods/services identified in the Notice of Allowance.

☐ Those goods/services identified in the Notice of Allowance except: (Identify goods/services to be **deleted** from application)

_____

_____

_____

This is the_____ request for an Extension of Time following mailing of the Notice of Allowance.
        (Specify: First - Fifth)

If this is not the first request for an Extension of Time, check one box below. If the first box is checked explain the circumstance(s) of the non-use in the space provided:

☐   Applicant has not used the mark in commerce yet on all goods/services specified in the Notice of Allowance; however, applicant has made the following ongoing efforts to use the mark in commerce on or in connection with each of the goods/services specified above:

_____

_____

If additional space is needed, please attach a separate sheet to this form

☐   Applicant believes that it has made valid use of the mark in commerce, as evidenced by the Statement of Use submitted with this request; however, if the Statement of Use does not meet minimum requirements under 37 CFR 2.88(e), applicant will need additional time in which to file a new statement.

The undersigned being hereby warned that willful false statements and the like so made are punishable by fine or imprisonment, or both, under 18 U.S.C. 1001, and that such willful false statements may jeopardize the validity of the application or any resulting registration, declares that he/she is properly authorized to execute this Request for an Extension of Time to File a Statement of Use on behalf of the applicant; and that all statements made of his/her own knowledge are true and all statements made on information and belief are believed to be true.

_____   _____
Date   Signature

_____   _____
Telephone Number   Type or Print Name and Position

☐   **Check here if Request to Divide is being submitted with this statement** (if Applicant wishes to proceed to publication or registration with certain goods/services on or in connection with which it has used the mark in commerce and retain an active application for any remaining goods/services, a divisional application and fee are required. 37 C.F.R. §2.87)

PTO Form 1581 (REV. 6-96)   U.S. Department of Commerce/Patent and Trademark Office
OMB No. 0651-0009
Exp. (06/30/98)   There is no requirement to respond to this collection of information unless a currently valid OMB Number is displayed.

e. Request to Divide

This only applies to original applications that listed more than one good or service. If your mark has been used with one but not all of the products and/or services listed in your application, see Section C9, above, about dividing your application.

f. Continued Bona Fide Intention to Use

If you still intend to use the mark in connection with the same goods and/or services described in your application, check the first box.

If you decide to limit use of your mark to, for example, only two of three products, check the second box. Then list any products or services you want deleted from your application.

In the blank provided, indicate whether it is your first, second, third, fourth or fifth request for an extension. (As mentioned, no extension of time will be granted beyond 36 months after the Notice of Allowance was issued.)

If this is your first request, leave the next two boxes blank. If it is your 2nd, 3rd, 4th or 5th request, you must check one of the next two boxes. Check the first one if you still have not used the mark in commerce that Congress may regulate. Then explain what you have done to get ready to use the mark in such commerce. Your explanation need not be lengthy; a sentence or two will do. Some possible explanations include the following:

- the need for more research or development of your product or service
- the need for more research about your market, including where and how to sell the product or service

- a delay in efforts to arrange for product manufacturing
- the need for more time to develop advertising or promotional activities
- attempts to get government approval are still in progress
- attempts to set up marketing networks are still in progress
- a prolonged illness
- destruction of vital records of your factory due to fire or other disaster, or
- any other reasonable explanation for why you haven't done any of the above.

The last box applies if you have, in fact, used the mark in commerce that Congress may regulate, and are planning to submit your Allegation of Use during the upcoming six-month period.

The declaration is the same as the one you signed in your application.

2. Filing Your Extension

You should send your extension request to this address:

Assistant Commissioner for Trademarks
BOX ITU
2900 Crystal Drive
Arlington, Virginia 22202-3513.

Pay special attention to the deadline for filing this document. Your request for an extension of time will be considered filed on the day it arrives at the PTO. You will not be able to use Express Mail through the U.S. Postal Service to move the filing date up to the day it was left with the Express Mail service (as was the case when you filed your application for registration). ■

Publication, Opposition and Registration

Congratulations! If you have received notice that your application has been approved for publication, rest assured that you have successfully passed through the most difficult and risky part of the registration process. This chapter discusses:

- the publication process
- oppositions (when someone opposes your registration during the publication period of 30 days), and
- certificates of registration.

A. Publication

If all goes well, the Examiner will authorize the publication of your mark in the PTO's *Official Gazette*, which means the PTO has made a preliminary decision that your mark qualifies for registration. The *Official Gazette* is a weekly PTO publication available by subscription (which is very expensive) or at your local Patent and Trademark Depository Library (a list is in the Appendix). Among other things, the purpose of the *Official Gazette* in trademark terms is to display all of the marks being considered for registration by the PTO at the time that particular volume of the *Gazette* is published. This puts the public on notice that these marks may be registered if no one comes forward to oppose the registration. Opposers have 30 days to file their oppositions with the PTO. If someone requests more time in which to decide whether to oppose the mark, the PTO will usually give them at least another 30 days.

B. Oppositions

An opposition is a formal proceeding held by a body of the PTO in which a decision is made whether the registration of a particular trademark should be blocked. Oppositions are filed against only 3% of marks published in the *Official*

Gazette. If an opposition is filed against your pending mark, carefully weigh the benefits of sticking with your mark against the high cost of fighting the opposition (usually tens of thousands of dollars).

A good idea of what is in store for you should you end up in an opposition can be gleaned from the table of contents for the *Trademark Trial and Appeal Board's Manual of Procedures*:

Table of Contents

Chapter 0100 General Information
Chapter 0200 Extensions of Time to Oppose
Chapter 0300 Pleadings
Chapter 0400 Discovery
Chapter 0500 Stipulations and Motions
Chapter 0600 Withdrawal; Settlement
Chapter 0700 Introduction of Evidence
Chapter 0800 Briefs on Case, Oral Hearing, Final Decision
Chapter 0900 Review Decision of Board
Chapter 1000 Interferences
Chapter 1100 Concurrent Use Proceedings
Chapter 1200 Ex Parte Appeals

Opposers are typically large companies that pay a lawyer or trademark monitoring service to review the *Official Gazette* and bring to their attention any marks that potentially conflict with marks used by the company. Of course, any marks that appear in the *Official Gazette* have already been approved by the Examiner as likely not to conflict with other registered marks. Therefore, opposition is often based on either an unregistered mark (on the basis of the mark's prior use) or on a registered mark that the Examiner did not initially believe was conflicting.

Your mark is subject to challenge even if no opposition is filed. The fact that the owner of an existing mark has the right to oppose your registration doesn't mean that it must do so. Even if your mark is unopposed after publication, the existing mark owner still can file an infringement action in court. If that occurs, the fact that the plaintiff did not oppose the registration of your mark will not strengthen your legal position in the lawsuit. However, if your mark remains on the federal register for five years without challenge and you file the proper form with the PTO, your mark can be made "incontestable," which greatly strengthens it against a later challenge based on infringement. (See Chapter 13.)

Since most marks are unopposed, and since oppositions can become quite complicated, we do not deal with them in any detail in this book. If you need more information on oppositions, see Chapter 14, Help Beyond This Book.

C. Receiving Your Certificate of Registration

After your mark is published and the time for opposition has expired, your mark will be registered and the certificate sent to you if:

- you filed a use application or
- you filed an intent-to-use application and you also filed an Allegation of Use form before you received a Notice of Publication (see Chapter 11 on filing the Allegation of Use).

If you have filed an intent-to-use application, but plan to file an Allegation of Use form after you receive your Notice of Allowance, your certificate will be sent to you once the PTO has received and approved your Allegation of Use.

Depending on the backlog of paperwork at the PTO, it can take as long as three months from the expiration of the opposition date for you to receive the certificate. If you want to know the status of your application before the certificate is received, call the PTO Status Line at 703-305-8747 or visit the PTO's website at http://www.upto.gov/ and look for the pilot project called TARR.

Certificate of Registration on Principal Register

The Certificate of Registration reproduces the mark and sets out the date of first use in commerce. In addition, it indicates the particular product or service on which the mark is used, the number and date of registration, the term of registration, the date on which the application for registration was received at the Patent and Trademark Office and any conditions and limitations that may be imposed on the registration, such as disclaimed words.

Put your certificate in a safe place after making a few copies for your records. By now, you should have a file for all of your trademark papers. This would be a natural place to keep your certificate.

100% Colombian Coffee

Certificate of Registration

The United States of America

CERTIFICATE OF REGISTRATION
PRINCIPAL REGISTER

The Mark shown in this certificate has been registered in the United States Patent and Trademark Office to the named registrant.

The records of the United States Patent and Trademark Office show that an application for registration of the Mark shown in this Certificate was filed in the Office, that the application was examined and determined to be in compliance with the requirements of the law and with the regulations prescribed by the Commissioner of Patents and Trademarks, and that the Applicant is entitled to registration of the Mark under the Trademark Act of 1946, as Amended.

A copy of the Mark and pertinent data from the application are a part of this certificate.

This registration shall remain in force for TEN (10) years, unless terminated earlier as provided by law, and subject to compliance with the provisions of Section 8 of the Trademark Act of 1946, as Amended.

Commissioner of Patents and Trademarks

D. Avoiding the Sections 8 and 15 Trap

While you are entitled to hearty congratulations upon receiving your Certificate of Registration, you need to be aware of a sneaky rule that may trap you in the future. Between five and six years after your registration date, you will be required to file some additional paperwork with the PTO. This additional paperwork is known as a Sections 8 and 15 Affidavit (the numbers refer to the trademark statute section numbers that require this filing). The purpose of the Sections 8 and 15 Affidavit is to inform the PTO that you are still using the mark five years after you first registered it. If you fail to accomplish this filing (which, incidentally costs $100), all your previous registration efforts will be for naught.

What makes this rule sneaky is that the PTO doesn't send you notice when your filing is due. And if you miss the six-year deadline, your registration lapses and you'll have to start all over again. See Chapter 13 for instructions on how to complete the Sections 8 and 15 Affidavit and some suggestions for a reminder system.

Having to start over won't affect your ownership of the mark, or your right to prevent others from using it in a context that might lead to customer confusion. As we pointed out in Chapter 1, trademark ownership in the U.S. is based on first use. However, until you get the mark re-registered, you will not have available to you the very benefits that you sought by registering in the first place—including the nationwide presumption an infringer acted willfully when adopting a conflicting mark (see Chapter 1, Section A).

Also, when your mark turns up in a search of the federal register, it will carry a cancelled designation, which may actually encourage others to use the mark without first checking to see whether you are still using it. While you will be able to go to court to stop the user—assuming there is a likelihood of customer confusion (see Chapter 10, Section B, for an explanation of likelihood of customer confusion)—the basic idea of federal registration is to scare off would-be users, thereby preempting the need to go to court. ∎

Keeping Your Registration Valid and Your Mark Strong

At last, you've achieved federal registration for your trademark. Is that the end of the story? Not exactly. Ownership of the mark can be lost if you don't use the mark correctly. And your registration may lapse if you fail to take certain required follow-up steps. This chapter identifies the formal follow-up tasks you need to complete to keep your registration valid. Plus, we suggest some easy strategies for keeping your mark strong against all potential copiers.

Maintenance of a registered trademark is an ongoing process, involving the continuous use of your mark in commerce and the filing of certain forms to actually increase your rights and renew your registration once the registration period has expired.

A. File Your Sections 8 and 15 Affidavit

Between the fifth and sixth year after federally registering your mark, you must complete and file with the PTO an important form called the "Sections 8 and 15 Affidavit." By filing this single document, you'll protect your mark in two extremely important ways. The Sections 8 and 15 Affidavit officially advises the PTO that:

- your mark is still in use and that your registration should continue in force, and
- your mark has been in continuous use from the date of registration and therefore deserves extra protection against potential challengers. In PTO jargon, you're requesting "incontestability status" for your mark.

More specifically, your mark can become "incontestable" if all of the following apply:

- Your mark was placed on the Principal Register at least five years ago and you have used the mark continuously—without a lapse—since that registration date, and that you have used your mark in the same manner and on the same goods or services for which it was originally registered. (If you

are using the mark for some of those original goods or services but not for others, it may become incontestable for the goods and services you are still using.)
- No court has rendered a final decision (that is, one that is not on appeal) that affects your ownership claim since the date of registration.
- No court or PTO challenge to your ownership claim is pending.
- You file the Sections 8 and 15 Affidavit on time (see Section A1, below).
- The mark is not and has not become generic.

Incontestability status makes it more difficult—but not impossible—for anyone to challenge the validity of your mark should a conflict arise down the road. The result is that it will be easier for you to protect your mark from infringement. Even though an incontestable mark can still be challenged in a number of ways (see sidebar below), it is safe from attack on the basis that it lacks distinctiveness. This is a key benefit—once a mark is considered distinctive beyond argument, it gets very strong protection.

EXAMPLE: Park 'N Fly, Inc., sued Dollar Park and Fly, Inc., for trademark infringement. Dollar Park and Fly defended on the ground that the Park 'N Fly mark was too weak to deserve protection. But the U.S. Supreme Court ruled that the Park 'N Fly mark had obtained incontestability status and couldn't be challenged on that ground.

Of course, even after the mark attains incontestability status, if you stop using it for a sufficiently long time, the mark may be considered abandoned and dropped from the federal register. (See Section C, below, for more information about abandonment.)

EXAMPLE: In 1996, Frank Brown invents an inexpensive but highly accurate blood pressure testing kit and starts distributing it under the trademark F/B Stresstest. After five years have passed, in 2001, the mark will be entitled to incontestable status if Frank keeps the mark in continuous use for this five-year period. But if he stops using it for two years or more, he'll not only possibly give up the incontestable status but may abandon his federal registration altogether.

"Incontestable" Really Means "Harder to Contest"

Paradoxically, you *can* contest (or challenge the validity of) an incontestable trademark in quite a few ways. The upshot is that "incontestable" really means "harder to contest."

An incontestable mark may be challenged on any of the following grounds:

- the mark's registration or its incontestability was obtained fraudulently
- the mark has been abandoned by the registrant
- the mark is being used to misrepresent the source of the goods or services with which it is being used (for instance, use of the mark involves the unfair trade practice known as "palming off")
- the infringing mark is an individual's name being used in his own business (that is, a trade name and so not registrable)
- the use of the infringing mark is prohibited or reserved under the Lanham Act
- the infringing mark was used in interstate commerce before the incontestable mark, and before its registration
- the infringing mark was registered before the incontestable mark, or
- the mark is being used to violate the antitrust laws of the United States. (37 USC Sec. 1115(b).)

---

1. How to Qualify for a Sections 8 and 15 Affidavit

You'll need to briefly evaluate the use of your mark to make sure you're eligible to file the important Sections 8 and 15 Affidavit. Ask yourself the following questions:

- **Is your mark still in use?** You must still be using your mark in the manner described in your registration certificate; otherwise your registration for the mark will be canceled. This means that you must still be using it, at a minimum, on the same products or services and in the same way (on packaging or pamphlets, for example) as you originally stated, and be able to come up with samples of this continued use.
- **Has your mark been in continuous use for five years?** You'll qualify for incontestable status if your mark has been in continuous use for five years after being placed on the Principal Register.
- **Can you file on time?** The form must be signed and filed with the PTO between the fifth and sixth years of registration. Your timing is crucial because there are no extensions. For that reason, it should be filed well before the six-year deadline. That way you'll have time to clear up questions or provide the PTO with more information, if needed.

EXAMPLE: If your mark was registered on May 15, 1995, you must sign and file your Sections 8 and 15 Affidavit between May 15, 2000, and May 14, 2001. It would be best to file it in June or July of 2000 so there is plenty of time to make corrections.

The importance of filing on time. Failure to file the Sections 8 and 15 Affidavit on time will result in your federal registration being canceled. This means you will have to reregister if you still want the benefit of federal registration. It also means that you will not be able to obtain incontestable status for the mark until an additional five years have passed from your re-registration date. Clearly, it is in your interest to make sure this document is filed on time. You should also know that the PTO will not remind you to file this affidavit. So it's up to you to calendar it and make sure it happens.

2. How to Complete the Sections 8 and 15 Affidavit

The form for filing a Sections 8 and 15 Affidavit is in the Appendix. The official form name is "Combined Declaration of Use and Incontestability Under Sections 8 and 15 of the Trademark Act of 1946, as Amended." Additional forms may be obtained from the Patent and Trademark Office if needed. (See Chapter 14, Help Beyond This Book.)

Mark: Enter the mark exactly as it appears on your trademark registration certificate. If you don't have a copy of your registration, request one from the PTO in plenty of time before it is due.

Registration Number: Enter the registration number which also appears on your trademark registration certificate.

Registration Date: Enter the registration date for your mark. This will appear on the Certificate of Registration you received from the PTO—usually several months after the mark was published for opposition.

Name of Registrant: If you are the current owner of the mark, your name goes here. If you own the mark with another person, both your names go in this blank. If the mark is owned by a corporation, partnership or other business entity, the entity's name goes here. If the names here are not the same as those entered in the registration, use an attachment page to explain why (for instance, ownership changed by assignment or sale of a business). (See Chapters 4 or 5 for more details about how company names must be stated in full.)

Registrant's Current Mailing Address: Enter the mailing address for the registrant. If there are more than two registrants, enter the address of the registrant who will be handling communication with the PTO if any is needed.

Registration Number: Enter the registration number again.

Type of Commerce: Enter the type of commerce the mark has been used in during the previous five years. This will be interstate, territorial, foreign or a combination. If you have any questions about this, or how to describe the type of commerce, see Chapters 4 or 5. The back of the form also gives some suggestions about how to describe the type of commerce.

Identify Goods and/or Services: If you are still using the mark on all the goods and services identified on your certificate of registration, enter "N.A." in this blank. If there are some goods and services that were listed but which are no longer carrying the registered mark, describe those goods and services here.

Specimen: As we've explained in earlier chapters, "Specimen" is the word the PTO uses for a sample showing how your mark is being used. The specimen you send must be in use at or near the time you are filing the Sections 8 and 15 Affidavit. (See Chapter 3, for a description of suggested specimens for goods and services.)

In your original registration you listed goods or services in one or more international classes. If you registered in more than one of these classes (and paid an extra application fee) you will need to submit one specimen of goods or services for each class that:

1. you included in your original registration, and
2. you wish to maintain as part of your registration.

For example, assume you registered your mark under two classes: one class for your products (fanciful shaped wicker baskets) and a separate class for a service that your business provides (basket repair). If you are still using the mark for your products and service, you will need to submit two specimens—one for each use.

Affidavit of Use and Incontestability (Page 1)

COMBINED DECLARATION OF USE AND INCONTESTABILITY UNDER **SECTIONS 8 & 15'** OF THE TRADEMARK ACT OF 1946, AS AMENDED	MARK (Identify the mark)	
	REGISTRATION NO.	DATE OF REGISTRATION:

TO THE ASSISTANT SECRETARY AND COMMISSIONER OF PATENTS AND TRADEMARKS:

REGISTRANT'S NAME:[2]

REGISTRANT'S CURRENT MAILING ADDRESS: _____

_____

_____

GOODS AND/OR SERVICES AND USE IN COMMERCE STATEMENT:

The mark shown in Registration No. _____, owned by the above-identified registrant, has been in

continuous use in _____ commerce for five consecutive years from the date of registration or the
   (type of)[3]

date of publication under § 12(c)[4] to the present, on or in connection with all of the goods and/or services

identified in the registration, (*except* for the following)[5]_____

_____ ;

as evidenced by the attached specimen(s)[6] showing the mark as currently used. There has been no final

decision adverse to registrant's claim of ownership of such mark for such goods or services, or to registrant's

right to register the same or to keep the same on the register; and there is no proceeding involving said

rights pending and not disposed of either in the Patent and Trademark Office or in the courts.

DECLARATION

The undersigned being hereby warned that willful false statements and the like so made are punishable by fine or imprisonment, or both, under 18 U.S.C. 1001, and that such willful false statements may jeopardize the validity of this document, declares that he/she is properly authorized to execute this document on behalf of the registrant; he/she believes the registrant to be the owner of the above identified registration; the trademark/service mark is in use in commerce; and all statements made of his/her own knowledge are true and all statements made on information and belief are believed to be true.

_____
Date

_____
Signature

_____
Telephone Number

_____
Print or Type Name and Position
[if applicable][7]

If you are continuing registration for less than the total number of classes in your original registration, make sure you specify in your transmittal letter the classes for which the declaration is being submitted.

One specimen needs to be submitted for each class of goods and/or services that will be covered by the Sections 8 and 15 affidavit.

Declaration: Before signing, carefully read the entire declaration. The PTO wants to make sure you still have the right to use the mark, that your right has not been taken away by a court or the PTO, and that your right is not being formally challenged. A complete discussion of all this is beyond the scope of this book. The odds are that you have used the mark without fighting about it in court or through the PTO system. If you are not sure whether you can truthfully sign the form, consult a trademark lawyer. (See Chapter 14, Help Beyond This Book.)

If the present owner is an individual, the individual should sign the declaration. If the present owner is a partnership, the declaration should be signed by a general partner. If the present owner is a corporation or similar entity, the declaration should be signed by an officer of the corporation/entity. Print or type the officer title of the person signing the declaration.

Add the telephone number of one of the persons signing the application and enter the date of signature.

3. How to File the Sections 8 and 15 Affidavit With the PTO

Before mailing your completed Sections 8 and 15 Affidavit to the PTO, make at least two complete copies for your records. If the document is lost in the mail or misplaced by the PTO, you will have another copy to send. You should send your completed Sections 8 and 15 Affidavit to the PTO within a few days of when it was signed and dated. If you're nearing the six-year deadline, follow the mailing instructions on the back of the

form. Your Sections 8 and 15 Declaration package should be mailed to:

Assistant Commissioner for Trademarks
P.O. Box Reg Fee
2900 Crystal Drive
Arlington, VA 22202-3513
Include the following:

- A transmittal letter.
- Original Sections 8 and 15 Affidavit. Keep a copy for your records.
- Specimen.
- Fee. As of November 1998, the PTO charges, for filing a Sections 8 and 15 Affidavit, a fee of $200 for each class under which the mark is being used. Read Chapter 7, Section B1, to learn how to confirm the fee if you are filing at a later date. Also, read the box on fees on the back of the form.
- Return postcard. Send a return-receipt postcard as described in Chapters 4 and 5. This allows you to keep track of when your paper was filed.

Once again, file on time. Don't let the six years expire without being sure your affidavit was filed! As you can see, we can't emphasize this enough. The time period within which the form must be filed is rigid, so if you don't receive your postcard within several weeks, contact the PTO. You may have to send a duplicate affidavit if it was lost in the mail or misplaced.

If the PTO finds your affidavit acceptable, you will eventually receive a notice saying they received it and have accepted it.

B. Renew Your Registration

In addition to filing a Sections 8 and 15 Affidavit, you must renew your registration at the end of the registration period if you don't want it to expire. If your registration does expire because of your failure to renew it on a timely basis, you will lose all the benefits of federal registration—

including the right to use the ® symbol—unless and until you reregister it.

1. When to File Your Application for Renewal

If your mark was registered on or after November 16, 1989, it must be renewed within ten years. If it was registered before November 16, 1989, it will last 20 years before renewal is necessary.

The renewal application should be filed within the six-month period directly preceding the ten- or 20-year anniversary of your mark's registration. For an additional per-class filing fee, however, the renewal may be filed within three months after the ten- or 20-year anniversary date. No renewal application will be accepted after that date. For instance, if your registration expires on May 15, 1999, your renewal application 1) must be dated after November 15, 1998, and 2) may be filed between November 16, 1998, and May 15, 1999 (or between May 16 and August 15, 1999, if you pay the extra fee).

Small inconsistencies in the information you provide the PTO on this form may cause a delay in getting the renewal filed. For this reason, we strongly recommend that you file your renewal application as soon as possible, to allow the maximum time possible for curing glitches. If you file early (before the six-month period preceding the date your renewal is due), the PTO will send back your application but hold onto your money if there are problems with your application. If you don't file your application on time, the PTO will refund your money.

2. How to Complete the Application for Renewal

The renewal form in the Appendix is identical to the Sections 8 and 15 Declaration (Section A above). For that reason, the following instructions direct you to instructions for that form.

Mark: Enter the mark exactly as it appears on your trademark registration certificate.

Registration Number: Use the registration number that also appears on your certificate.

Date of Registration: Follow the directions in Section A2 above.

Registrant's Name: Usually the renewal applicant and original registrant are the same person. However, if ownership of the mark has changed since registration, the original registrant will be different from the renewal applicant. For example, suppose Roxanne registered her mark Lollipops for children's toy catalog sales as an individual applicant. If she later formed a corporation to handle her quickly growing business, and transferred ownership of the mark to the corporation by assignment (as discussed in Section C, below), then she is the original registrant, and the corporation is the renewal applicant.

Registrant's Current Mailing Address: Follow the instructions in Section A2 above.

Registration Number: Enter the registration number again.

Type of Commerce: Follow the instructions in Section A2 above.

Identify Goods and Services: Follow the instructions in Section A2 above.

Specimen: In your original registration you listed goods or services in one or more international classifications. If you registered in more than one of these classifications (and paid an extra registration fee) you will need to submit one specimen of goods or services for each classification:

1. that you included in your original registration, and
2. that you wish to maintain as part of your renewed registration.

EXAMPLE: Eduardo was renewing the mark Easy Street for his massage services (Class 42) and massage oils (Class 3). He would need to submit two specimens (such as a current advertisement for the massage services and a current label for the oils).

For general information about appropriate specimens, see Chapter 3.

If you are continuing registration for less than the total number of classes in your original registration, make sure you specify in your transmittal letter the classes for which the declaration is being submitted.

Declaration: Before signing, carefully read the entire Application for Renewal. The PTO wants to make sure that the registrant is still the owner of the mark, that the mark is still in use and that all other information in the form is true. If the registrant/owner is an individual, the individual should sign the declaration. If the registrant/owner is a partnership, the declaration should be signed by a general partner. If the registrant/owner is a corporation or similar juristic entity, the declaration should be signed by an officer of the corporation/entity. Print or type the officer title of the person signing the declaration. If the registration is owned by two or more parties as joint owners, each owner must sign.

Add the telephone number of one of the persons signing the application and enter the date of signature.

File within the six-month period preceding the expiration date. Under no circumstances may the form be dated more than six months before the registration would expire. If it is dated too early, the PTO will send it back and you will have to do a new renewal application.

Fee: As of November 1998, the PTO charges $300 per class for filing a renewal application. If you are filing at a later date, review Chapter 7, Section B1, for how to confirm the correct fee.

3. How to File the Application for Renewal

You should send your completed Application for Renewal to the PTO within a few days of when it was signed and dated. If you're nearing the expiration period, follow the mailing instructions on the back of the form. Your renewal package should be mailed to:

BOX POST REG FEE
Assistant Commissioner for Trademarks
2900 Crystal Drive
Arlington, Virginia 22202-3513
Include the following in the package:

- a transmittal letter.
- Original Application for Renewal (of Registration of a Mark Under Section 9 of the Trademark Act of 1946, as Amended.) Keep a copy for your records.
- Specimen(s).
- Fees.
- Return postcard. Send a stamped self-addressed receipt postcard as described in Chapters 4 and 5. This allows you to keep track of when your Application for Renewal was filed.

If you don't hear from the PTO within six months as to whether your Application for Renewal has been accepted or rejected, call the Trademark Status Line at 703-305-8747 or the Post Registration Division at 703-308-9500.

4. After the Renewal Application is Filed

If the PTO thinks something is wrong with your renewal application, it will write you a letter very similar to the action letters discussed in Chapter 8, Dealing With the PTO After You've Filed Your Application. You must respond within six months; if you don't, the mark will expire without renewal. If you have any questions about their letter, call the PTO and talk with the Examiner who sent it. Usually the questions can be cleared up if you write one simple response letter.

Once the PTO is satisfied, the renewal certificate will be sent to you.

C. Ongoing Care to Keep Your Mark Strong and Protected

Beyond registration, follow-up forms and renewals, there are some other things you should keep in mind on a day-to-day basis to protect your trademark. This section will explain how to use trademark symbols, how to use your mark (or risk losing it), how to maintain tight control of your mark, how to use your mark properly and keep track of your ownership.

1. Use of Trademark Symbols

If your mark is federally registered on either the Principal or Supplemental Register, you have the right to use the symbol for a registered trademark —®—with your mark and should begin doing so immediately. The mark puts others on notice that the mark is federally registered. If your mark is not on either of the federal trademark registers, you may not use the ® symbol.

The ® symbol is usually printed in very tiny type to the right of the mark. By placing the ® next to your mark, you improve your chances of collecting damages or defendant's profits if it is ever necessary to take an infringer to court. This is because the ® symbol places all would-be infringers on notice that the mark is registered. If they knowingly infringe, they are classified as willful infringers. Willful infringers are subject to

more severe legal penalties. However you won't lose ownership of the mark by omitting this notice.

EXAMPLE: While searching for a name for his new word processing program, Phil sees an advertisement in a trade magazine for a new program called Sorcerer's Apprentice that allows the user to construct databases for hobby collections. No notice of registration is displayed in the advertisement, so Phil foolishly decides the mark is probably not registered and proceeds to use it as a trademark for his program. The work is in fact registered. While the owners of the mark Sorcerer's Apprentice could sue Phil for infringement because the goods are so closely related (they're both software) and can probably force him to stop using the mark, they might have trouble collecting the damages allowed for willful infringement (triple damages, the defendant's profits and possibly attorneys' fees) because they didn't use the ® symbol.

It is enough that the symbol appears at least once on each label, tag or advertisement. You don't need to use the symbol on every occurrence of your mark. There is no rule for how often the symbol should be used; common sense—and a healthy sense of aesthetics—should do fine. The main idea to using these symbols is to make sure you get the message across once, or if there are many pages, at least once on every page. It can be quite distracting to see the same word appear over and over again on a page with a little ® or ™ mark appearing next to it every time.

Incidentally, instead of using the ® symbol, you may state that "[Your Mark] is a registered trademark of [Your Name]." This has the same legal effect as the ® symbol, but takes up much more space.

Be sure to specify how you want the symbol used when hiring advertising services or printers; it is your responsibility to make sure the world knows your mark is registered.

Use of ® if Your Federal Registration Is Canceled

Federal trademark registrations are canceled by the PTO if the registrants fail to file certain required follow-up documents after the initial registration (discussed above). Because the PTO doesn't notify the registrant of this cancellation action, it is easy to inadvertently continue using the ® on a mark that is no longer technically registered. Obviously the easiest way to prevent this from happening is to meet the follow-up requirements. But if you slip up—and many do—use your best efforts to stop using the ® unless and until you reregister the mark.

If your mark is unregistered, you may use ^{TM} (for trademarks) or ^{SM} (for service marks) next to the mark to show that you claim ownership and intend to assert your rights against copiers. While use of the ^{TM} or ^{SM} symbols provides no statutory legal benefits, in practice it reminds would-be copiers that the name or other device is already being claimed as a mark and, in most instances, will cause them to stay away from it. As with the ® symbol, it's usually wise to limit your use of the ^{TM} or ^{SM} symbol. It is enough that the symbol appears at least once on each label, tag or advertisement.

2. Use It or Risk Losing It

Although this may seem like an overly simple principle, you must continuously use your mark in order to maintain your rights. First, you won't be able to file your Sections 8 and 15 Affidavit (see Section A, above) and achieve incontestability unless you continuously used your mark for five years following the date of registration. Second, a mark must be in continuous use for the owner to be able to keep others from using it. If the mark falls out of continuous use, it is said to be "abandoned." Even a mark that has been registered with the PTO, if not used for three years or more, will be presumed abandoned if challenged. Presumed abandonment means that the owner of the mark will have the burden of proving that the mark was not abandoned or that there was a good reason for the non-use. In this situation, if the mark's original owner brings a court action against someone who began using it later, the original owner will lose the suit without a good explanation of why the three years of non-use did not constitute an "intent to abandon."

In cases where a mark is challenged as abandoned, contingencies such as temporary financial difficulty, bankruptcy proceedings and the need for a product revision may all qualify as satisfactory explanations for non-use of a mark.

3. Maintain Tight Control of Your Mark

As we explain in other parts of the book, trademarks serve the primary function of identifying a particular product or service in the marketplace. If a mark owner allows others to use the trademark without restricting what product or service it represents, the mark no longer serves as a meaningful indicator of a particular product's or service's origin and will be considered abandoned. For instance, if a fast food hamburger chain allows its franchise operators to have complete discretion as to the food, decor and type of service they offer under the company logo, the logo quickly loses its ability to indicate a particular type of food service. In this situation, the logo is considered abandoned since it doesn't serve its original function of product or service identification and anyone will be free to use it.

The way that McDonald's controls its marks exemplifies the type of vigilance over the product or service that is necessary to avoid the possibility of abandonment. This company uses its service mark not only to distinguish its service from its competitors generally, but also to call to a consumer's mind such characteristics as a specific level of service, a specific type of meal at a specific price, and a specific level of cleanliness. It does this by requiring every owner of a McDonald's franchise to operate the franchise under tight rules and restrictions, designed to insure that the characteristics associated with the McDonald's mark are always present. Without such restrictions, the McDonald's service mark soon would stand for nothing, since each McDonald's operation would soon cease to provide the consumer with meaningful information about its products and service, and would therefore be considered abandoned, just as if it were no longer used.

Another aspect of controlling your mark is to police its use by others. Even if you don't particularly care whether some others use your mark, your failure to assert your exclusive ownership rights means that the mark may be considered abandoned. Policing your mark might mean annual checks of the trade literature applicable to your business, weekly scrutiny of the *Official Gazette* for new trademark applications or even periodic full trademark searches. You can find the complete collection of the *Official Gazette* (including all the current editions) in your local Patent and Trademark Depository Library (the list is in the Appendix). You might also check with your local public law library or the law library at your local university. You could subscribe to the *Official Gazette*, but the cost is quite prohibitive. Unless you are planning on applying for lots and lots of trademarks, it makes little sense to buy a subscription. The *Official Gazette* is not yet published online.

To learn more about how to properly police your mark and respond to possible infringers, see *Trademark: Legal Care for Your Business & Product Name*, by Stephen Elias and Kate McGrath (Nolo).

Authorized Uses of Your Trademark

Not all uses of your trademark by others place it in jeopardy. For example, it is common for stores to use marks belonging to other companies to tell their customers that the goods or services identified by the marks can be purchased at that store. When using marks in this way, however, the stores must make it clear that the marks belong to their owners, not to the store. Usually this fact is clear from the context ("Levi's sold here," or, "An authorized distributor of Apple Computer products"). Often you will see on labels of goods that incorporate others' products, like a sofa, a message like "Wear-Dated ® is a trademark of the Monsanto Company," to indicate that the name of the sofa's fabric is a trademark of another company.

Such uses become a problem only when it is not clear that the trademark belongs to the rightful trademark owner. For example, if the trademark does not look like it normally does, that may be a confusing use of the mark.

Generally, use of a trademark that is simply typed is not a problem, but if the advertisement employs special designs, the mark must have the same typeface and logo as used by the original mark owner, or a disclaimer specifying who the owner of the mark is.

4. Use the Mark Properly— Avoid Genericide

A few businesses—almost always large ones— have the apparent good fortune of owning a mark that has become a household word. But paradoxically, once the mark becomes so much of household word that it becomes synonymous with any product or service of the sort it originally represented, it ceases to be a mark—it becomes generic. For example, some people refer to all facial paper tissues as Kleenex, and all acetaminophen analgesics as Tylenol. These marks would be in danger of becoming lost through "genericide" if the companies did not protest such improper uses of the marks.

The problem is this: the more well-known a particular mark becomes, the more the public is prone to equate the mark with the underlying product rather than view it as one brand name among many. This is just another way of saying that the mark loses its ability to identify a particular brand and becomes generic. Only a tiny number of companies will face this problem—it tends to arise with revolutionary new products that the public comes to associate with the name their first manufacturer gives them, like Roller Blades for in-line skates. But because genericide is avoidable, you ought to know how to prevent your mark from going generic if that ever seems to be even a remote a possibility.

The best way to keep a mark from becoming generic is to:

- accompany every use of the mark with the generic product or service name (for example, Kleenex tissues).
- never use the mark as a verb (for instance, you never go "roller blading," you skate on Roller Blade skates).
- always capitalize your mark (Tylenol).
- never use the mark as a general noun (for instance, don't call a photocopy a "Xerox").
- If you become aware that your mark is being used improperly, you must remind the public that it is a mark and not a generic name. For instance, Xerox has spent millions advising the public that Xerox is a registered mark that must always be capitalized and used as a proper adjective describing a

noun (for instance, a Xerox brand photocopier). If later on someone challenges the Xerox Corporation's right to the exclusive use of the word "Xerox," on the ground it has become generic, Xerox will prevail if it can show that people understood these advertisements and that most use the term "Xerox" as a brand name—not a generic one.

5. Keep Track of the Mark's Ownership

You should consider your registered mark as property with a title, the same as a house or car. The title document is your Certificate of Registration. If for any reason you sell your business or rights in the products you manufacture or distribute, you will also need to sell the marks used to identify the business and products in the marketplace. The complete transfer of ownership in a mark to another person or entity is called an "assignment." An assignment of a registered mark must be in writing to be valid. It can—and should—be filed with the U.S. Patent and Trademark Office. The new owner can obtain a new Certificate of Registration in his or her name. If you anticipate a sale (assignment) of your mark, see a trademark attorney (see Chapter 14, Help Beyond This Book).

If you are selling a business, the chances are you are also selling any trademarks associated with it. If so, it makes sense to assign your ownership of the marks in a document that is separate from the contract of sale. This enables the new mark owner to record only the transfer of mark ownership with the U.S. Patent and Trademark Office, while keeping private the many details of the deal that do not affect the transfer of trademark rights. ■

Help Beyond This Book

We hope that this book provides all the information you will need to register your trademark. But you may need additional help, either in the form of more advanced legal resources or a trademark attorney's assistance.

In Section A, we introduce you to many sources that offer more information on trademark law. Written for law students and lawyers, these resources include books and websites which discuss recent legal trends and developments, and provide citations (references) to substantive trademark law, including statutes, court decisions and PTO rules. In Section B, we provide some tips for finding a good trademark lawyer.

Don't Be Afraid of Legal Research

Looking up the law for yourself needn't be scary. By reading this book you will have already learned the basic trademark vocabulary necessary to understand the more technical legal materials we discuss in Section A. In addition, Nolo publishes a basic legal research guide, *Legal Research: How to Find and Understand the Law,* by Stephen Elias & Susan Levinkind, and an excellent two-hour video, *Legal Research Made Easy,* by law librarian Robert Berring, which teach you how to do basic legal research efficiently. If you have access to the web, you can visit Nolo's website at http://www.nolo.com and use Nolo's legal research tutorial to learn how to do legal research on the web. You will also find most law librarians to be of great help.

Application Fee Updates

To obtain the most current information on trademark application fees, try either of the following sources:

- The PTO's website at http://www.uspto. gov. From the home page, choose "PTO Fees" from the menu on the left side of the home page. Click on "Trademark Processing Fees" and locate the fee for the Application for Registration. As of the date of this book's publication, the fee is $245 per application.
- Call the Trademark Assistance Center at 703-308-9000 (office hours are 8:30 a.m. to 5:00 p.m., Monday through Friday, except federal holidays), or the PTO's automated information system for patents and trademarks (available 24 hours a day, seven days a week, including holidays) at 703-557-INFO.

A. Doing Your Own Research

When seeking answers in a law library, you will find useful the three-step approach that we describe below:

Step 1: Read one or more discussions by experts in the field to get a background and overview of the topic being researched. In this case, you will already have a basic background from this book and will be looking for additional details on whatever particular topic you're researching.

Step 2: Read the law itself (cases and statutes) upon which the experts base their opinions. Reading primary materials such as these can be confusing without first digesting an expert's analysis (Step 1).

Step 3: Make sure the law you read is completely up-to-date (it is the most current legal information available).

1. Read One or More Discussions by Experts

The following are some recommended publications written by trademark law experts. You can find others via your law library's card catalog. It is usually most efficient to call your local libraries ahead of time to make sure they have the resources you want. Once you are at the library, check with the library's card catalog, online catalog or the law librarian for a book's location. Most of these books will be non-circulating (which means you can't check them out and take them home), so you may want to make sure you bring enough money to photocopy pages you find particularly important.

a. Federal Trademark Law

The most authoritative book on trademark law is the two-volume set entitled *McCarthy on Trademarks and Unfair Competition*, by J. Thomas McCarthy, published by Clark Boardman Callaghan. McCarthy, a law professor at the University of San Francisco, is the most widely respected trademark law expert in the United States. His book is so comprehensive and well-respected that judges often consult it and refer to it in their decisions. You can find this treatise, with its annual supplements, in most public and academic law libraries.

Trademarks and Unfair Competition includes discussions of virtually every issue that has arisen with respect to the trademark and unfair competition areas of law. Each point that McCarthy makes is supported by footnote references to court cases and statutes—the primary sources that you may want to consult next as part of your overall legal research plan.

You can find your topic of interest in *Trademarks and Unfair Competition* by consulting the detailed table of contents, the extensive index or the headings that precede each chapter.

Don't overlook the handy appendices in Volume 2, which include the complete text of the Lanham Act (the federal trademark statute), other statutes related to trademark law, and the Trademark Rules of Practice of the U.S. Patent and Trademark Office.

As a companion to McCarthy's treatise on trademark law, *Trademark Law Practice Forms (Volume I),* by Barry Kramer and Allen D. Brufsky, published by Clark Boardman Callaghan, is a four-volume set of books containing many sample forms that are particularly useful if you plan to amend your application or otherwise respond to an office action. You will find almost all of the forms dealing with filing or amending an application or responding to an office action in *Volume 1: Rules of Practice in the Patent and Trademark Office.* This resource might be difficult to find. Check with your local public law library first, making sure you have the librarian first check the shelves for Volume 1 of the four-volume set before you go over there. Next, check the college or university law libraries nearest you.

Although very comprehensive, McCarthy's material may not give you enough detail on how to apply trademark law to real-life situations, such as rules on using the ®, or filing and prosecuting a trademark action in the U.S. Patent and Trademark Office (PTO). Probably the best resource for questions of this type is the *Trademark Manual of Examining Procedures (TMEP),* published by the PTO and available for purchase from the Superintendent of Documents, U.S. Government Printing Office, Washington, D.C., or, usually, from whatever source in your area sells U.S. government publications. You can also find the *TMEP* in browsable form on the PTO's website, listed below.

Also, there are two respected resources that provide how-to information. They are:

- *Trademark Law—A Practitioner's Guide,* by Siegrun D. Kane, published by the Practicing Law Institute, and
- *Trademark Registration Practice,* by James E. Hawes, published by Clark Boardman Callaghan.

The first of these resources provides practical advice for lawyers about the practice and litigation of trademark cases, which may prove helpful if you end up in court or you want a better idea of what lies ahead should a lawsuit loom. The second resource is a fairly good guide to the registration process, although not always up-to-date. Your local law libraries should also have these resources.

b.   State Trademark Law

A good source of information on state trademark law is *State Trademark and Unfair Competition Law*, a publication of the International Trademark Association (see sidebar below). It has chapters discussing trademark and unfair competition laws of every state. At the end it has a chart listing the registration requirements for each state. It is updated one or more times a year. You can find this resource in most major law libraries.

c.   Law Review Articles

If you have a very unusual trademark problem that is not covered by the resources already mentioned (for example, how to register a distinctive sound as a trademark), or a problem in an area in which the law has changed very recently (perhaps because of a new Supreme Court case), the best sources of available information may be articles appearing in scholarly journals called "law reviews." You can find citations (references) to all the law review articles on a particular topic by looking under "trademark" or "unfair competition" in the *Index to Legal Periodicals,* the *Current Law Index* or one of the cumulative electronic indexes that are with increasing frequency found in law libraries. A key to the abbreviations used in these indexes is located at the front of each index volume. Substantial collections of law reviews are usually located in large public law libraries or university libraries.

Trademark Associations and Legal Publishers

Two associations of trademark lawyers and one general legal publisher offer other materials that you might find helpful. You can get a list of their publications by writing or calling them.

International Trademark Association (INTA)
1133 Avenue of the Americas
New York, NY 10036
212-768-9887
http://www.inta.org/

Among other materials, the INTA publishes an annual paperback, *Trademark Law Handbook,* which analyzes current trademark issues, and *The Trademark Reporter,* a bimonthly law review that discusses recent trademark cases and issues. Only members can subscribe to it, but law libraries carry it for the public's use.

American Intellectual Property Law
   Association (AIPLA)
Suite 203, 2001 Jefferson Davis Highway
Arlington, VA 22202
703-415-0780
http://www.aipla.org/aipla

The AIPLA is an association of lawyers that conducts scholarly studies and publishes articles by its members. Materials by AIPLA are available only in libraries or through members of the association.

Clark Boardman Callaghan
155 Pfingsten Road
Deerfield, IL 60015-4998
800-323-1336

Clark Boardman Callaghan is the principal publisher of trademark materials for lawyers. You can get a list of their publications or order them by phone.

2. Read the Law Itself (Cases and Statutes)

Following are explanations of the main types of law that you may encounter if you do your own legal research.

a. Statutes

The main law governing trademarks in the United States is the Lanham Act, also known as the Federal Trademark Act of 1946 (as amended in 1988). It is codified at Title 15, Chapters 1051 through 1127, of the United States Code. You can find it in either of two series of books, United States Code Annotated, (U.S.C.A.) or United States Code Service, Lawyers Edition (U.S.C.S.). All law libraries carry at least one of these series. To find a specific section of the Lanham Act, consult either the index at the end of Title 15, or the index at the end of the entire code.

b. Regulations

The regulations implementing the Lanham Act consist of the specific rules that govern registration of a trademark. They are found in Title 37, Chapter 1, of the Code of Federal Regulations (C.F.R.). It comes in paperback form, which you can purchase from the Superintendent of Documents, U.S. Government Printing Office, Washington, DC 20402. It also is available in most law libraries.

c. Court Decisions

There are several ways to find the pertinent court decisions on a particular trademark issue. As we discussed, an excellent way to get started is to consult *Trademarks and Unfair Competition,* by J. Thomas McCarthy, a law review or one of the other secondary sources we mentioned above.

These will list ("cite" in legal parlance) and usually discuss all the significant pertinent cases. In addition, the U.S. Code Annotated and U.S. Code Service both refer to and briefly summarize all the decisions relevant to each section of the Lanham Act. These "case notes" are located just after each section of the Act.

You can also get cites to cases from a series of books by the West Publishing Company called Federal Practice Digest. If you look under the term "trademark," in the detailed table of contents, or under a more specific topic in the very detailed subject matter index, you will find short summaries of trademark law decisions.

3. Finding Trademark Laws and Information on the World Wide Web

The World Wide Web offers convenient access to an enormous amount of trademark materials, including:

- the federal trademark statutes and regulations
- informative articles by trademark experts
- the federal trademark database (for a reasonable fee), and
- recent changes in PTO trademark examination procedures.

Here is a brief list of sites that will either have the information you are looking for or will provide you with links to other sites that do.

- **http://www.uspto.gov/** The U.S. Patent and Trademark Office is the place to go to find the PTO's trademark publications. You will find the following publications: *Trademark Manual of Examining Procedure (TMEP); Trademark Acceptable Identification of Goods and Services Manual; U.S. Trademark Law: Rules of Practice & Federal Statutes;* a PTO paper on Trademark Registration of Internet Domain Names; and many other useful resources. The PTO's website also handles online trademark applications, as discussed in Chapters 4 (for use applications) and Chapter 5 (for intent-to-use applications), as well as a pilot project called TARR, which allows you to check on the status of your filed trademark application. You can also find recent policy and statutory changes and transcripts of hearings on various trademark law issues. This site also links to other useful trademark-related sites.

- **http://www.findlaw.com/** This search engine offers an excellent collection of trademark-related materials on the web, including trademark statutes, regulations, classification manuals and articles of general interest.
- **http://www.ggmark.com/** This site, maintained by a trademark lawyer, provides basic trademark information and a fine collection of links to other trademark resources.
- **http://www.sci3.com/** This site, maintained by the Sunnyvale Center for Innovation, Invention and Ideas (a Patent and Depository Library), provides information about their excellent, low-cost trademark search service conducted by the Center's librarians.
- **http://www.micropat.com/ trademarkwebindex.html** This site, maintained by Micropatent, lets you do your own search of the federal trademark register for $20 a day (text) and $30 a day (text and images). You can get a lot of searching done within a 24-hour period if you're adequately prepared.
- **http: //www.kuesterlaw.com/** This site, maintained by an Atlanta, Georgia, intellectual property law firm, also is an excellent springboard for finding trademark statutes, regulations, court cases and articles on such recent trademark law developments as domain name disputes.

4. Make Sure the Law You Read Is Completely Up-to-Date

Once you have found a statute or case that seems to address your research question, you will need to check that it is still good law. A statute or case is still "good law" if it hasn't been superceded by another, more current, statute or overturned by a more recent case in a jurisdiction that matters. For statutes this usually means checking the back of the volume you are using for an insert called a "pocket part." Pocket parts are published annually and include any recent changes in the statute. Updating the status of rules announced in cases means using a tool that is known throughout the legal research world as Shepard's Case Citations.

Explaining how to use this valuable tool is beyond the scope of this book. We recommend *Legal Research: How to Find and Understand the Law,* by Stephen Elias and Susan Levinkind (Nolo) for a crash course on the subject.

If you intend to do legal research yourself, be aware that interpreting statutes and cases can be difficult even for those with legal training and a specific background in the area you are researching. Before you act in reliance on anything you find in the law library, it usually makes sense to double check with a knowledgeable attorney. (Section B below.)

B. Finding a Lawyer

If you become involved in a trademark dispute, are having trouble getting your mark registered or simply want some advice from a professional about a trademark issue, you will want to consult a trademark lawyer—but not just any trademark lawyer. Start by understanding that if you have read substantial portions of this book you already know more about trademarks than most lawyers. This puts you in the difficult position of finding someone who knows more than you do and yet is willing to acknowledge the considerable competence that you've now gained in this area. You want a trademark lawyer who:

- knows the trademark field well
- is willing to acknowledge your competence gained from using this book, and
- is honest and conscientious.

Fortunately, by arming yourself with the information in this book, you have a good shot at finding a lawyer with all of these characteristics. Unfortunately, we know of no sure-fire way to do so, but here are some suggestions.

1. Find a Lawyer Who Knows the Trademark Field Well

Trademark lawyers usually advertise in the Yellow Pages and legal journals as intellectual property specialists, able to handle patent, trademark, copyright and trade secret cases. Such ads can be misleading, because most intellectual property law specialists tend to be very knowledgeable in one or two of these areas, and only passingly familiar with the others.

For instance, it is common for patent lawyers to be far more knowledgeable in that area than in trademark law, even though both patents and trademarks involve practice before the U.S. Patent and Trademark Office. Similarly, some lawyers specialize in trademarks and do little or no patent work.

The point of knowing this, of course, is that you want a trademark lawyer who really knows trademarks, not someone willing to brush up on trademarks at your expense.

When you call on the intellectual property specialist, ask these questions:

- What percentage of your practice involves trademark work?
- How many trademarks have you prosecuted?
- Are you a member of the International Trademark Association or the American Intellectual Property Law Association?

The first two inquiries will help you find a true specialist in this area, while the third will help you find a lawyer who is involved enough with trademark issues to join an association of trademark specialists.

Beyond the Yellow Pages, you should call the state bar association in your state and ask about any intellectual property attorney rosters it may have. Many cities and counties have local bar associations with rosters of member attorneys and their specialties.

2. Find a Lawyer Who Is Willing to Acknowledge Your Competence

In addition to satisfying yourself that a lawyer is competent, you want to find someone who is reasonably congenial to work with. You don't need us to tell you that lawyers tend to look down on laypersons when it comes to the lawyer's area of expertise. This means that many of the lawyers you initially encounter are likely to be turned off by your expertise. Fortunately, however, some lawyers are willing to respect their clients' knowledge and know how to work with it rather than against it. It is this type of lawyer you should be looking for.

You can find a lawyer who isn't intimidated by a competent client if you:

- explain over the phone that you have been using this book
- articulate exactly what you want the lawyer to do; and
- carefully monitor the lawyer's reaction.

If the lawyer scoffs at the idea of a self-help law book or you get a whiff of, "Don't tell me what you need, I'm the lawyer," go on to the next name on the list. If the response appears to respect your self-help efforts and admits to the possibility that you are a competent human being, make an appointment.

3. Find a Lawyer Who Is Honest and Conscientious

If you are just seeking advice, then you needn't worry much about the lawyer's character. But if you are looking for someone to represent you, the human being you are dealing with becomes paramount. The best analytical trademark lawyer in the world can bring you to financial and emotional ruin, if he or she lacks the ability to understand your needs and to represent you with your best interests in mind.

a. Honesty

While some would argue that there's no such thing as an honest lawyer, we maintain that it is possible to have honest dealings with your lawyer. Start by clearly understanding that the lawyer's financial interest—to run up lots of billable hours over a period of time—is the opposite of yours—which is to arrive at a fast, cost-efficient and reasonably livable resolution of the problem.

Once you understand this, you'll also understand that it is essential that you and your lawyer agree up front about what the lawyer is to do and the amount of control you are to have over the lawyer's activities. Rule one is that the lawyer is working for you, not vice versa; and rule two is that you have a right to understand the reason for every minute of the lawyer's time that will be billed to you.

b. Conscientiousness

Your lawyer must be willing to agree to have you regularly consulted on all phases of the case and to promptly return your phone calls. Although nothing leads to a ruinous relationship faster than bad communication, too few lawyers keep their clients well posted. Lawyers faced with complaints about their lousy client contact habits often reply that many clients call or expect too much. But since the client is paying for the lawyer's time, this seems like a pretty weak excuse. Our experience tells us that the usual reason lawyers don't return phone calls is that they have neglected some facet of the case and simply don't want to face the client.

Your lawyer must also be willing to follow through on your case to its completion. This one is tricky to monitor, since it involves predicting the future. However, as long as good communication is established at the outset, there's an improved chance that your lawyer will give you good service. ■

State Trademark Agencies and Statutes

Alabama

Ala. Code §§ 8-12-1 to 8-12-44
Secretary of State
Lands & Trademark Division
Room 528, State Office Building
Montgomery, AL 36130-7701
334-242-5324

Alaska

Alaska Stat. §§ 45.50.101 et seq.
Department of Commerce and Economic
 Development, Corporations Section
P.O. Box 110808
Juneau, AK 99811
BSC@commerse.state.ak.us.
907-465-2530

Arizona

Ariz. Rev. Stat. §§ 44-1441 et seq.
Office of Secretary of State
1700 W. Washington St.
Phoenix, AZ 85007
www.sosaz.com
602-542-6187

Arkansas

Ark. Code A. §§ 4-71-101 through 4-71-114
Secretary of State
256 State Capitol Building
Little Rock, AR 72201-1094
www.sosweb.state.ar.us
501-682-3405
FAX 501-682-3481

California

Cal. Bus. & Prof. Code §§ 14200 et seq.
Secretary of State
Trademark/Service Marks
1500 11th St., Ste. 345
Sacramento, CA 95814
www.ss.ca.gov/business/ts/ts.htm
916-653-4984

Colorado

Colo. Rev. Stat. §§ 7-70-102 to 7-70-113
Colorado Secretary of State
Corporations Office
1560 Broadway, Suite 200
Denver, CO 80202
303-894-2251

Connecticut

Conn. Gen. Stats, 621a §§ 35-11a et seq.
 and 622a §§ 35-18a et seq.
Secretary of State
Division of Corporations, UCC & Trademarks
Attn: Trademarks
State of Connecticut
30 Trinity St.
Hartford, CT 06106
860-566-1721

Delaware

6 Del. C. §§ 3301 et seq.
State of Delaware
Department of State
Division of Corporations
Attn: Trademark Filings
Townsend Building
P.O. Box 898
Dover, DE 19903
www.state.de.us./corp
302-739-3073

Florida

Fla. Stat. ch. 495.011 et seq.
Corporation Records Bureau,
Division of Corporations
Department of State
P.O. Box 6327
Tallahassee, FL 32301
www.dos.state.fl.us
850-487-6051

Georgia

O.C.G.A. §§ 10-1-440 et seq.
Office of Secretary of State
State of Georgia
306 W. Floyd Towers
2 MLK Drive
Atlanta, GA 30334
www.sos.state.ga.us/corporations/trademarks.htm
404-656-2861

Hawaii

Hawaii Revised Stats. §§ 482 et seq.
Department of Commerce and Consumer Affairs
Business Registration Division
1010 Richards St.
Honolulu, HA 96813
808-586-2730

Idaho

Idaho Code §§ 48-501 et seq. (1979)
Secretary of State
Room 203
Statehouse
Boise, ID 83720
www.idsos.state.id.us
208-334-2300
FAX 208-334-2282

Illinois

Ill. Rev. Stat. 1987, ch. 140, §§ 8-22
Illinois Secretary of State
The Index Dept., Trademark Division
111 E. Monroe
Springfield, IL 62756
www.sos.state.il.us
217-782-7017

Indiana

Indiana Code §§ 24-2-1-1 et seq.
Secretary of State of Indiana
Trademark Division
302 W. Washington, Rm. E.111
Indianapolis, IN 46204
trademarks@sos.state.in.us
317-232-6540

Iowa

Iowa Code ch. 548
Secretary of State
Corporate Division
Hoover Bldg.
Des Moines, IA 50319
www.sos.state.ia.us
515-281-5204

Kansas

K.S.A. §§ 81-111 et seq.
Secretary of State

300 S.W. 10th Ave.
2nd Fl. State Capitol
Topeka, KS 66612
www.ksos.org
785-296-2034

Kentucky

K.R.S. §§ 365.560 to 365.625
Office of Kentucky Secretary of State
Frankfort, KY 40601
www.sos.state.ky.us
502-564-2848

Louisiana

La. Rev. Stat. Ann. §§ 51:211 et seq.
Secretary of State
Corporation Division
P.O. Box 94125
Baton Rouge, LA 70804-9125
www.sec.state.la.us
225-925-4704

Maine

10 M.R.S.A. §§ 1521-1532
State of Maine
Department of State
Division of Public Administration
101 State House Station, Rm. 221
Augusta, ME 04333
www.state.me.us/sos/cec
207-287-4195

Maryland

Md. Ann. Code Art. 41, §§ 3-101 through 3-114
Secretary of State
State House
Annapolis, MD 21404
410-974-5521

Massachusetts

Mass. Laws Ann., Ch. 110 B, §§ 1-16.
Office of Secretary of State
Trademark Division
Rm. 1711
One Ashburton Place
Boston, MA 02108
www.state.ma.us/sec/cor
617-727-8329

Michigan

MSA §§ 18.638(21) through 18.638 (36)

Michigan Department of Commerce

Corporations, Securities and Land
  Development Bureau

Corporation Division

P.O. Box 30054

Lansing, MI 48909-7554

www.cis.state.mi.us./corp/

517-334-6302

Minnesota

M.S.A. §§ 333.001-333.54

Secretary of State of Minnesota

Corporations Division

180 State Office Bldg.

100 Constitution Ave.

St. Paul, MN 55155-1299

www.sos.state.mn.us

651-296-2803

Mississippi

Miss. Code Ann., §§ 75-25-1 through 75-25-27

Office of Secretary of State

P.O. Box 136

Jackson, MS 39201

www.sos.state.ms.us

601-359-1350

FAX 601-359-6344

Missouri

Missouri Rev. Stat. 1978 §§ 417.005 et seq.

Office of Secretary of State

Attn: Trademark Division

P.O. Box 784

Jefferson City, MO 65101

http://mosl.sos.state.mo.us

573-751-4756

Montana

Mont. Code Ann., §§ 30-13-301 et seq. (1985)

Office of Secretary of State

Montana State Capitol

P.O. Box 202801

Helena, MT 59620

www.state.mt.us/sos

406-444-3665

FAX 406-444-3976

Nebraska

R.R.S. 1943, ch. 87 §§ 87.101 et seq.

Secretary of State

State Capitol Bldg.

Lincoln, NE 68509

www.nol.org/home/sos

402-471-4079

Nevada

Nev. Rev. Stat. §§ 600.040 et seq.

Secretary of State of Nevada

Capitol Complex

101 N. Carson St., Ste. #3

Carson City, NV 89701-4786

http://sos.state.nv.us

775-684-5708

New Hampshire

RSA 350-A

Corporation Division

Office of Secretary of State

State House Annex

Concord, NH 03301

603-271-3244

New Jersey

N. J. Stat. §§ 56:3-13.1 through 56:3-13.19

Secretary of State

State House

P.O. Box 300

West State Street

Trenton, NJ 08625

www.state.nj.us/state

609-984-1900

New Mexico

N.M.S.A. §§ 57-3-1 through 57-3-14

Secretary of State

Capitol Bldg. Rm. 420

Santa Fe, NM 87503

www.sos.state.nm.us

or 164.64.217.55

505-827-3600

New York

N. Y. Gen. Bus. Law §§ 360 et seq.
Secretary of State
Department of State
Miscellaneous Records
41 State St.
Albany, NY 12231
www.dos.state.ny.us/corp/corpwww.html
518-473-2492

North Carolina

N.C.G.S. §§ 80-1 et seq.
Trademark Division
Office of Secretary of State
300 N. Salisbury Street
Raleigh, NC 27611
www.state.nc.us/secstate/
919-733-4161

North Dakota

N.D.C.C., ch. 47-22 through 47-22-13
Secretary of State
600 E. Blvd. Ave., Dept. 108
Bismarck, ND 58505-0500
www.state.nd.us/sec/
701-328-4284
FAX 701-328-2992

Ohio

ORC, ch. 1329.54 through 1329.68
Secretary of State
Corporations Department
30 E. Broad St., 14th Floor
Columbus, OH 43215-0418
614-466-3910

Oklahoma

78 Okla. St. Ann. §§ 21 through 34
Office of the Secretary of State
State of Oklahoma
2300 N. Lincoln Blvd., Room 101
Oklahoma City, OK 73105-4897
405-521-3911

Oregon

ORS §§ 647.005 through 647.105(i) and 647.115
Director, Corporation Division

Office of Secretary of State
255 Capitol St., NE, Ste. 151
Salem, OR 97310
www.sos.state.or.us
503-986-2200

Pennsylvania

54 Pa. Cons. Stat. Ann. §§ 1101-1126
  (Purdon 1987 Supp.)
Department of State
Corporation Bureau
308 North Office Bldg.
Harrisburg, PA 17120
www.state.pa.us
717-787-1057

Puerto Rico

Title 10, Laws of P. R. Ann. §§ 191 through 215
Secretary of State of Puerto Rico
P.O. Box 3271
San Juan, PR 00904
809-722-2121, Ext. 337

Rhode Island

R. I. Gen. Laws §§ 6-2-1 through 6-2-18
Secretary of State
The Trademarks Division
100 No. Main St.
Providence, RI 02903
www.state.ri.us
401-222-2340

South Carolina

S. C. Code Ann. §§ 39-15-1105 et seq.
Office of Secretary of State
P.O. Box 11350
Columbia, SC 29211
803-734-2158

South Dakota

SDCL ch. 37-6-1 through 37-6-32
Secretary of State
State Capitol Bldg.
500 East Capitol
Pierre, SD 57501
www.state.sd.us/state/executive/sos/sos.htm
605-773-3537

Tennessee

Tenn. Code Ann. §§ 47-25-501 et seq.
Secretary of State
Suite 1800
James K. Polk Bldg.
Nashville, TN 37243
www.state.tn.us/sos
615-741-0531

Texas

Tex. Bus. & Com. Code §§ 16.01 through 16.28
Secretary of State
Corporations Section, Trademark Office
Box 13697, Capitol Station
Austin, TX 78711-3697
www.sos.state.tx.us/
512-463-5576

Utah

U.C.A. §§ 70-3-1 et seq.
Division of Corporations & Commercial Code
Heber M. Wells Bldg.
160 E. 300 South
Salt Lake City, UT 84111
 or P.O. Box 146705
Salt Lake City, UT 84114-6705
www.commerce.state.ut.us
801-530-4849

Vermont

§ 9 V.S.A. §§ 2521 through 2532
Vermont Secretary of State
Corporations Division
Mail: State Office Bldg.
109 State St.
Montpelier, VT 05609-1104
www.sec.state.vt.us
802-828-2386

Virginia

Va. Code §§ 59.1-77 et seq.
State Corp. Commission

Division of Securities and Retail Franchises
1220 Bank Street
Richmond, VA 23209
804-786-2441

Washington

R.C.W. §§ 19.77.010 et seq.
Corporations Division
Office of Secretary of State
505 E. Union St., 2nd Floor
P.O. Box 40234
Olympia, WA 98504-0234
www.secstate.wa.gov/corps/default.htm
360-753-7115

West Virginia

W. Va. Code §§ 47-2-1- et seq. and §§ 47-3-1 et seq.
Secretary of State
Corporations Division
State Capitol, Bldg. 1, Rm. W139
Charleston, WV 25305
304-558-8000

Wisconsin

Wisconsin Stat. §§ 132.01 et seq.
Secretary of State
Trademark Records
P.O. Box 7848
Madison, WI 53707
http://badger.state.wi.us/agencies/sos
608-266-5653

Wyoming

W.S. §§ 40-1-101 et seq.
Office of Secretary of State
Corporation Division
Capitol Bldg.
Cheyenne, WY 82002
http://soswy.state.wy.us
307-777-7311

Patent and Trademark Depository Libraries

Reprinted with permission, from *Patent It Yourself,* by David Pressman (Nolo).

Alabama
Auburn University Libraries
334-844-1747

Birmingham Public Library
205-226-3620

Alaska
Anchorage: Z.J. Loussac Public Library
907-562-7323

Arizona
Tempe: Noble Library, Arizona State University
602-965-7010

Arkansas
Little Rock: Arkansas State Library
501-682-2053

California
Los Angeles Public Library
213-228-7220

Sacramento: California State Library
916-654-0069

San Diego Public Library
619-236-5813

San Francisco Public Library
415-557-4500

Santa Rosa: Bruce Sawyer Center
(not a PTDL, but useful)
707-524-1773

Sunnyvale Center for Innovation
408-730-7290

Colorado
Denver Public Library
303-640-6220

Connecticut
Hartford: Hartford Public Library
860-543-8628

New Haven: New Haven Free Public Library
203-946-8130

Delaware
Newark: University of Delaware Library
302-831-2965

District of Columbia
Washington: Howard University Libraries
202-806-7252

Florida
Fort Lauderdale: Broward County Main Library
954-357-7444

Miami: Dade Public Library
305-375-2665

Orlando: Univ. of Central Florida Libraries
407-823-2562

Tampa: Tampa Campus Library,
University of South Florida
813-974-2726

Georgia
Atlanta: Price Gilbert Memorial Library,
Georgia Institute of Technology
404-894-4508

Hawaii
Honolulu: Hawaii State Public Library System
808-586-3477

Idaho
Moscow: University of Idaho Library
208-885-6235

Illinois
Chicago Public Library
312-747-4450

Springfield: Illinois State Library
217-782-5659

Indiana
Indianapolis: Marion County Public Library
317-269-1741

West Lafayette: Purdue University Libraries
317-494-2872

Iowa
Des Moines: State Library of Iowa
515-281-4118

Kansas
Wichita: Ablah Library, Wichita State University
316-978-3155

Kentucky
Louisville Free Public Library
502-574-1611

Louisiana
Baton Rouge: Troy H. Middleton Library,
Louisiana State University
504-388-8875

Maine
Orono: Raymond H. Fogler Library,
University of Maine
207-581-1678

Maryland
College Park: Engineering and Physical Sciences
Library, University of Maryland
301-405-9157

Massachusetts
Amherst: Physical Sciences Library,
University of Massachusetts
413-545-1370

Boston Public Library
617-536-5400, Ext. 265

Michigan
Ann Arbor: Media Union Library,
University of Michigan
313-647-5735

Big Rapids: Abigail S. Timme Library,
Ferris State University
616-592-3602

Detroit Public Library
313-833-3379

Minnesota
Minneapolis Public Library and Information Center
612-630-6120

Mississippi
Jackson: Mississippi Library Commission
601-359-1036

Missouri
Kansas City: Linda Hall Library
816-363-4600

St. Louis Public Library
314-241-2288, Ext. 390

Montana
Butte: Montana College of Mineral
Science & Technology Library
406-496-4281

Nebraska
Lincoln: Engineering Library,
University of Nebraska
402-472-3411

Nevada
Reno: University of Nevada-Reno Library
702-784-6500, Ext. 257

New Hampshire
Concord: New Hampshire State Library
603-271-2239

New Jersey
Newark Public Library
973-733-7779

Piscataway: Library of Science & Medicine,
Rutgers University
732-445-2895

New Mexico
Albuquerque: University of New Mexico
General Library
505-277-4412

New York
Albany: New York State Library
518-474-5355

Buffalo and Erie County Public Library
716-858-7101

New York Science, Industry & Business Library
212-592-7000

Stony Brook: Engineering Library, SUNY
516-632-7148

North Carolina
Raleigh: D.H. Hill Library,
North Carolina State University
919-515-2935

North Dakota
Grand Forks: Chester Fritz Library,
University of North Dakota
701-777-4888

Ohio
Akron: Summit County Public Library
330-643-9075

Cincinnati and Hamilton County,
Public Library of
513-369-6971

Cleveland Public Library
216-623-2870

Columbus: Ohio State University Libraries
614-292-6175

Toledo/Lucas County Public Library
419-259-5212

Oklahoma
Stillwater: Oklahoma State University Library
405-744-7086

Oregon
Portland: Paul L. Boley Law Library,
Lewis & Clark College
503-768-6786

Pennsylvania
Philadelphia, The Free Library of
215-686-5331

Pittsburgh, Carnegie Library of
412-622-3138

University Park: Pattee Library,
Pennsylvania State University
814-865 4861

Puerto Rico
Mayaguez General Library, University of Puerto Rico
787-832-4040, Ext. 3459

Rhode Island
Providence Public Library
401-455-8027

South Carolina
R.M. Cooper Library, Clemson University
864-656-3024

South Dakota
Rapid City: Devereaux Library,
South Dakota School of Mines and Technology
605-394-1275

Tennessee
Memphis & Shelby County Public Library and
Information Center
901-725-8877

Nashville: Stevenson Science Library,
Vanderbilt University
615-322-2717

Texas
Austin: McKinney Engineering Library,
University of Texas at Austin
512-495-4500

College Station: Sterling C. Evans Library,
Texas A & M University
409-845-3826

Dallas Public Library
214-670-1468

Houston: The Fondren Library, Rice University
713-527-8101, Ext. 2587

South Central Intellectual Property Partnership at
Rice University (SCIPPR)
713-285-5196

Lubbock: Texas Tech University
806-742-2282

Utah
Salt Lake City: Marriott Library, University of Utah
801-581-8394

Vermont
Burlington: Bailey/Howe Library,
University of Vermont
802-656-2542

Virginia
Richmond: James Branch Cabell Library,
Virginia Commonwealth University
804-828-1104

Washington
Seattle: Engineering Library,
University of Washington
206-543-0740

West Virginia
Morgantown: Evansdale Library,
West Virginia University
304-293-2510, Ext. 5113

Wisconsin
Madison: Kurt F. Wendt Library,
University of Wisconsin
608-262-6845

Milwaukee Public Library
414-286-3051

Wyoming
Casper: Natrona County Public Library
307-237-4935

C

Class Descriptions

International Schedule of Classes of Goods and Services

Goods

1. Chemical products used in industry, science, photography, agriculture, horticulture, forestry; artificial and synthetic resins; plastics in the form of powders, liquids or pastes, for industrial use; manures (natural and artificial); fire extinguishing compositions; tempering substances and chemical preparations for soldering; chemical substances for preserving foodstuffs; tanning substances; adhesive substances used in industry.

2. Paints, varnishes, lacquers; preservatives against rust and against deterioration of wood; colouring matters, dyestuffs; mordants; natural resins; metals in foil and powder form for painters and decorators.

3. Bleaching preparations and other substances for laundry use; cleaning, polishing, scouring and abrasive preparations; soaps; perfumery, essential oils, cosmetics, hair lotions; dentifrices.

4. Industrial oils and greases (other than oils and fats and essential oils); lubricants; dust laying and absorbing compositions; fuels (including motor spirit) and illuminants; candles, tapers, night lights and wicks.

5. Pharmaceutical, veterinary, and sanitary substances; infants' and invalids' foods; plasters, material for bandaging; material for stopping teeth, dental wax, disinfectants; preparations for killing weeds and destroying vermin.

6. Unwrought and partly wrought common metals and their alloys; anchors, anvils, bells, rolled and cast building materials; rails and other metallic materials for railway tracks; chains (except driving chains for vehicles); cables and wires (nonelectric); locksmiths' work; metallic pipes and tubes; safes and cash boxes; steel balls; horseshoes; nails and screws; other goods in nonprecious metal not included in other classes; ores.

7. Machines and machine tools; motors (except for land vehicles); machine couplings and belting (except for land vehicles); large size agricultural implements; incubators.

8. Hand tools and instruments; cutlery, forks and spoons; side arms.

9. Scientific, nautical, surveying and electrical apparatus and instruments (including wireless), photographic, cinematographic, optical, weighing, measuring, signalling, checking (supervision), life-saving and teaching apparatus and instruments; coin or counterfreed apparatus; talking machines; cash registers; calculating machines; fire extinguishing apparatus.

10. Surgical, medical, dental, and veterinary instruments and apparatus (including artificial limbs, eyes and teeth).

11. Installations for lighting, heating, steam generating, cooking, refrigerating, drying, ventilating, water supply, and sanitary purposes.

12. Vehicles; apparatus for locomotion by land, air or water.

13. Firearms; ammunition and projectiles; explosive substances; fireworks.

14. Precious metals and their alloys and goods in precious metals or coated therewith (except cutlery forks and spoons); jewelry, precious stones, horological and other chronometric instruments.

15. Musical instruments (other than talking machines and wireless apparatus).

16. Paper and paper articles, cardboard and cardboard articles; printed matter, newspaper and periodicals, books; bookbinding material; photographs; stationery, adhesive materials (stationery); artists' materials; paint brushes; typewriters and office requisites (other than furniture); instructional and teaching material

(other than apparatus); playing cards; printers' type and cliches (stereotype).

17. Gutta-percha, india rubber, balata and substitutes, articles made from these substances and not included in other classes; plastics in the form of sheets, blocks and rods, being for use in manufacture; materials for packing, stopping or insulating; asbestos, mica and their products; hose pipes (nonmetallic).

18. Leather and imitations of leather, and articles made from these materials and not included in other classes; skins, hides; trunks and travelling bags; umbrellas, parasols and walking sticks; whips, harness and saddlery.

19. Building materials, natural and artificial stone, cement, lime, mortar, plaster and gravel; pipes or earthenware or cement; roadmaking materials; asphalt, pitch and bitumen; portable buildings; stone monuments; chimney pots.

20. Furniture, mirrors, picture frames; articles (not included in other classes) of wood, cork, reeds, cane, wicker, horn, bone, ivory, whalebone, shell, amber, mother-of-pearl, meerschaum, celluloid, substitutes for all these materials, or of plastics.

21. Small domestic utensils and containers (not of precious metals, or coated therewith); combs and sponges; brushes (other than paint brushes); brushmaking materials; instruments and material for cleaning purposes, steel wool; unworked or semi-worked glass (excluding glass used in building); glassware, porcelain and earthenware, not included in other classes.

22. Ropes, string, nets, tents, awnings, tarpaulins, sails, sacks; padding and stuffing materials (hair, kapok, feathers, seaweed, etc.); raw fibrous textile materials.

23. Yarns, threads.

24. Tissues (piece goods); bed and table covers; textile articles not included in other classes.

25. Clothing, including boots, shoes and slippers.

26. Lace and embroidery, ribbons and braid; buttons, press buttons, hooks and eyes, pins and needles; artificial flowers.

27. Carpets, rugs, mats and matting; linoleums and other materials for covering existing floors; wall hangings (nontextile).

28. Games and playthings; gymnastic and sporting articles (except clothing); ornaments and decorations for Christmas trees.

29. Meats, fish, poultry and game; meat extracts; preserved, dried and cooked fruits and vegetables; jellies, jams; eggs, milk and other dairy products; edible oils and fats; preserves, pickles.

30. Coffee, tea, cocoa, sugar, rice, tapioca, sago, coffee substitutes; flour, and preparations made from cereals; bread, biscuits, cakes, pastry and confectionery, ices; honey, treacle; yeast, baking powder; salt, mustard, pepper, vinegar, sauces, spices; ice.

31. Agricultural, horticultural and forestry products and grains not included in other classes; living animals; fresh fruits and vegetables; seeds; live plants and flowers; foodstuffs for animals, malt.

32. Beer, ale and porter; mineral and aerated waters and other nonalcoholic drinks; syrups and other preparations for making beverages.

33. Wines, spirits and liqueurs.

34. Tobacco, raw or manufactured; smokers' articles; machines.

Services

35. Advertising and business.

36. Insurance and financial.

37. Construction and repair.

38. Communication.

39. Transportation and Storage.

40. Material treatment.

41. Education and entertainment.

42. Miscellaneous.

Descriptions of Goods and Services (From USTA—International Classes)*

Goods

Class 1: Chemicals

Chemicals used in industry, science and photography as well as in agriculture, horticulture and forestry; unprocessed artificial resins, unprocessed plastics; manures; fire extinguishing compositions; tempering and soldering preparations; chemical substances for preserving foodstuffs; tanning substances; adhesives used in industry.

This class includes mainly chemical products used in industry, science and agriculture, including those which go to the making of products belonging to other classes.

Includes, in particular: compost; salt for preserving other than for foodstuffs.

Does not include, in particular: chemical products for use in medical science (Cl. 5); fungicides, herbicides and preparations for destroying vermin (Cl. 5); raw natural resins (Cl. 2); salt for preserving foodstuffs (Cl. 30); adhesives for stationery purposes (Cl. 16); straw mulch (Cl. 31).

Class 2: Paints

Paints, varnishes, lacquers; preservatives against rust and against deterioration of wood; colourants; mordants; raw natural resins; metals in foil and powder form for painters, decorators, printers and artists.

This class includes mainly paints, colourants and preparations used for the protection against corrosion.

Includes, in particular: paints, varnishes and lacquers for industry, handicrafts and arts; dye-stuffs for clothing; colourants for foodstuffs and beverages.

Does not include, in particular: laundry blueing (Cl. 3); cosmetic dyes (Cl. 3); insulating paints and varnishes (Cl. 17); paint boxes (articles for use in school) (Cl. 16); unprocessed artificial resins (Cl. 1); mordants for seed (Cl. 5).

Class 3: Cosmetics and cleaning preparations

Bleaching preparations and other substances for laundry use; cleaning, polishing, scouring and abrasive preparations; soaps; perfumery, essential oils, cosmetics, hair lotions; dentifrices.

This class includes mainly cleaning preparations and toilet preparations.

Includes, in particular: deodorants for personal use; sanitary preparations being toiletries.

Does not include, in particular: chemical chimney cleaners (Cl. 1); de-greasing preparations for use in manufacturing processes (Cl. 1); sharpening stones and grindstones (handtools) (Cl. 8); deodorants other than for personal use (Cl. 5).

Class 4: Lubricants and fuels

Industrial oils and greases; lubricants; dust absorbing, wetting and binding compositions; fuels (including motor spirit) and illuminants; candles, wicks.

This class includes mainly industrial oils and greases, fuels and illuminants.

Does not include, in particular: certain special industrial oils and greases (consult the Alphabetical List of Goods).

Class 5: Pharmaceuticals

Pharmaceutical, veterinary and sanitary preparations; dietetic substances adapted for medical use, food for babies; plasters, materials for dressings; material for stopping teeth, dental wax; disinfectants; preparations for destroying vermin; fungicides, herbicides.

---

* Adapted from *The Trademark Manual of Examining Procedure,* published by the U.S. Trademark and Patent Office.

This class includes mainly pharmaceuticals and other preparations for medical purposes.

Includes, in particular: sanitary preparations for medical purposes and for personal hygiene; deodorants other than for personal use; cigarettes without tobacco, for medical purposes.

Does not include, in particular: sanitary preparations being toiletries (Cl. 3); deodorants for personal use (Cl. 3); supportive bandages (Cl. 10).

Class 6: Metal goods

Common metals and their alloys; metal building materials; transportable buildings of metal; materials of metal for railway tracks; non-electric cables and wires of common metal; ironmongery, small items of metal hardware; pipes and tubes of metal; safes; goods of common metal not included in other classes; ores.

This class includes mainly unwrought and partly wrought common metals as well as simple products made of them.

Does not include, in particular: mercury, antimony, alkaline and alkaline-earth metals (Cl. 1); metals in foil and powder form for painters, decorators, printers and artists (Cl. 2); bauxite (Cl. 1).

Class 7: Machinery

Machines and machine tools; motors (except for land vehicles); machine coupling and belting (except for land vehicles); agricultural implements; incubators for eggs.

This class includes mainly machines, machine tools, engines and motors.

Does not include, in particular: certain special machines and machine tools (consult the Alphabetical List of Goods); motors for land vehicles and their parts (Cl. 12); hand tools and implements, hand operated (Cl. 8).

Class 8: Hand tools

Hand tools and implements (hand operated); cutlery, forks and spoons; side arms; razors.

This class includes mainly hand operated implements used as tools in the respective professions.

Includes, in particular: cutlery of precious metals; electric razors and clippers (hand instruments).

Does not include, in particular: certain special instruments (consult the Alphabetical List of Goods); machine tools and implements driven by a motor (Cl. 7); surgical cutlery (Cl. 10); paper-knives (Cl. 16); fencing weapons (Cl. 28).

Class 9: Electrical and scientific apparatus

Scientific, nautical, surveying, electric, photographic, cinematographic, optical, weighing, measuring, signalling, checking (supervision), life-saving and teaching apparatus and instruments; apparatus for recording, transmission or reproduction of sound or images; magnetic data carriers, recording discs; automatic vending machines and mechanisms for coin-operated apparatus; cash registers, calculating machines and data processing equipment; fire-extinguishing apparatus.

Includes, in particular: apparatus and instruments for scientific research in laboratories; apparatus and instruments for controlling ships, such as apparatus and instruments, for measuring and for transmitting orders; the following electrical apparatus and instruments:

    a. certain electrothermic tools and apparatus, such as electric soldering irons, electric flat irons which, if they were not electric, would belong to Class 8;

    b. apparatus and devices which, if not electrical, would be listed in various classes, i.e., electrically heated cushions (not for medical purposes), electric kettles, electrically heated clothing and other articles worn on the body, cigar-lighters for automobiles;

    c. electrical apparatus for the household, used for cleaning (electric suction-cleaners and floor polishers for domestic use) which, if not electrical, would belong to Class 21;

protractors; punched card office machines; amusement apparatus adapted for use with television receivers only.

Does not include, in particular: the following electrical apparatus and instruments:

a. electromechanical apparatus for the kitchen (grinders and mixers for foodstuffs, fruitpresses, electrical coffee mills, etc.), and certain other apparatus and instruments driven by an electrical motor, all coming under Class 7;

b. electric razors and clippers (hand instruments) (Cl. 8); electric toothbrushes and combs (Cl. 21);

c. electrically heated blankets (Cl. 10); electrical apparatus for space heating or for the heating of liquids, for cooking, ventilating, etc. (Cl. 11);

clocks and watches and other chronometric instruments (Cl. 14); control clocks (Cl. 14).

Class 10: Medical apparatus

Surgical, medical, dental and veterinary apparatus and instruments, artificial limbs, eyes and teeth; orthopedic articles; suture materials.

This class includes mainly medical apparatus, instruments and articles.

Includes, in particular: special furniture for medical use; hygienic rubber articles (consult the Alphabetical List of Goods); supportive bandages.

Class 11: Environmental control apparatus

Apparatus for lighting, heating, steam generating, cooking, refrigerating, drying, ventilating, water supply and sanitary purposes.

Includes, in particular: air conditioning apparatus; electric foot-warmers; electric cooking utensils.

Does not include, in particular: steam producing apparatus (parts of machines) (Cl. 7); electric kettles (Cl. 9).

Class 12: Vehicles

Vehicles; apparatus for locomotion by land, air or water.

Includes, in particular: engines for land vehicles; transmission couplings and belting for land vehicles; air cushion vehicles.

Does not include, in particular: certain parts of vehicles (consult the Alphabetical List of Goods); railway material of metal (Cl. 6); engines, transmission couplings and belting other than for land vehicles (Cl. 7).

Class 13: Firearms

Firearms; ammunition and projectiles; explosives; fireworks.

This class includes mainly firearms and pyrotechnical products.

Does not include, in particular: matches (Cl. 34).

Class 14: Jewelry

Precious metals and their alloys and goods in precious metals or coated therewith, not included in other classes; jewelry, precious stones; horological and chronometric instruments.

This class includes mainly precious metals, goods in precious metals and, in general jewelry, clocks and watches.

Includes, in particular: jewelry (i.e., imitation jewelry and jewelry of precious metal and stones); cuff links, tie pins; objects of art fashioned in bronze.

Does not include, in particular: certain goods in precious metals (classified according to their function or purpose), for example: metals in foil and powder form for painters, decorators, printers and artists (Cl. 2); amalgam of gold for dentists (Cl. 5); cutlery (Cl. 8); electric contacts (Cl. 9); writing pens of gold (Cl. 16); objects of art not in precious metal nor in bronze are classified according to the material of which they consist.

Class 15: Musical Instruments

Musical instruments.

Includes, in particular: mechanical pianos and their accessories; musical boxes; electrical and electronical musical instruments.

Does not include, in particular: apparatus for the recording, transmission, amplification and reproduction of sound (Cl. 9).

Class 16: Paper goods and printed matter

Paper, cardboard and goods made from these materials, not included in other classes; printed matter; bookbinding material, photographs; stationery; adhesives for stationery or household purposes; artists' materials; paint brushes; type-writers and office requisites (except furniture); instructional and teaching material (except apparatus); plastic materials for packaging (not included in other classes); playing cards; printers' type; printing blocks.

This class includes mainly paper, goods made from that material and office requisites.

Includes, in particular: paper-knives; duplicators; plastic sheets, sacks and bags for wrapping and packaging.

Does not include, in particular: certain goods made of paper and cardboard (consult the Alphabetical List of Goods); colours (Cl. 2); hand tools for artists (for example: spatulas, sculptors' chisels) (Cl. 8).

Class 17: Rubber goods

Rubber, gutta-percha, gum, asbestos, mica and goods made from these materials and not in-cluded in other classes; plastics in extruded form for use in manufacture; packing, stopping and insulating materials; flexible pipes, not of metal.

This class includes mainly electrical, thermal and acoustic insulating materials and plastics, being for use in manufacture in the form of sheets, blocks and rods.

Includes, in particular: rubber material for recapping tyres; padding and stuffing materials of rubber or plastics; floating anti-pollution barriers.

Class 18: Leather goods

Leather and imitations of leather, and goods made of these materials and not included in other classes; animal skins, hides; trunks and travelling bags; umbrellas, parasols and walking sticks; whips; harness and saddlery.

This class includes mainly leather, leather imitations, travel goods not included in other classes and saddlery.

Does not include, in particular: clothing, footwear, headgear (consult the Alphabetical List of Goods).

Class 19: Non-metallic building materials

Building materials (non-metallic); non-metallic rigid pipes for building; asphalt, pitch and bitumen; non-metallic transportable buildings; monuments, not of metal.

This class includes mainly non-metallic building materials.

Includes, in particular: semi-worked woods (for example: beams, planks, panels); veneers; building glass (for example: floor slabs, glass tiles); glass granules for marking out roads; letter boxes of masonry.

Does not include, in particular: cement preser-vatives and cement-waterproofing preparations (Cl. 1); fireproofing preparations (Cl. 1).

Class 20: Furniture and articles not otherwise classified

Furniture, mirrors, picture frames; goods (not included in other classes) of wood, cork, reed, cane, wicker, horn, bone, ivory, whalebone, shell, amber, mother-of-pearl, meerschaum and substitutes for all these materials, or of plastics.

This class includes mainly furniture and its parts and plastic goods, not included in other classes.

Includes, in particular: metal furniture and furniture for camping; bedding (for example: mattresses, spring mattresses, pillows); looking glasses and furnishing or toilet mirrors; registra-tion number plates not of metal; letter boxes not of metal or masonry.

Does not include, in particular: certain special types of mirrors, classified according to their function or purpose (consult the Alphabetical List of Goods); special furniture for laboratories (Cl. 9); special furniture for medical use (Cl. 10); bedding linen (Cl. 24); eiderdowns (Cl. 24).

Class 21: Housewares and glass

Household or kitchen utensils and containers (not of precious metal or coated therewith); combs and sponges; brushes (except paint brushes); brush-making materials; articles for cleaning purposes; steel wool; unworked or semi-worked glass (except glass used in building); glassware, porcelain and earthenware not included in other classes.

This class includes mainly small, hand-operated, utensils and apparatus for household and kitchen use as well as toilet utensils, glassware and articles in porcelain.

Includes, in particular: utensils and containers for household and kitchen use, for example: kitchen utensils, pails, and pans of iron, aluminum, plastics and other materials, small hand-operated apparatus for mincing, grinding, pressing, etc.; candle extinguishers, not of precious metal; electric combs; electric toothbrushes; dish stands and decanter stands.

Does not include, in particular: small apparatus for mincing, grinding, pressing, etc., driven by electricity (Cl. 7); cooking utensils, electric (Cl. 11); razors and shaving apparatus, clippers (hand instruments), metal implements and utensils for manicure and pedicure (Cl. 8); cleaning preparations, soaps, etc. (Cl. 3); certain goods made of glass, porcelain and earthenware (consult the Alphabetical List of Goods); toilet mirrors (Cl. 20).

Class 22: Cordage and fibers
Ropes, string, nets, tents, awnings, tarpaulins, sails, sacks and bags (not included in other classes); padding and stuffing materials (except of rubber or plastics); raw fibrous textile materials.

This class includes mainly rope and sail manufacture products, padding and stuffing materials and raw fibrous textile materials.

Includes, in particular: cords and twines in natural or artificial textile fibres, paper or plastics.

Does not include, in particular: strings for musical instruments (Cl. 15); certain nets, sacs and bags (consult the Alphabetical List of Goods).

Class 23: Yarns and threads
Yarns and threads, for textile use.

Class 24: Fabrics
Textiles and textile goods, not included in other classes; bed and table covers.

This class includes mainly textiles (piece goods) and textile covers for household use.

Includes, in particular: bedding linen of paper.

Does not include, in particular: certain special textiles (consult the Alphabetical List of Goods); electrically heated blankets (Cl. 10); table linen of paper (Cl. 16); horse blankets (Cl. 18).

Class 25: Clothing
Clothing, footwear, headgear.

Does not include, in particular: certain clothing and footwear for special use (consult the Alphabetical List of Goods).

Class 26: Fancy goods
Lace and embroidery, ribbons and braid; buttons, hooks and eyes, pins and needles; artificial flowers.

This class includes mainly dressmakers' articles.

Includes, in particular: slide fasteners.

Does not include, in particular: certain special types of hooks (consult the Alphabetical List of Goods); certain special types of needles (consult the Alphabetical List of Goods); yarns and threads for textile use (Cl. 23).

Class 27: Floor coverings
Carpets, rugs, mats and matting, linoleum and other materials for covering existing floors; wall hangings (non-textile).

This class includes mainly products intended to be added as furnishings to previously constructed floors and walls.

Class 28: Toys and sporting goods
Games and playthings; gymnastic and sporting articles not included in other classes; decorations for Christmas trees.

Includes, in particular: fishing tackle; equipment for various sports and games.

Does not include, in particular: playing cards (Cl. 16); diving equipment (Cl. 9); clothing for gymnastics and sports (Cl. 25); fishing nets (Cl. 22); Christmas tree candles (Cl. 4); electrical lamps (garlands) for Christmas trees (Cl. 11); confectionery and chocolate decorations for Christmas trees (Cl. 30); amusement apparatus adapted for use with television receivers only (Cl. 9).

Class 29: Meat and processed foods
Meat, fish, poultry and game; meat extracts; preserved, dried and cooked fruits and vegetables; jellies, jams; eggs, milk and milk products; edible oils and fats; salad dressings; preserves.

This class includes mainly foodstuffs of animal origin as well as vegetables and other horticultural comestible products which are prepared for consumption or conservation.

Includes, in particular: mollusca and crustacea (living as well as not living); milk beverages (milk predominating).

Does not include, in particular: living animals (Cl. 31); certain foodstuffs of plant origin (consult the Alphabetical List of Goods); baby food (Cl. 5); dietetic substances adapted for medical use (Cl. 5); fertilized eggs for hatching (Cl. 31); foodstuffs for animals (Cl. 31).

Class 30: Staple foods
Coffee, tea, cocoa, sugar, rice, tapioca, sago, artificial coffee; flour and preparations made from cereals, bread, pastry and confectionery, ices; honey, treacle; yeast, baking-powder; salt, mustard; vinegar, sauces (except salad dressings); spices; ice.

This class includes mainly foodstuffs of plant origin prepared for consumption or conservation as well as auxiliaries intended for the improvement of the flavour of food.

Includes, in particular: beverages with coffee, cocoa or chocolate base, cereals prepared for human consumption (for example: oat flakes and those made of other cereals).

Does not include, in particular: certain foodstuffs of plant origin (consult the Alphabetical List of Goods); salt for preserving other than for foodstuffs (Cl. 1); medicinal teas and dietetic substances adapted for medical use (Cl. 5); baby food (Cl. 5); raw cereals (Cl. 31); foodstuffs for animals (Cl. 31).

Class 31: Natural agricultural products
Agricultural, horticultural and forestry products and grains not included in other classes; living animals; fresh fruits and vegetables; seeds, natural plants and flowers; foodstuffs for animals, malt.

This class includes mainly land products not having been subjected to any form of preparation for consumption, living animals and plants as well as foodstuffs for animals.

Includes, in particular: raw woods; raw cereals; fertilized eggs for hatching.

Does not include, in particular: semi-worked woods (Cl. 19); rice (Cl. 30); tobacco (Cl. 34); cultures of micro-organisms and leeches for medical purposes (Cl. 5); fishing bait (Cl. 28); mollusca and crustacea (living as well as not living) (Cl. 29).

Class 32: Light beverages
Beers; mineral and aerated waters and other non-alcoholic drinks; fruit drinks and fruit juices; syrups and other preparations for making beverages.

This class includes mainly non-alcoholic beverages, as well as beer.

Includes, in particular: de-alcoholised drinks.

Does not include, in particular: beverages for medical purposes (Cl. 5); milk beverages (milk predominating) (Cl. 29); beverages with coffee, cocoa or chocolate base (Cl. 30).

Class 33: Wine and spirits
Alcoholic beverages (except beers).

Does not include, in particular: medicinal drinks (Cl. 5); de-alcoholised drinks (Cl. 32).

Class 34: Smokers' articles
Tobacco; smokers' articles; matches.

Includes, in particular: tobacco substitutes (not for medical purposes).

Does not include, in particular: certain smokers' articles in precious metal (Cl. 14) (consult the Alphabetical List of Goods); cigarettes without tobacco, for medical purposes (Cl.5).

Services

Class 35: Advertising and business

This class includes mainly services rendered by persons or organizations principally with the object of:

1. help in the working or management of a commercial undertaking, or
2. help in the management of the business affairs or commercial functions of an industrial or commercial enterprise, as well as services rendered by advertising establishments primarily undertaking communications to the public, declarations or announcements by all means of diffusion and concerning all kinds of goods or services.

Includes, in particular: services consisting of the registration, transcription, composition, compilation, transmission or systematization of written communications and registrations, and also the exploitation or compilation of mathematical or statistical data; services of advertising agencies and services such as the distribution of prospectuses, directly or through the post, or the distribution of samples. This class may refer to advertising in connection with other services, such as those concerning bank loans or advertising by radio.

Does not include, in particular: activity of an enterprise the primary function of which is the sale of goods, i.e., of a so-called commercial enterprise; services such as evaluations and reports of engineers which do not directly refer to the working or management of affairs in a commercial or industrial enterprise (consult the Alphabetical List of Services); professional consultations and the drawing up of plans not connected with the conduct of business (Cl. 42).

Class 36: Insurance and financial

This class includes mainly services rendered in financial and monetary affairs and services rendered in relation to insurance contracts of all kinds.

Includes, in particular: services relating to financial or monetary affairs comprise the following:

a. services of all the banking establishments, or institutions connected with them such as exchange brokers or clearing services;
b. services of credit institutions other than banks such as co-operative credit associations, individual financial companies, lenders, etc.;
c. services of "investment trusts," of holding companies;
d. services of brokers dealing in shares and property;
e. services connected with monetary affairs vouched for by trustees;
f. services rendered in connection with the issue of travelers' cheques and letters of credit; services of realty administrators of buildings, i.e., services of letting or valuation, or financing; services dealing with insurance such as services rendered by agents or brokers engaged in insurance, services rendered to insurers and insured, and insurance underwriting services.

Class 37: Construction and repair

This class includes mainly services rendered by contractors or subcontractors in the construction or making of permanent buildings, as well as services rendered by persons or organisations engaged in the restoration of objects to their original condition or in their preservation without altering their physical or chemical properties.

Includes, in particular: services relating to the construction of buildings, roads, bridges, dams or transmission lines and services of undertakings specializing in the field of construction such as those of painters, plumbers, heating installers or roofers; services auxiliary to construction services like inspections of construction plans; services consisting of hiring of tools or building materials; repair services, i.e. services which undertake to put any object into good condition after wear, damage, deterioration or partial destruction (restoration of an existing building or another object that has become imperfect and is to be restored to its original condition); various repair services such as those in the fields of electricity, furniture, instruments, tools, etc.; services of maintenance for preserving an object in its original condition without changing any of its properties (for the difference between this class and Class 40 see the explanatory note of Class 40).

Does not include, in particular: services consisting of storage of goods such as clothes or vehicles (Cl. 39); services connected with dyeing of cloth or clothes (Cl. 40).

Class 38: Communication

This class includes mainly services allowing at least one person to communicate with another by a sensory means. Such services include those which:

1. allow a person to talk to another,
2. transmit messages from one person to another, and
3. place a person in oral or visual communication with another (radio and television).

Includes, in particular: services which consist essentially of the diffusion of radio or television programmes.

Does not include, in particular: radio advertising services (Cl. 35).

Class 39: Transportation and storage

This class includes mainly services rendered in transporting people or goods from one place to another (by rail, road, water, air or pipeline) and services necessarily connected with such transport, as well as services relating to the storing of goods in a warehouse or other building for their preservation or guarding.

Includes, in particular: services rendered by companies exploiting stations, bridges, railroad ferries, etc., used by the transporter; services connected with the hiring of transport vehicles; services connected with maritime tugs, unloading, the functioning of ports and docks and the salvaging of wrecked ships and their cargoes; services connected with the functioning of air-

ports; services connected with the packaging and parcelling of goods before dispatch; services consisting of information about journeys or the transport of goods by brokers and tourist agencies, information relating to tariffs, timetables and methods of transport; services relating to the inspection of vehicles or goods before transport.

Does not include, in particular: services relating to advertising transport undertakings such as the distribution of prospectuses or advertising on the radio (Cl. 35); services relating to the issuing of travelers' cheques or letters of credit by brokers or travel agents (Cl. 36); services relating to insurances (commercial, fire or life) during the transport of persons or goods (Cl. 36); services rendered by the maintenance and repair of vehicles, nor the maintenance or repair of objects connected with the transport of persons or goods (Cl. 37); services relating to reservation of rooms in a hotel by travel agents or brokers (Cl. 42).

Class 40: Material treatment

This class includes mainly services not included in other classes, rendered by the mechanical or chemical processing or transformation of objects or inorganic or organic substances.

For the purposes of classification, the mark is considered a service mark only in cases where processing or transformation is effected for the account of another person. A mark is considered a trademark in all cases where the substance or object is marketed by the person who processed or transformed it.

Includes, in particular: services relating to transformation of an object or substance and any process involving a change in its essential properties (for example, dyeing a garment); consequently, a maintenance service, although usually in Class 37, is included in Class 40 if it entails such a change (for example, the chroming of motor vehicle bumpers); services of material treatment which may be present during production of any substance or object other than a building; for example, services which involve shaping, polishing by abrasion or metal coating.

Does not include, in particular: repair services (Cl. 37).

Class 41: Education and entertainment

This class contains mainly services rendered by persons or institutions in the development of the mental faculties of persons or animals, as well as services intended to entertain or to engage the attention.

Includes, in particular: services consisting of all forms of education of persons or training of animals; services having the basic aim of the entertainment, amusement or recreation of people.

Class 42: Miscellaneous

This class contains all services which could not be placed in other classes.

Includes, in particular: services rendered in procuring lodgings, rooms and meals, by hotels, boarding houses, tourist camps, tourist houses, dude ranches, sanatoria, rest homes and convalescence homes; services rendered by establishments essentially engaged in procuring food or drink prepared for consumption; such services can be rendered by restaurants, self-service restaurants, canteens, etc.; personal services rendered by establishments to meet individual needs; such services may include social escorts, beauty salons, hairdressing salons, funeral establishments or crematoria; services rendered by persons, individually or collectively, as a member of an organisation, requiring a high degree of mental activity and relating to theoretical or practical aspects of complex branches of human effort; the services rendered by these persons demand of them a deep and extensive university education or equivalent experience; such services rendered by representatives of professions such as engineers, chemists, physicists, etc., are included in this class; services of travel agents or brokers ensuring hotel accommodation for travelers; services of engineers engaged in valuing, estimates, research and reports; services (not included in other classes) rendered by associations to their own members.

Does not include, in particular: professional services giving direct aid in the operations or functions of a commercial undertaking (Cl. 35); services for travelers rendered by travel agencies (Cl. 39); performances of singers or dancers in orchestras or operas (Cl. 41).

1401.02(b)   Short Titles for International Trademark Classes [R-6]

The United States Patent and Trademark Office associates the following word titles with the respective international trademark class numbers:

Goods

1. Chemicals
2. Paints
3. Cosmetics and cleaning preparations
4. Lubricants and fuels
5. Pharmaceuticals
6. Metal goods
7. Machinery
8. Hand tools
9. Electrical and scientific apparatus
10. Medical apparatus
11. Environmental control apparatus
12. Vehicles
13. Firearms
14. Jewelry
15. Musical instruments
16. Paper goods and printed matter
17. Rubber goods
18. Leather goods
19. Non-metallic building materials
20. Furniture and articles not otherwise classified
21. Housewares and glass
22. Cordage and fibers
23. Yarns and threads
24. Fabrics
25. Clothing
26. Fancy goods
27. Floor coverings
28. Toys and sporting goods

29. Meats and processed foods
30. Staple foods
31. Natural agricultural products
32. Light beverages
33. Wine and spirits
34. Smokers' articles

Services

35. Advertising and business
36. Insurance and financial
37. Construction and repair
38. Communication
39. Transportation and storage
40. Material treatment
41. Education and entertainment
42. Miscellaneous

These short titles are not an official part of the international classification. Their purpose is to provide a means by which the general content of numbered international classes can be quickly identified. Therefore the titles selected consist of short terms which generally correspond to the major content of each class but which are not intended to be more than merely suggestive of the content. Because of their nature these titles will not necessarily disclose the classification of specific items. The titles are not designed to be used for classification but only as information to assist in the identification of numbered classes. For determining classification of particular goods and services and for full disclosure of the contents of international classes, it is necessary to refer to the Alphabetical List of Goods and Services and to the names of international classes and the Explanatory Notes in the volume entitled "International Classification of Goods and Services for the Purposes of the Registration of Marks" (4th ed. 1983), published by the World Intellectual Property Organization (WIPO). The full names of

international classes appear in Section 6.1 of the Trademark Rules of Practice. 37 CFR § 6.1.

The short titles are printed in the OFFICIAL GAZETTE in association with the international class numbers under MARKS PUBLISHED FOR OPPOSITION, Sections 1 and 2, under TRADE-MARK REGISTRATIONS ISSUED, PRINCIPAL REGISTER, Section 1, and under SUPPLEMENTAL REGISTER, Sections 1 and 2.

The international trademark classification was adopted by the United States as its system of classification as of September 1, 1973 (see TMEP section 1401.02 and 911 O.G. TM 210, June 26, 1973).

The use of short titles was announced in the *Official Gazette* of July 16, 1974 (924 O.G. TM 155).

1401.03   Marking Classification on Copies in Search Library (R-5]

Beginning September 1, 1973, all published marks, registrations and renewals will be assigned not only an international class number but also a class number according to prior United States classification.

By placing a prior United States class number, as well as an international class number, on copies of registrations which are placed in the Trademark Search Library after the international classification becomes official, searching may continue to be conducted on the basis of the prior United States classification. Registration copies placed in the Search Library prior to September 1, 1973, bear prior United States class numbers, so that placing prior United States class numbers on registration copies on and after September 1, 1973, will provide continuity in the identification of classes on copies of registrations.

D

Tear-Out Forms

Trademark/Service Mark Application, Principal Register, With Declaration

Allegation of Use for Intent-to-Use Application, With Declaration

Request for Extension of Time to File a Statement of Use, With Declaration

Combined Declaration of Use and Incontestability Under Sections 8 & 15 of the Trademark Act of 1946, As Amended

Application for Renewal of Registration of a Mark Under Section 9 of the Trademark Act of 1946, As Amended

Request to Divide Application

TRADEMARK/SERVICE MARK APPLICATION, PRINCIPAL REGISTER, WITH DECLARATION	MARK (Word(s) and/or Design)	CLASS NO. (If known)

TO THE ASSISTANT COMMISSIONER FOR TRADEMARKS:

APPLICANT'S NAME:

APPLICANT'S MAILING ADDRESS:

(Display address exactly as it should appear on registration)

APPLICANT'S ENTITY TYPE: (**Check one** and supply requested information)

	Individual - Citizen of (Country)
	Partnership - State where organized (Country, if appropriate):_____ Names and Citizenship (Country) of General Partners:_____
	Corporation - State (Country, if appropriate) of Incorporation:
	Other (Specify Nature of Entity and Domicile):

GOODS AND/OR SERVICES:

Applicant requests registration of the trademark/service mark shown in the accompanying drawing in the United States Patent and Trademark Office on the Principal Register established by the Act of July 5, 1946 (15 U.S.C. 1051 et. seq., as amended) for the following goods/services (SPECIFIC GOODS AND/OR SERVICES MUST BE INSERTED HERE) :

BASIS FOR APPLICATION: (Check boxes which apply, **but never both the first AND second boxes,** and supply requested information related to each box checked in.)

[ ]	Applicant is using the mark in commerce on or in connection with the above identified goods/services. (15 U.S.C. 1051(a), as amended.) Three specimens showing the mark as used in commerce are submitted with this application. • Date of first use of the mark in commerce which the U.S. Congress may regulate (for example, interstate or between the U.S. and a foreign country):_____ • Specify the type of commerce:_____ (for example, interstate or between the U.S. and a specified foreign country) • Date of first use anywhere (the same as or before use in commerce date):_____ • Specify manner or mode of use of mark on or in connection with the goods/services:_____ (for example, trademark is applied to labels, service mark is used in advertisements)
[ ]	Applicant has a bona fide intention to use the mark in commerce on or in connection with the above identified goods/services.(15 U.S.C. 1051(b), as amended.) • Specify intended manner or mode of use of mark on or in connection with the goods/services:_____ (for example, trademark will be applied to labels, service mark will be used in advertisements)
[ ]	Applicant has a bona fide intention to use the mark in commerce on or in connection with the above identified goods/services, and asserts a claim of priority based upon a foreign application in accordance with 15 U.S.C. 1126(d), as amended. • Country of foreign filing:_____ •Date of foreign filing:_____
[ ]	Applicant has a bona fide intention to use the mark in commerce on or in connection with the above identified goods/services and, accompanying this application, submits a certification or certified copy of a foreign registration in accordance with 15 U.S.C 1126(e), as amended. • Country of registration:_____ • Registration number:_____

NOTE: Declaration, on Reverse Side, MUST be Signed

PTO Form 1478 (REV 6/96)

U.S. DEPARTMENT OF COMMERCE/Patent and Trademark Office

OMB No. 0651-0009 (Exp. 06/30/98) There is no requirement to respond to this collection of information unless a currently valid OMB Number is displayed.

DECLARATION

The undersigned being hereby warned that willful false statements and the like so made are punishable by fine or imprisonment, or both, under 18 U.S.C. 1001, and that such willful false statements may jeopardize the validity of the application or any resulting registration, declares that he/she is properly authorized to execute this application on behalf of the applicant; he/she believes the applicant to be the owner of the trademark/service mark sought to be registered, or if the application is being filed under 15 U.S.C. 1051(b), he/she believes the applicant to be entitled to use such mark in commerce; to the best of his/her knowledge and belief no other person, firm, corporation, or association has the right to use the above identified mark in commerce, either in the identical form thereof or in such near resemblance thereto as to be likely, when used on or in connection with the goods/services of such other person, to cause confusion, or to cause mistake, or to deceive; and that all statements made of his/her own knowledge are true and that all statements made on information and belief are believed to be true.

_____   _____

DATE   SIGNATURE

_____   _____

TELEPHONE NUMBER   PRINT OR TYPE NAME AND POSITION

INSTRUCTIONS AND INFORMATION FOR APPLICANT

TO RECEIVE A FILING DATE, THE APPLICATION MUST BE COMPLETED AND SIGNED BY THE APPLICANT AND SUBMITTED ALONG WITH:

1. The prescribed **FEE ($245.00)** for each class of goods/services listed in the application;
2. A **DRAWING PAGE** displaying the mark in conformance with 37 CFR 2.52;
3. If the application is based on use of the mark in commerce, **THREE (3) SPECIMENS** (evidence) of the mark as used in commerce for each class of goods/services listed in the application. All three specimens may be the same. Examples of good specimens include: (a) labels showing the mark which are placed on the goods; (b) photographs of the mark as it appears on the goods, (c) brochures or advertisements showing the mark as used in connection with the services.
4. An **APPLICATION WITH DECLARATION** (this form) - The application must be signed in order for the application to receive a filing date. Only the following persons may sign the declaration, depending on the applicant's legal entity: (a) the individual applicant; (b) an officer of the corporate applicant; (c) one general partner of a partnership applicant; (d) all joint applicants.

SEND APPLICATION FORM, DRAWING PAGE, FEE, AND SPECIMENS (IF APPROPRIATE) TO:

Assistant Commissioner for Trademarks
Box New App/Fee
2900 Crystal Drive
Arlington, VA 22202-3513

Additional information concerning the requirements for filing an application is available in a booklet entitled **Basic Facts About Registering a Trademark,** which may be obtained by writing to the above address or by calling: (703) 308-HELP.

ALLEGATION OF USE FOR INTENT-TO-USE APPLICATION, WITH DECLARATION (Amendment To Allege Use/Statement Use)	MARK (Identify the mark)
	SERIAL NO.

TO THE ASSISTANT COMMISSIONER FOR TRADEMARKS:

APPLICANT NAME:

Applicant requests registration of the above-identified trademark/service mark in the United States Patent and Trademark Office on the Principal Register established by the Act of July 5, 1946 (15 U.S.C. §1051 *et seq.*, as amended). Three specimens per class showing the mark as used in commerce and the prescribed fees are submitted with this statement.

Applicant is using the mark in commerce on or in connection with the following goods/services (CHECK ONLY ONE):

☐ (a) those in the application or Notice of Allowance; **OR**

☐ (b) those in the application or Notice of Allowance **except** (if goods/services are to be deleted, list the goods/services to be **deleted**): _____

_____

_____

Date of first use in commerce which the U.S. Congress may regulate:_____
Specify type of commerce: _____
(for example, interstate and/or commerce between the U.S. and a foreign country)
Date of first use anywhere: _____

Specify manner or mode of use of mark on or in connection with the goods/services: (for example, trademark is applied to labels, service mark is used in advertisements):_____

_____

_____

The undersigned, being hereby warned that willful false statements and the like so made are punishable by fine or imprisonment, or both, under 18 U.S.C. §1001, and that such willful false statements may jeopardize the validity of the application or any resulting registration, declares that he/she is properly authorized to execute this Amendment to Allege Use or Statement of Use on behalf of the applicant; he/she believes the applicant to be the owner of the trademark/service mark sought to be registered; the trademark /service mark is now in use in commerce; and all statements made of his/her own knowledge are true and all statements made on information and belief are believed to be true.

_____   _____
Date   Signature

_____   _____
Telephone Number   Type or Print Name and Position

☐ **Check here if Request to Divide is being submitted with this statement** (if Applicant wishes to proceed to publication or registration with certain goods/services on or in connection with which it has used the mark in commerce and retain an active application for any remaining goods/services, a divisional application and fee are required. 37 C.F.R. §2.87)

PLEASE SEE REVERSE FOR MORE INFORMATION

INSTRUCTIONS AND INFORMATION FOR APPLICANT

In an application based upon a bona fide intention to use a mark in commerce, **the Applicant must use its mark in commerce before a registration will be issued.** After use begins, the applicant must file the Allegation of Use. If the Allegation of Use is filed before the mark is approved for publication in the *Official Gazette* it is treated under the statute as **an Amendment to Allege Use (AAU).** If it is filed after the Notice of Allowance is issued, it is treated under the statute as **a Statement of Use (SOU).** The Allegation of Use cannot be filed during the time period between approval of the mark for publication in the *Official Gazette* and the issuance of the Notice of Allowance. The difference between the AAU and SOU is the time at which each is filed during the process.

Additional requirements for filing this Allegation of Use:

1) the fee of $100.00 per class of goods/services **(please note that fees are subject to change, usually on October 1 of each year)**; and
2) three (3) specimens of the mark as used in commerce for each class of goods/services (for example, photographs of the mark as it appears on the goods, labels for affixation on goods, advertisements showing the mark as used in connection with services).

•   The Applicant may list dates of use for one item in each class of goods/services identified in the Allegation of Use. The Applicant must have used the mark in commerce on all the goods/services in the class, however, it is only necessary to list the dates of use for one item in each class.

•   Only the following persons may sign the verification on this form: (a) the individual applicant; (b) an officer of a corporate applicant; (c) one general partner of a partnership applicant; (d) all joint applicants.

•   The goods/services in the Allegation of Use must be the same as those specified in the application or Notice of Allowance. The Applicant may limit or clarify the goods/services, but cannot add to or otherwise expand the identification specified in the application or Notice of Allowance. If goods/services are deleted, they may **not** be reinserted at a later time.

•   Amendments to Allege Use are governed by Trademark Act §1(c), 15 U.S.C. §1051(c) and Trademark Rule 2.76, 37 C.F.R. §2.76. Statements of Use are governed by Trademark Act §1(d), 15 U.S.C. §1051(d) and Trademark Rule 2.88, 37 C.F.R. §2.88.

> **MAIL COMPLETED FORM TO:**
>
> **ASSISTANT COMMISSIONER FOR TRADEMARKS**
> **BOX AAU/SOU**
> **2900 CRYSTAL DRIVE**
> **ARLINGTON, VIRGINIA 22202-3513**

Please note that the filing date of a document in the Patent and Trademarks Office is the date of receipt in the Office, not the date of deposit of the mail. 37 C.F.R. §1.6. To avoid lateness due to mail delay, use of the certificate of mailing set forth below, is encouraged.

COMBINED CERTIFICATE OF MAILING/CHECKLIST

Before filing this form, please make sure to complete the following:

☐ three specimens, per class have been enclosed;
☐ the filing fee of $100 (subject to change as noted above), per class has been enclosed; and
☐ the declaration has been signed by the appropriate party

CERTIFICATE OF MAILING

I do hereby certify that the foregoing are being **deposited** with the United States Postal Service as first class mail, postage prepaid, in an envelope addressed to the Assistant Commissioner for Trademarks, 2900 Crystal Drive, Arlington, VA 22202-3513, on _____ (date).

_____   _____
Signature   Date of Deposit

_____
Print or Type Name of Person Signing Certificate

This form is estimated to take 15 minutes to complete including time required for reading and understanding instructions, gathering necessary information, record keeping and actually providing the information. Any comments on the amount of time you require to complete this form should be sent to the Office of Management and Organization, U.S. Patent and Trademark Office, U.S. Department of Commerce, Washington, D.C. 20231. Do not send forms to this address.

REQUEST FOR EXTENSION OF TIME TO FILE A STATEMENT OF USE, WITH DECLARATION	MARK (Identify the mark)
	SERIAL NO.

TO THE ASSISTANT SECRETARY AND COMMISSIONER OF PATENTS AND TRADEMARKS:

APPLICANT NAME:

NOTICE OF ALLOWANCE MAILING DATE:

Applicant requests a six-month extension of time to file the Statement of Use under 37 CFR 2.89 in this application.

Applicant has a continued bona fide intention to use the mark in commerce on or in connection with the following goods/services: (Check One below)

☐ Those goods/services identified in the Notice of Allowance.

☐ Those goods/services identified in the Notice of Allowance except: (Identify goods/services to be **deleted** from application)

_____

_____

_____

This is the_____ request for an Extension of Time following mailing of the Notice of Allowance.
      (Specify: First - Fifth)

If this is not the first request for an Extension of Time, check one box below. If the first box is checked explain the circumstance(s) of the non-use in the space provided:

☐   Applicant has not used the mark in commerce yet on all goods/services specified in the Notice of Allowance; however, applicant has made the following ongoing efforts to use the mark in commerce on or in connection with each of the goods/services specified above:

_____

_____

If additional space is needed, please attach a separate sheet to this form

☐   Applicant believes that it has made valid use of the mark in commerce, as evidenced by the Statement of Use submitted with this request; however, if the Statement of Use does not meet minimum requirements under 37 CFR 2.88(e), applicant will need additional time in which to file a new statement.

The undersigned being hereby warned that willful false statements and the like so made are punishable by fine or imprisonment, or both, under 18 U.S.C. 1001, and that such willful false statements may jeopardize the validity of the application or any resulting registration, declares that he/she is properly authorized to execute this Request for an Extension of Time to File a Statement of Use on behalf of the applicant; and that all statements made of his/her own knowledge are true and all statements made on information and belief are believed to be true.

_____
Date

_____
Signature

_____
Telephone Number

_____
Type or Print Name and Position

☐   **Check here if Request to Divide is being submitted with this statement** (if Applicant wishes to proceed to publication or registration with certain goods/services on or in connection with which it has used the mark in commerce and retain an active application for any remaining goods/services, a divisional application and fee are required. 37 C.F.R. §2.87)

PTO Form 1581 (REV. 6-96)
OMB No. 0651-0009
Exp. (06/30/98)   There is no requirement to respond to this collection of information unless a currently valid OMB Number is displayed.

U.S. Department of Commerce/Patent and Trademark Office

INSTRUCTIONS AND INFORMATION FOR APPLICANT

Applicant must file a Statement of Use within six months after the mailing of the Notice of Allowance based upon a bona fide intention to use a mark in commerce, UNLESS, within that same period, applicant submits a request for a six-month extension of time to file the Statement of Use. The written request **must**:

    (1)   be received in the PTO within six months after the issue date of the Notice of Allowance,

    (2)   include applicant's verified statement of continued bona fide intention to use the mark in commerce,

    (3)   specify the goods/services to which the request pertains as they are identified in the Notice of Allowance, and

    (4)   include a fee of $100 for each class of goods/services **(please note that fees are subject to change, usually on October 1 of each year).**

Applicant may request four further six-month extensions of time. No extensions may extend beyond 36 months from the issue date of the Notice of Allowance. Each further request must be received in the PTO within the previously granted six-month extension period and must include, in addition to the above requirements, a showing of **GOOD CAUSE**. This good cause showing must include:

    (1)   applicant's statement that the mark has not been used in commerce yet on all the goods or services specified in the Notice of Allowance with which applicant has a continued bona fide intention to use the mark in commerce, **and**

    (2)   applicant's statement of ongoing efforts to make such use, which may include the following: (a) product or service research or development, (b) market research, (c) promotional activities, (d) steps to acquire distributors, (e) steps to obtain required governmental approval, or (f) similar specified activity.

Applicant may submit one additional six-month extension request during the existing period in which applicant files the Statement of Use, unless the granting of this request would extend the period beyond 36 months from the issue date of the Notice of Allowance. As a showing of good cause for such a request, applicant should state its belief that applicant has made valid use of the mark in commerce, as evidenced by the submitted Statement of Use, but that if the Statement is found by the PTO to be defective, applicant will need additional time in which to file a new statement of use.

Only the following person may sign the declaration of the Request for Extension of Time: (a) the individual applicant; (b) an officer of corporate applicant: (c) one general partner of partnership applicant; (d) all joint applicants.

MAILING INSTRUCTIONS

MAIL COMPLETED FORM TO:

ASSISTANT COMMISSIONER FOR TRADEMARKS
BOX ITU
2900 CRYSTAL DRIVE
ARLINGTON, VIRGINIA 22202-3513

Please note that the filing date of a document in the Patent and Trademarks Office is the date of receipt in the Office, not the date of deposit of the mail. 37 C.F. R. §1.6. To avoid lateness due to mail delay, use of the certificate of mailing set forth below is encouraged.

CERTIFICATE OF MAILING

I do hereby certify that this correspondence is being **deposited** with the United States Postal Service as first class mail, postage prepaid, in an envelope addressed to the Assistant Commissioner for Trademarks, 2900 Crystal Drive, Arlington, VA 22202-3513, on _____ (date).

_____
Signature

_____
Date of Deposit

_____
Print or Type Name of Person Signing Certificate

<table>
<tr>
<td>

COMBINED DECLARATION OF USE AND INCONTESTABILITY UNDER SECTIONS 8 & 15[1] OF THE TRADEMARK ACT OF 1946, AS AMENDED

</td>
<td colspan="2">

MARK (Identify the mark)

</td>
</tr>
<tr>
<td></td>
<td>

REGISTRATION NO.

</td>
<td>

DATE OF REGISTRATION:

</td>
</tr>
</table>

TO THE ASSISTANT SECRETARY AND COMMISSIONER OF PATENTS AND TRADEMARKS:

REGISTRANT'S NAME:[2]

REGISTRANT'S CURRENT MAILING ADDRESS: _____

_____

_____

GOODS AND/OR SERVICES AND USE IN COMMERCE STATEMENT:

The mark shown in Registration No. _____, owned by the above-identified registrant, has been in

continuous use in _____ commerce for five consecutive years from the date of registration or the

(type of)[3]

date of publication under § 12(c)[4] to the present, on or in connection with all of the goods and/or services

identified in the registration, (*except* for the following)[5]_____

_____ ;

as evidenced by the attached specimen(s)[6] showing the mark as currently used. There has been no final

decision adverse to registrant's claim of ownership of such mark for such goods or services, or to registrant's

right to register the same or to keep the same on the register; and there is no proceeding involving said

rights pending and not disposed of either in the Patent and Trademark Office or in the courts.

DECLARATION

The undersigned being hereby warned that willful false statements and the like so made are punishable by fine or imprisonment, or both, under 18 U.S.C. 1001, and that such willful false statements may jeopardize the validity of this document, declares that he/she is properly authorized to execute this document on behalf of the registrant; he/she believes the registrant to be the owner of the above identified registration; the trademark/service mark is in use in commerce; and all statements made of his/her own knowledge are true and all statements made on information and belief are believed to be true.

_____   _____
Date   Signature

_____   _____
Telephone Number   Print or Type Name and Position
                                                      [if applicable][7]

FOOTNOTES

1. If you do not have five years of continuous use, you should file a Section 8 affidavit only. Please see PTO Form #1583.

2. The present owner of the registration must file this form between the 5th and 6th year after registration. If ownership of the registration has changed since the registration date, provide supporting documentation if available or a verified explanation. The present owner should refer to itself as the registrant.

3. "Type of Commerce" must be specified as "interstate," "territorial," "foreign," or such other commerce as may lawfully be regulated by Congress. Foreign registrants must specify commerce which Congress may regulate, using wording such as "foreign commerce between the U.S. and a foreign country."

4. Use this combined form only when the five year period of continuous use, required for Section 15, (1) occurs between the 5th and 6th year after registration on the **Principal Register**, or (2) after publication under § 12(c) as is required for Section 8.

5. List only those goods and/or services for which registrant is no longer using the mark. You should fill in this blank **only** if you are no longer using the mark on all the goods or services in the registration.

6. A specimen showing current use of the registered mark for at least one product or service in each class of the registration must be submitted with this form. Examples of speciments are tags or labels for goods, and advertisements for services. The registration number should be printed directly on the specimen.

7. If the present owner is an individual, the individual should sign the declaration.

8. If the present owner is a partnership, the declaration should be signed by a General Partner.

9. If the present owner is a corporation or similar juristic entity, the declaration should be signed by an officer of the corporation/entity. Please print or type the officer title of the person signing the declaration.

NOTE: If the registration is owned by more than one party, as joint owners, each owner must sign this declaration.

PTO Notification

You should receive written notification from the PTO of either the acceptance or rejection of this post registration document. If you do not receive written notification from the PTO within six months after filing, you may wish to telephone the Trademark Status Line at (703) 305-8747 or the Post Registration Division at (703) 308-9500.

FEES

For each declaration under Sections 8 & 15, the required fee is $200.00 per international class. Please be aware that our fees may change. Changes, if any, are normally effective October 1 of each year. If this declaration is intended to cover less than the total number of classes in the registration, please specify the classes for which the declaration is submitted. The declaration, with appropriate fee(s), should be sent to:

BOX POST REG
FEE
Assistant Commissioner for Trademarks
2900 Crystal Drive
Arlington, Virginia 22202-3513

MAILING INSTRUCTION BOX

You can ensure timely filing of this form by following the procedure described in 37 CFR 1.10 as follows: (1) on or before the due date for filing this form, deposit the completed form with the U.S. Post Office using the "Express Mail Post Office to Addressee" Service; (2) include a certificate of "Express Mail" under 37 CFR 1.10. Papers properly mailed under 37 CFR 1.10 are considered received by the PTO on the date that they are deposited with the Post Office.

When placing the certificate directly on the correspondence, use the following language:

Certificate of Express Mail Under 37 CFR 1.10

"Express Mail" mailing label number: _____
Date of Deposit: _____
I hereby certify that this paper and fee is being deposited with the United States Postal Service "Express Mail Post Office to Addressee" service under 37 CFR 1.10 on the date indicated above and is addressed to the Assistant Commissioner for Trademarks, 2900 Crystal Drive, Arlington, Virginia 22202-3513.

_____   _____
(Typed or printed name of person mailing paper & fee)   (Signature of person mailing paper & fee)

This form is estimated to take 15 minutes to complete. Time will vary depending upon the needs of the individual case. Any comments on the amount of time you require to complete this form should be sent to the Office of Management and Organization, U.S. Patent and Trademark Office, U.S. Department of Commerce, Washington, D.C. 20231, and to the Office of Information and Regulatory Affairs, Office of Management and Budget, Washington, D.C. 20503. **DO NOT SEND FORMS TO EITHER OF THESE ADDRESS.**

<table>
<tr><td>APPLICATION FOR RENEWAL OF REGISTRATION OF A MARK UNDER **SECTION 9** OF THE TRADEMARK ACT OF 1946, AS AMENDED</td><td colspan="2">MARK (Identify the mark)</td></tr>
<tr><td></td><td>REGISTRATION NO.</td><td>DATE OF REGISTRATION:</td></tr>
</table>

TO THE ASSISTANT SECRETARY AND COMMISSIONER OF PATENTS AND TRADEMARKS:

REGISTRANT'S NAME:[1]

REGISTRANT'S CURRENT MAILING ADDRESS: _____

_____

_____

GOODS AND/OR SERVICES AND USE IN COMMERCE STATEMENT:

The mark shown in Registration No. _____ owned by the above-identified registrant is still in use in

_____ commerce on or in connection with all of the goods and/or services identified in the
 (type of)[2]

registration, (*except* for the following)[3] _____

_____

as evidenced by the attached specimen(s)[4] showing the mark as currently used.

DECLARATION

The undersigned being hereby warned that willful false statements and the like so made are punishable by fine or imprisonment, or both, under 18 U.S.C. 1001, and that such willful false statements may jeopardize the validity of this document, declares that he/she is properly authorized to execute this document on behalf of the registrant; he/she believes the registrant to be the owner of the above identified registration; the trademark/service mark is in use in commerce; and all statements made of his/her own knowledge are true and all statements made on information and belief are believed to be true.

_____

Date

_____

Telephone Number

_____

Signature

_____

Print or Type Name and Position
[if applicable][5]

PTO Form 4.13a (Rev. 1/93)
OMB No. 0651-0009 (Exp. 6/30/95)

U.S. DEPARTMENT OF COMMERCE/Patent and Trademark Office

FOOTNOTES

1.   The present owner of the registration must file this form within 6 months prior to the expiration of the registration term. The form may also be filed within a 3 month grace period following the expiration of the registration term upon payment of the late fee. If ownership of the registration has changed since the registration date, provide supporting documentation if available or a verified explanation. The present owner should refer to itself as the registrant.

2.   "Type of Commerce" must be specified as "interstate," "territorial," "foreign," or such other commerce as may lawfully be regulated by Congress. Foreign registrants must specify commerce which Congress may regulate, using wording such as "foreign commerce between the U.S. and a foreign country."

3.   List only those goods and/or services for which registrant is no longer using the mark. You should fill in this blank only if you are no longer using the mark on all the goods or services in the registration.

4.   A specimen showing current use of the registered mark for at least one product or service in each class of the registration must be submitted with this form. Examples of specimens are tags or labels for goods, and advertisements for services. The registration number should be printed directly on the specimen.

5.   If the present owner is an individual, the individual should sign the declaration.

6.   If the present owner is a partnership, the declaration should be signed by a General Partner.

7.   If the present owner is a corporation or similar juristic entity, the declaration should be signed by an officer of the corporation/entity. Please print or type the officer title of the person signing the declaration.

NOTE: If the registration is owned by more than one party, as joint owners, each owner must sign this declaration.

PTO Notification

You should receive written notification from the PTO of either the acceptance or rejection of this post registration document. If you do not receive written notification from the PTO within six months after filing, you may wish to telephone the Trademark Status Line at (703) 305-8747 or the Post Registration Division at (703) 308-9500.

FEES

For each renewal application under Section 9, the required fee is $300.00 per class. Please be aware that our fees may change. Changes, if any, are normally effective October 1 of each year. If filed during the three month grace period a late fee of $100.00 per class must also be submitted. If this renewal application is intended to cover less than the total number of classes in the registration, please specify the classes for which the renewal application is submitted. The renewal application, with appropriate fee(s), should be sent to:

BOX POST REG
FEE
Assistant Commissioner for Trademarks
2900 Crystal Drive
Arlington, Virginia 22202-3513

MAILING INSTRUCTION BOX

You can ensure timely filing of this form by following the procedure described in 37 CFR 1.10 as follows: (1) on or before the due date for filing this form, deposit the completed form with the U.S. Post Office using the "Express Mail Post Office to Addressee" Service; (2) include a certificate of "Express Mail" under 37 CFR 1.10. Papers properly mailed under 37 CFR 1.10 are considered received by the PTO on the date that they are deposited with the Post Office.

When placing the certificate directly on the correspondence, use the following language:

Certificate of Express Mail Under 37 CFR 1.10

"Express Mail" mailing label number: _____

Date of Deposit: _____

I hereby certify that this paper and fee is being deposited with the United States Postal Service "Express Mail Post Office to Addressee" service under 37 CFR 1.10 on the date indicated above and is addressed to the Assistant Commissioner for Trademarks, 2900 Crystal Drive, Arlington, Virginia 22202-3513.

_____   _____
(Typed or printed name of person mailing paper & fee)   (Signature of person mailing paper & fee)

TRADEMARK

Request to Divide

United States Department of Commerce
Patent and Trademark Office

Applicant _____

Mark _____   Trademark Law Office _____

Serial Number _____   Trademark Attorney _____

Filed _____

Assistant Commissioner for Trademarks
Box ITV
2900 Crystal Drive
Arlington, VA 22202-3513

Request to Divide Application

The applicant hereby requests that the application identified above be divided as follows:

Please retain in the original application the following goods/services—(use the language of the original application insofar as possible).

Please include in the new, divided application the following goods/services—(they should be different from and should not overlap, those remaining in the original application).

(Check one)

☐ Enclosed is a check in payment of the filing fee for the divided application.

☐ The divided application includes all goods or services in a single class presented in the original, parent application; therefore the applicant submits that no filing fee is due or required.

DATED: _____   Respectfully,

_____

Telephone Number: _____

Address: _____

_____

_____

Index

■

CATALOG

...more from nolo.com

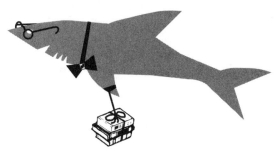

		PRICE	CODE

BUSINESS

		PRICE	CODE
⊙	The CA Nonprofit Corp Kit (Binder w/CD-ROM)	$39.95	CNP
▣	Consultant & Independent Contractor Agreements (Book w/Disk—PC)	$24.95	CICA
▣	The Corporate Minutes Book (Book w/Disk—PC)	$69.95	CORMI
	The Employer's Legal Handbook	$31.95	EMPL
▣	Form Your Own Limited Liability Company (Book w/Disk—PC)	$34.95	LIAB
▣	Hiring Independent Contractors: The Employer's Legal Guide (Book w/Disk—PC)	$29.95	HICI
▣	How to Create a Buy-Sell Agreement and Control the Destiny of your Small Business (Book w/Disk—PC)	$49.95	BSAG
▣	How to Form a California Professional Corporation (Book w/Disk—PC)	$49.95	PROF
▣	How to Form a Nonprofit Corporation (Book w/Disk —PC)—National Edition	$39.95	NNP
	How to Form a Nonprofit Corporation in California	$34.95	NON
▣	How to Form Your Own California Corporation (Binder w/Disk—PC	$39.95	CACI
▣	How to Form Your Own California Corporation (Book w/Disk—PC)	$34.95	CCOR
▣	How to Form Your Own Florida Corporation (Book w/Disk—PC)	$39.95	FLCO
▣	How to Form Your Own New York Corporation (Book w/Disk—PC)	$39.95	NYCO
▣	How to Form Your Own Texas Corporation (Book w/Disk—PC)	$39.95	TCOR
	How to Write a Business Plan	$24.95	SBS
	The Independent Paralegal's Handbook	$29.95	PARA
	Legal Guide for Starting & Running a Small Business, Vol. 1	$24.95	RUNS
▣	Legal Guide for Starting & Running a Small Business, Vol. 2: Legal Forms (Book w/Disk—PC)	$29.95	RUNS2
	Marketing Without Advertising	$19.00	MWAD
▣	Music Law (Book w/Disk—PC)	$29.95	ML
	Nolo's California Quick Corp (Quick & Legal Series)	$19.95	QINC
⊙	Open Your California Business in 24 Hours (Book w/CD-ROM)	$24.95	OPEN
▣	The Partnership Book: How to Write a Partnership Agreement (Book w/Disk—PC)	$34.95	PART
	Sexual Harassment on the Job	$18.95	HARS
	Starting & Running a Successful Newsletter or Magazine	$24.95	MAG
	Take Charge of Your Workers' Compensation Claim (California Edition)	$29.95	WORK
	Tax Savvy for Small Business	$29.95	SAVVY
	Trademark: Legal Care for Your Business and Product Name	$34.95	TRD
	Wage Slave No More: Law & Taxes for the Self-Employed	$24.95	WAGE
	Your Rights in the Workplace	$21.95	YRW

CONSUMER

		PRICE	CODE
	Fed Up with the Legal System: What's Wrong & How to Fix It	$9.95	LEG
	How to Win Your Personal Injury Claim	$26.95	PICL
	Nolo's Everyday Law Book	$24.95	EVL
	Nolo's Pocket Guide to California Law	$12.95	CLAW
	Trouble-Free Travel...And What to Do When Things Go Wrong	$14.95	TRAV

▣ Book with disk

⊙ Book with CD-ROM

	PRICE	CODE

ESTATE PLANNING & PROBATE

	PRICE	CODE
8 Ways to Avoid Probate (Quick & Legal Series)	$15.95	PRO8
9 Ways to Avoid Estate Taxes (Quick & Legal Series)	$22.95	ESTX
How to Probate an Estate (California Edition)	$39.95	PAE
Make Your Own Living Trust	$24.95	LITR
Nolo's Law Form Kit: Wills	$14.95	KWL
▣ Nolo's Will Book (Book w/Disk—PC)	$29.95	SWIL
Plan Your Estate	$24.95	NEST
Quick & Legal Will Book (Quick & Legal Series)	$15.95	QUIC

FAMILY MATTERS

	PRICE	CODE
Child Custody: Building Parenting Agreements That Work	$26.95	CUST
The Complete IEP Guide	$24.95	IEP
Divorce & Money: How to Make the Best Financial Decisions During Divorce	$26.95	DIMO
Do Your Own Divorce in Oregon	$19.95	ODIV
Get a Life: You Don't Need a Million to Retire Well	$18.95	LIFE
The Guardianship Book (California Edition)	$39.95	GB
How to Adopt Your Stepchild in California	$34.95	ADOP
How to Raise or Lower Child Support in California (Quick & Legal Series)	$19.95	CHLD
A Legal Guide for Lesbian and Gay Couples	$25.95	LG
The Living Together Kit	$29.95	LTK
Nolo's Pocket Guide to Family Law	$14.95	FLD
Using Divorce Mediation: Save Your Money & Your Sanity	$21.95	UDMD

GOING TO COURT

	PRICE	CODE
Beta Your Ticket: Go To Court and Win! (National Edition)	$19.95	BEYT
Collect Your Court Judgment (California Edition)	$29.95	JUDG
The Criminal Law Handbook: Know Your Rights, Survive the System	$24.95	KYR
Everybody's Guide to Small Claims Court (National Edition)	$18.95	NSCC
Everybody's Guide to Small Claims Court in California	$18.95	CSCC
Fight Your Ticket ... and Win! (California Edition)	$19.95	FYT
How to Change Your Name in California	$34.95	NAME
How to Mediate Your Dispute	$18.95	MEDI
How to Seal Your Juvenile & Criminal Records (California Edition)	$24.95	CRIM
How to Sue For Up to $25,000...and Win!	$29.95	MUNI
Mad at Your Lawyer	$21.95	MAD
Represent Yourself in Court: How to Prepare & Try a Winning Case	$29.95	RYC

HOMEOWNERS, LANDLORDS & TENANTS

	PRICE	CODE
▣ Contractors' and Homeowners' Guide to Mechanics' Liens (Book w/Disk—PC)	$39.95	MIEN
The Deeds Book (California Edition)	$24.95	DEED
Dog Law	$14.95	DOG
▣ Every Landlord's Legal Guide (National Edition, Book w/Disk—PC)	$34.95	ELLI
Every Tenant's Legal Guide	$26.95	EVTEN
For Sale by Owner in California	$24.95	FSBO
How to Buy a House in California	$24.95	BHCA
The Landlord's Law Book, Vol. 1: Rights & Responsibilities (California Edition)	$34.95	LBRT
The Landlord's Law Book, Vol. 2: Evictions (California Edition)	$34.95	LBEV
Leases & Rental Agreements (Quick & Legal Series)	$18.95	LEAR
Neighbor Law: Fences, Trees, Boundaries & Noise	$17.95	NEI
Renters' Rights (National Edition—Quick & Legal Series))	$15.95	RENT
Stop Foreclosure Now in California	$29.95	CLOS
Tenants' Rights (California Edition)	$21.95	CTEN

HUMOR

	PRICE	CODE
29 Reasons Not to Go to Law School	$9.95	29R
Poetic Justice	$9.95	PJ

▣ Book with disk

◉ Book with CD-ROM

CALL 800-992-6656 OR USE THE ORDER FORM IN THE BACK OF THE BOOK

		PRICE	CODE

IMMIGRATION

	PRICE	CODE
How to Get a Green Card: Legal Ways to Stay in the U.S.A.	$24.95	GRN
U.S. Immigration Made Easy	$44.95	IMEZ

MONEY MATTERS

	PRICE	CODE
▣ 101 Law Forms for Personal Use (Quick & Legal Series, Book w/disk—PC)	$24.95	SPOT
Bankruptcy: Is It the Right Solution to Your Debt Problems? (Quick & Legal Series)	$15.95	BRS
Chapter 13 Bankruptcy: Repay Your Debts	$29.95	CH13
Credit Repair (Quick & Legal Series)	$15.95	CREP
▣ The Financial Power of Attorney Workbook (Book w/disk—PC)	$24.95	FINPOA
How to File for Chapter 7 Bankruptcy	$26.95	HFB
IRAs, 401(k)s & Other Retirement Plans: Taking Your Money Out	$21.95	RET
Money Troubles: Legal Strategies to Cope With Your Debts	$19.95	MT
Nolo's Law Form Kit: Personal Bankruptcy	$16.95	KBNK
Stand Up to the IRS	$24.95	SIRS
Take Control of Your Student Loans	$19.95	SLOAN

PATENTS AND COPYRIGHTS

	PRICE	CODE
▣ The Copyright Handbook: How to Protect and Use Written Works (Book w/disk—PC)	$29.95	COHA
Copyright Your Software	$24.95	CYS
How to Make Patent Drawings Yourself	$29.95	DRAW
The Inventor's Notebook	$19.95	INOT
▣ License Your Invention (Book w/Disk—PC)	$39.95	LICE
Patent, Copyright & Trademark	$24.95	PCTM
Patent It Yourself	$46.95	PAT
Patent Searching Made Easy	$24.95	PATSE
◉ Software Development: A Legal Guide (Book with CD-ROM)	$44.95	SFT

RESEARCH & REFERENCE

	PRICE	CODE
◉ Government on the Net (Book w/CD-ROM—Windows/Macintosh)	$39.95	GONE
◉ Law on the Net (Book w/CD-ROM—Windows/Macintosh)	$39.95	LAWN
Legal Research: How to Find & Understand the Law	$24.95	LRES
Legal Research Made Easy (Video)	$89.95	LRME
Legal Research Online & in the Library (Book w/CD-ROM—Windows/Macintosh)	$39.95	LRO

SENIORS

	PRICE	CODE
Beat the Nursing Home Trap	$21.95	ELD
The Conservatorship Book (California Edition)	$44.95	CNSV
Social Security, Medicare & Pensions	$21.95	SOA

SOFTWARE

Call or check our website at www.nolo.com for special discounts on Software!

	PRICE	CODE
◉ LeaseWriter CD—Windows/Macintosh	$99.95	LWD1
◉ Living Trust Maker CD—Windows/Macintosh	$79.95	LTD2
◉ Small Business Legal Pro 3 CD—Windows/Macintosh	$79.95	SBCD3
◉ Personal RecordKeeper 5.0 CD—Windows/Macintosh	$59.95	RKD5
◉ Patent It Yourself CD—Windows	$229.95	PPC12
◉ WillMaker 7.0 CD—Windows/Macintosh	$69.95	WMD7

▣ Book with disk

◉ Book with CD-ROM

ORDER FORM

Code	Quantity	Title	Unit price	Total
		Subtotal		
		California residents add Sales Tax		
		Basic Shipping ($3.95)		
		UPS RUSH delivery $8.00–any size order*		
		TOTAL		

Name

Address

(UPS to street address, Priority Mail to P.O. boxes)

* Delivered in 3 business days from receipt of order.
S.F. Bay Area use regular shipping.

FOR FASTER SERVICE, USE YOUR CREDIT CARD AND OUR TOLL-FREE NUMBERS

Order 24 hours a day   1-800-992-6656

Fax your order   1-800-645-0895

Online   www.nolo.com

METHOD OF PAYMENT

☐ Check enclosed

☐ VISA   ☐ MasterCard   ☐ Discover Card   ☐ American Express

Account #   Expiration Date

Authorizing Signature

Daytime Phone

PRICES SUBJECT TO CHANGE.

VISIT OUR OUTLET STORE!   VISIT US ONLINE!

BERKELEY
950 Parker Street
Berkeley, CA 94710
1-510-704-2248

on the Internet
www.nolo.com

You'll find our complete line of books and software, all at a discount.

Nolo.com 950 PARKER ST., BERKELEY, CA 94710

Take 2 Minutes & Give Us Your 2 cents

Your comments make a big difference in the development and revision of Nolo books and software. Please take a few minutes and register your Nolo product—and your comments—with us. Not only will your input make a difference, you'll receive special offers available only to registered owners of Nolo products on our newest books and software. Register now by:

PHONE
1-800-992-6656

FAX
1-800-645-0895

EMAIL
cs@nolo.com

or **MAIL** us
this registration card

REMEMBER:
Little publishers have big ears. We really listen to you.

- - - - - - - - - - - - - - - - - - - fold here - - - - - - - - - - - - - - - - - - -

 **REGISTRATION CARD**

NAME	DATE
ADDRESS	

CITY	STATE	ZIP
PHONE	E-MAIL	

WHERE DID YOU HEAR ABOUT THIS PRODUCT?

WHERE DID YOU PURCHASE THIS PRODUCT?

DID YOU CONSULT A LAWYER? (PLEASE CIRCLE ONE)   YES   NO   NOT APPLICABLE

DID YOU FIND THIS BOOK HELPFUL?   (VERY)   5   4   3   2   1   (NOT AT ALL)

COMMENTS

WAS IT EASY TO USE?   (VERY EASY)   5   4   3   2   1   (VERY DIFFICULT)

DO YOU OWN A COMPUTER? IF SO, WHICH FORMAT? (PLEASE CIRCLE ONE)   WINDOWS   DOS   MAC

❑ If you do not wish to receive mailings from these companies, please check this box.

❑ You can quote me in future Nolo.com promotional materials. Daytime phone number _____.

TREG 1.0

NOLO IN THE NEWS

"Nolo helps lay people perform legal tasks without the aid—or fees—of lawyers."
—USA TODAY

Nolo books are ..."written in plain language, free of legal mumbo jumbo, and spiced with witty personal observations."
—ASSOCIATED PRESS

"...Nolo publications...guide people simply through the how, when, where and why of law."
—WASHINGTON POST

"Increasingly, people who are not lawyers are performing tasks usually regarded as legal work... And consumers, using books like Nolo's, do routine legal work themselves."
—NEW YORK TIMES

"...All of [Nolo's] books are easy-to-understand, are updated regularly, provide pull-out forms...and are often quite moving in their sense of compassion for the struggles of the lay reader."
—SAN FRANCISCO CHRONICLE

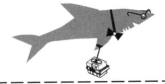

fold here

- -

Place
stamp here

nolo.com
950 Parker Street
Berkeley, CA 94710-9867

Attn: | TREG 1.0 |